Shameful Bodies

ALSO AVAILABLE FROM BLOOMSBURY

Capitalizing Religion, Craig Martin
Practical Spiritualities in a Media Age, Curtis Coats and Monica M. Emerich
Religion in Hip Hop, Monica R. Miller, Anthony B. Pinn, and Bernard
"Bun B" Freeman

Shameful Bodies

Religion and the culture of physical improvement

MICHELLE MARY LELWICA

Bloomsbury Academic
An imprint of Bloomsbury Publishing Plc

B L O O M S B U R Y
LONDON · OXFORD · NEW YORK · NEW DELHI · SYDNEY

Bloomsbury Academic

An imprint of Bloomsbury Publishing Plc

50 Bedford Square	1385 Broadway
London	New York
WC1B 3DP	NY 10018
UK	USA

www.bloomsbury.com

BLOOMSBURY and the Diana logo are trademarks of Bloomsbury Publishing Plc

First published 2017
© Michelle Mary Lelwica, 2017

British Library Cataloguing-in-Publication Data
A catalogue record for this book is available from the British Library.

ISBN: HB: 978-1-4725-9494-5
PB: 978-1-4725-9493-8
ePDF: 978-1-4725-9495-2
ePub: 978-1-4725-9496-9

Library of Congress Cataloging-in-Publication Data
A catalog record for this book is available from the Library of Congress.

Cover design by Clare Turner
Cover images: zakazpc / istock.com; Piotr Marcinski and arka38 / shutterstock.com

Typeset by Newgen Knowledge Works (P) Ltd., Chennai, India
Printed and bound in Great Britain

Contents

Illustrations

Preface

This book started in my hip. I realize that might sound strange, so let me explain.

About three years before the idea for *Shameful Bodies* was conceived, I was diagnosed with advanced osteoarthritis in my left hip. I'd been having pain there for quite some time, especially after jogging—which was not only my routine form of exercise but also my preferred method of stress reduction. Increasingly, though, the discomfort I felt afterward was more severe and longer lasting. Eventually, it never went away.

Reluctantly, I went to see an orthopedic doctor. He took one look at the x-ray and, raising his eyebrows, asked: "What did you do to your hip?" Before giving me a chance to respond, he went on: "It looks like the hip of a woman in her late eighties, not her late forties." He pointed to the x-ray to show me what he was talking about, but he didn't need to. Even without an ounce of medical training, I could see that the top of my femur—the part that's supposed to be round and smooth like the arch of a rainbow—looked more like the top of the Rocky Mountains, jagged and worn away. All that remained of the cartilage were fragments floating around that area.

My first reaction was relief. *Finally*, I thought somewhat triumphantly, *proof that the pain isn't just in my head*. But the satisfaction was short lived, as it dawned on me that this newly diagnosed hip problem was going to be a significant ordeal, hampering not just my therapeutic jogging but other parts of my life as well. "Bone and cartilage don't grow back, do they?" I was pretty sure I knew the answer, but figured it wouldn't hurt to ask.

"They do not," the doctor responded matter-of-factly. Then he asked again, this time more seriously, whether I'd ever injured my hip.

"Not that I know of." I quietly wondered whether knowing the cause of cartilage deterioration might somehow make the damage easier to fix. Unlikely, I decided. The doctor interrupted my thoughts by telling me the only way to fix the joint was a total hip replacement. "I'm only forty-seven," I pleaded. He nodded and assured me that I'd know when I was ready for surgery: at some point, the pain would interfere with my life so much that I wouldn't be able or willing to tolerate it anymore.

My sister-in-law, Amy, is an orthopedic surgeon, so naturally I called her. "What can I do short of surgery?" I asked. "Is there any way I can postpone such a drastic procedure?"

"You're not going to like this," she replied, "but I recommend using a cane."

A cane? I barely let the idea enter my mind before quickly chasing it out. "You're right," I responded. "I don't like that suggestion. Got any other ideas?"

Talking with Amy, I learned more about what hip replacement surgery entails. Basically, the doctor saws off the top of your femur—the largest bone in your body—and replaces it with a prosthetic that's inserted into the marrow of the remaining bone. The top of the artificial femur is fitted into a synthetic socket that's fastened to the pelvic frame. If all goes well, a person with a new hip can live for two decades or more without pain.

Though the procedure sounds dramatic, not to mention gory, today hip replacements are fairly routine. In fact, they're considered among the most successful joint surgeries. My older brother, John, had one a few years after my diagnosis, and so did my friend Richard not long after that. Both were happy to be done with the pain and had no regrets about going through with surgery.

The more people I talked to, the more stories I heard about hip replacements that had changed their lives for the better. "I only wish I hadn't waited so long" was the most common response. Despite these encouragements, the thought of going through with surgery terrified me. Imagining part of my body sawed apart made me feel fragile and broken. Surgically replacing the biggest bone in my body seemed so invasive, so unnatural. What if something went wrong? What if I was among the small percentage of patients who had postsurgical complications (e.g. infection, one leg shorter than the other, new or lingering pain)? What if my prosthetic hip didn't last as long as expected? I was, after all, in my late forties, not my late eighties, which meant I'd likely need at least one more replacement in my lifetime, assuming I was fortunate enough to live that long.

In addition to these fears, there were practical issues to consider, such as when in the world would I be able to simply check out of my overscheduled life for several weeks—the time necessary for surgery and recovery? I had a more-than-full-time job teaching college students and chairing a large department, on top of an ever-busy family life that revolved around my boys' sports practices and games, orchestra rehearsals and concerts, and endless homework—not to mention laundry, cooking, groceries, and other household chores. Moreover, despite being privileged enough to have good health insurance, the surgery would cost $3,500 out-of-pocket, which in my mind seemed like the equivalent of paying a lot of money for what seemed sure to be an all-around unpleasant experience.

By now, you have probably figured out that I postponed the surgery—for several years, actually, opting instead to manage the persistent discomfort with different forms of exercise and daily yoga, ibuprofen and glucosamine chondroitin, regular visits to the chiropractor and physical therapist, and an occasional massage. There was nothing brave about the decision to delay. Fear was my primary motivation. I wanted nothing more than for my body to be fixed and back to normal, to have the arthritis miraculously disappear, and, short of that, to avoid, deny, or fight the pain as best I could. I hated the feelings of anxiety, vulnerability, inadequacy, and frustration my troubled body surfaced in me.

Those years of living with chronic pain brought up questions I needed to explore—personally, intellectually, and spiritually. On a personal level, I'd already spent more than half my life learning to appreciate my body, which I'd all but abandoned in early adolescence when I was stuck in the prison of an eating disorder. How could I continue the journey of healing—of practicing peace with my body—when part of it constantly hurt? Intellectually, I couldn't help but wonder whether the same cultural ideologies and attitudes that encouraged me to loathe and abdicate my teenage flesh were now contributing to the overwhelming sense of betrayal and alienation I felt toward my body-in-pain. My desire to control my physicality was different now than it had been as a 15-year-old who was dangerously determined to be skinny. But was my longing to escape the pain also somehow connected to my adolescent effort to eradicate my flesh? Spiritually, I had long since relinquished the God-has-a-plan theology of my Catholic upbringing, despite its advantage of being able to explain pretty much everything. Yet I found myself searching for some larger lesson. What might the pain in my hip have to teach me?

The time I had to spend *on* my body, *with* my body, and *in* my body to manage the discomfort deepened my sense of continuity with it. I started every morning by alternating between exercise to keep the joint from getting stiff and stretching to keep the muscles around it from tightening. At work, I would close the door of my office and do yoga in between classes and meetings, bending and breathing into the hurt in the middle of a hectic day. During evenings, when my family was home unwinding in front of the television, I would sit on the floor massaging the muscles around my hip, attempting to relax before going to bed.

While chronic pain connected me to my physicality in ways that were hard to appreciate, the hurt also exposed assumptions I'd been making about my body, about myself, and about others. The self-discovery was not flattering and required some serious soul-searching. For example, why was I reluctant to use a cane? Did I unwittingly make judgments about people who did? Did I unknowingly see them as physically inferior? Defective? Weak? Why did I try so hard (unsuccessfully) to hide my limp? Was there something about limping that seemed unattractive, unfeminine, non-bourgeois? Did I unconsciously judge others whose bodies didn't look or perform as they were *supposed to*?

Examining these questions unsettled me, even as it opened me to new sensibilities and perceptions. I started correcting my boys when they used the word "lame" to describe something undesirable (as in: "Mom, that movie is totally *lame*"). At the same time, there was no denying that my arthritic hip limited my mobility and made me feel damaged, flawed, weak. The more I reflected on these internal judgments and feelings, the more inconsistencies I discovered in my thinking. I had no problem with the physical maladies and misfortunes of others. It was perfectly fine for *other* people to use a cane, a walker, or a wheelchair. Just *not me*. Intellectually, I knew this double-standard was untenable. But emotionally, I relied on it to keep a safe, if dubious, distance between me and people whose bodies had, in my mind, obviously failed them. I used this "not-me" mental strategy to *deny* the continuities between my own lame physicality and the nonconforming flesh of others.

In many ways, *Shameful Bodies* is an attempt to move beyond that denial, to bridge the distance and illuminate the resonances between different kinds of bodies that refuse to comply with dominant cultural standards for physical "normalcy," "health," and "beauty." The book challenges other boundaries as well, including the lines demarcating "mind" and "body," "religion" and "culture," "sacred" and "secular," "academic" and "personal," "concepts" and "experience," "individual" bodies and the "social body," "shameful bodies" and every body. *Shameful Bodies* encourages you to consider: What happens when your body doesn't feel the way it's *supposed to* feel? Or look how it's *supposed to* look? Or do what it's *supposed to* do? Who defines the ideals behind these expectations, anyway? What philosophical assumptions and religious narratives influence them? What are the psychic, physical, and spiritual consequences of efforts to "improve" your body? Who benefits from these efforts? How might stepping off the "better body" treadmill enable you to live more peacefully in the body you have?

Acknowledgments

One of my favorite spiritual teachers, the Zen-influenced, Austrian-born Benedictine monk David Steindl-Rast, emphasizes the link between gratitude and happiness—not the kind of happiness that comes and goes, but that deep, abiding sense of aliveness and well-being that can incorporate struggle and suffering.[1] I feel that gratitude/happiness connection when I think about the persons who have made this book possible.

In various courses I've taught at Concordia College, many students have joined me in reflecting on the issues I explore in these pages. Special thanks go to Karley Petersen and Stephanie Zoccatelli, who read early versions of the chapters in Part I and made helpful observations. I'm also tremendously grateful to my colleagues in Concordia's religion department for their indispensable encouragement and assistance as I worked on this project. Drs. David Creech and Elna Solvang directed me to biblical resources. Dr. Roy Hammerling shared his knowledge of Christian history and was always willing to discuss at length whatever chapter I was working on. Over the years, conversations with Drs. Ahmed Afzaal, Jacqueline Bussie, Stewart Herman, Hilda Koster, Anne Mocko, Jan Pranger, and Ernie Simmons have enriched my thinking about the relationship between religion, gender, culture, and body issues. Also at Concordia, Dr. Joan Kopperud was kind enough to read and discuss early versions of the chapters in Part I; Dr. Phillip LeMaster read and provided fruitful feedback on a late draft of the chapter on aging; Dr. Ellen Aho listened attentively for hours as I described the questions and epiphanies this project generated for me; and Dr. Affi Inberg took a break from her retirement to read a close-to-final version of the entire manuscript, generously offering keen insights and recommendations.

Beyond Concordia, I'd like to thank Dr. Julia Watts Belser for her reading recommendations for the chapter on disability and for her general encouragement of this project. I also acknowledge with gratitude and fondness my graduate school mentors—Drs. Margaret Miles, Elisabeth Schüssler Fiorenza, and the late Gordon Kaufman—whose atypical perspectives on religion continue to shape my thinking over 20 years later. Readers familiar with these scholars' works will see their ongoing influence in these pages. Finally, my editor at Bloomsbury Publishing, Lalle Pursglove, expressed unwavering faith in this project from start to finish, reading drafts of all the chapters and helping me with the somewhat daunting challenge of sticking to my word limit. While I take full responsibility for any of the book's shortcomings, the gratefulness I feel for all this support is a profound source of happiness.

Many people outside the academy supported my work on *Shameful Bodies*—too many to name individually here, but some of whom I'd like to publicly thank. Hannah Papenfuss and I became good friends not long after I'd started this project, and her reliable honesty, brilliant wit, poignant poetry, and unsanitized questions were an abiding source of inspiration to me on days when words were not flowing. My parents, Marge and Ted Lelwica, indulged me by regularly asking how the writing was going and (bless them) listening to my long-winded answers with genuine interest. They enriched my thinking about body issues with their knowledge as trained medical professionals, their experiences as elders with physical frailties, and their example of service to others as a source of meaning and healing. My husband, Robert Angotti, did his best to understand my endless fascination with—and passion for—the questions and issues explored in this book. And while our sons, Anthony and Giulio, were mostly oblivious to the work I was doing, they got glimpses of what I was up to when I shared with them my cultural critiques of some of their television and movie selections. Most importantly, my boys kept me sane by ensuring that I didn't spend my entire sabbatical tethered to my computer. Basketball tournaments, orchestra concerts, family dinners, and summer weekends camping at West Lake Olaf are just some of the ways in which I was constantly reminded that there's more to life than the world of ideas, however much I love that world, however much that world seeps into our lives and into our flesh. Thank you for helping me remember and experience just how *embodied* life really is.

Note

1 Brother David Steindl-Rast, "Grateful Living," in *David Steindl-Rast: Essential Writings*, ed. Clare Hallward (Maryknoll, NY: Orbis Books, 2010), 39–65

Introduction

Shameful Bodies explores the hidden role of religion in the popular but painful pursuit of physical improvement. I examine a variety of somatic (i.e. body-related) issues, including disability, weight, chronic pain and illness, and aging in light of the dominant cultural fantasy of the slender, able-bodied, pain-free, disease-free, wrinkle-free ideal. My own struggles with some these issues inform my analysis. I also engage the stories and views of others whose bodies refuse to live up to prevailing standards of health, normalcy, and beauty. Many of the authors I discuss have converted their corporeal "failures" into a prophetic critique of religious and cultural norms that encourage us to feel shame about our bodies and view our flesh as "the enemy." With the help of their perspectives, I analyze commercial and self-help messages that promote fear, judgment, and aggression toward unconventional bodies by insisting that they be supervised, controlled, and corrected. My analysis underscores the need for a fresh perspective on physical well-being—one that honors the diverse and tenuous nature of human bodies.

As a scholar of religion, I'm especially interested in the role religious narratives, beliefs, and practices play, however tacitly, in promoting the pursuit of a "better body" and in the shame that often shadows this quest. In *Shameful Bodies*, I explore this role in four ways (which I discuss in Chapters 2–4). First, I analyze how the widespread devotion to physical enhancement in developed Western societies serves what has historically been a religious function: the construction and pursuit of what Paul Tillich referred to as an "ultimate concern."[1] Second, I examine some traditional Christian narratives that are recycled in the salvation myth of somatic improvement, including the body's pivotal role in redemption, its long-standing association with women, and its anticipated perfection in the Resurrection. Third, I highlight how some aspects of the culture of physical improvement resemble certain features of traditional Christianity, including beliefs, images, rituals, and moral codes that encourage us to cultivate health, happiness, and healing ("salvation") by eradicating our physical "defects." Finally, I consider whether the popularity of the goal of a better body tells us something about our existential or spiritual needs, including the need for a sense of agency, purpose, and unconditional acceptance.

As we shall see, none of the body issues discussed in this book (i.e. aging, weight, illness, pain, disability) have been peripheral or neutral topics in the history of Christian theology. Moreover, since the modern period, traditional Christian views of "the body" as disobedient, unpredictable, and in need of taming have combined with Cartesian notions of the "self" as an unencumbered, autonomous individual to create a fantasy of the ideal body that is not just desirable, but achievable.

My analysis of the religious dimensions of the culture of physical improvement highlights the particular role Christianity plays because Christian traditions have had the most prominence and thus the most power to influence body norms in this context. Correspondingly, alternative views and values within Christianity can challenge our culture's devotion to a "better body" as defined by a singular, commercial ideal. I rely most heavily on the work of feminist scholars of religion to articulate this challenge. I also draw on the insights of several Western Buddhist teachers to construct a more supportive approach to the diversity, fragility, interconnection, and impermanence of embodied life.

Ultimately, two paradigms of religion emerge in the pages to come. One views religion as answer giving, rule oriented, individualistic, anti body, other worldly, triumphalist, exclusive, judgmental, and controlling. The other sees religion as question-raising, meaning seeking, diversely communal, this worldly, body affirming, earth loving, process oriented, and transformative. Whereas the *religion-as-controlling* paradigm promotes the energy of fight or flight (i.e. we must either conquer adversity or escape it), the *religion-as-transformative* paradigm fosters the energy of presence, which enables us to metabolize difficulty and loss in ways that open our hearts, sharpen our critical thinking, and deepen our sense of accountability to others. Religion's ambiguous potential to foster body shame or health and healing makes it part of the problem, and part of the solution.

Intersecting fields of study

My analysis draws on intellectual tools and insights from academic disciplines beyond the field of religion. Disability studies scholars have been exceptionally insightful in their critiques of the dominant culture's hierarchy of bodies and the harm this ranking system inflicts on those who don't cooperate with its symbolic authority. Engaging what Simi Linton calls "the vantage point of the atypical,"[2] their work reveals how this system renders some bodies desirable and others disgusting. Disability scholars show how the corporeal hierarchy is constructed through aesthetic, medical, and moral standards that associate beauty, health, and virtue with a specific form of physicality—the "normal" or "ideal" body that is seen to represent the well-ordered, sovereign "self."

By challenging the authority of the "normalizing gaze," disability studies scholars' analyses enable us to see nonconforming bodies as distinctive rather than defective, as extraordinary rather than shameful.[3] In interesting ways, their analyses support the critical questions scholars are exploring in the field of fat studies—questions that inform my analysis in Chapter 6, which focuses on weight issues. Insights from both fields challenge common assumptions about what it means to be healthy, happy, and whole, while prompting us to create a world in which all persons have the psychic and structural access they need to feel at home in their flesh. Such insights lead me to grant anomalous bodies a kind of epistemological privilege. This means I prioritize the knowledge of their experiences, not because their nonconformity makes them superior, but because it can create a different way of being and seeing— a way that questions assumptions about physical improvement, including the belief that every ailment has a cure.

I also draw on the work of postcolonial scholars whose analyses illuminate the crucial role race, class, gender, religion, and culture play in the construction of the somatic ideal and its internalized effects. Postcolonial critiques highlight the missionizing dynamic built into the normalizing plotline of the better body fiction—a dynamic that reflects the commercial interests embedded in this story. In both its masculine and feminine versions, the body that everybody is supposed to want to be is a *particular* fantasy—a white-Western, bourgeois ideal—masquerading as a universal norm,[4] serving the interests of transnational capitalism, and reflecting the same systemic injustices that enable some people to spend loads of money enhancing or fixing their flesh, while others have difficulty meeting their basic bodily needs. A postcolonial perspective illuminates how the iconography of corporeal perfection makes its way around the globe and into our imaginations, where it stirs our anxieties and sparks our aspirations to find happiness through physical improvement. This perspective reveals how commercial images colonize our self-perceptions not only through obvious channels such as advertisements, which are designed to make us feel bad so we'll buy the products they are promoting, but also through discourses that aim to make us feel better, including self-help enticements to "take charge" of our health, "blast" belly fat, "overcome" disability, "defy" aging, "fight" cancer, and "triumph over" pain. The language of conquest figures prominently in the culture of somatic improvement, revealing the colonial paradigm at its core. Ultimately, a postcolonial analysis exposes two key strategies in the pursuit of a better body: controlling the flesh and converting it to the normative ideal.

Finally, my analysis of body shame is indebted to the work of feminist scholars whose writings unmask and challenge intersecting social injustices and the superiority complexes supporting them. Building on the notion that "biology is not destiny,"[5] feminist scholars expose "femininity" and "masculinity" to be social scripts that are produced and performed in conjunction with race, class, sexuality, age, culture, religion, and related variables. Their work illuminates the imprisoning effects of normative gender narratives in the lives of diverse women and men. One such narrative depicts females as "closer" to the flesh than males (i.e. more defined by bodily processes and oriented by carnal desires), and thus as needing more bodily restraint and supervision than males. Because of women's historic association with physicality, and because feminine body norms are still central vehicles for patriarchal control, my discussion throughout *Shameful Bodies* focuses primarily on women, even as it includes multiple examples of the damage men experience when they internalize the gender/ body rules that underwrite the culture of physical improvement.

Despite my reliance on the frameworks, insights, and analytic tools of various academic disciplines, fellow scholars are not the main audience I have in mind for this book (although I'd be thrilled if they found it useful). I am most interested in engaging students like the ones I teach—male and female undergraduates with little or no formal training in the field of religion. My general hope is that my analysis of the culture of physical improvement will help them see the broad relevance of the study of religion beyond conventional religious topics and contexts. My more specific hope is that this analysis will help readers recognize the *social* (i.e. economic, historical, political, cultural) and *religious* roots of the seemingly private experience of body shame. Once we understand this shame not as a personal truth but as a culturally/religiously conditioned reaction to narratives and images that teach us to judge and rank corporeal diversity according to a normative ideal, we can begin the process of decolonizing our imaginations and consciously developing an alternative approach to physical improvement, one that affirms rather than denies the irreducible diversity, interconnection, and impermanence of embodied life. In so doing, we can redirect our energy to the momentum of contemporary liberation movements, whose central dynamic is the transformation of shame into self-love and empathy for others.

Nuancing criticism of the culture of physical improvement

My critique of the culture of physical improvement is not meant to be a totalizing rejection of *all* efforts to change how our bodies look, act, and feel.

My experience of chronic pain attests to the value of various remedies—from ibuprofen, to yoga, to surgery. Like me, many people appreciate the prosthetic devices that increase their access to a world designed for the nondisabled. Similarly, countless people with chronic diseases benefit from medical interventions—conventional and alternative. Some individuals report feeling more energetic after losing weight, and many enjoy extended longevity thanks to effective healthcare. While these scenarios can be seen as examples of physical improvement, none are necessarily predicated on controlling/conforming the body to a normative ideal, and that's where my critique is aimed.

This critique targets a particular story about physical improvement: one that serves the interests of global capitalism; one whose iconography constructs a symbolic hierarchy of bodies that reinforces social inequalities; one whose moral codes and unrealistic expectations foster judgment and aggression toward bodily configurations and conditions that don't resemble the singular ideal; one whose rhetoric and rituals encourage us to control and conform our one-of-a-kind bodies—to homogenize their eccentricities and deny their fragility—and leave us feeling alienated from our own flesh. I also challenge both the conception of selfhood that the salvation myth of physical perfection promotes—the self-willed, self-sufficient individual—and the fast-paced, productivity-driven, achievement-oriented culture this idealized body/self represents.

The drawback of a book that explores the cultural/religious norms and narratives that shape topics as broad-ranging as disability, weight, chronic pain and illness, and aging is that it will inevitably gloss over or omit any number of salient issues and concerns these topics raise. One could spend a lifetime deconstructing the fantasy of somatic perfection discussed in Part I; and one could write several books on any of the specific body issues examined in Part II—not to mention various other intersecting issues that are common sources of body shame, for example, sexual desire, skin tone, menstruation, and body hair. This book is far from exhaustive on the topics it seeks to examine. My aim is not to provide the final word on the culture of physical improvement, but to stimulate critical analysis of its prominent beliefs, images, rituals, and moral codes in relation to traditional religion. Ultimately, I hope to stir more conversation about the ways this culture affects our feelings about our particular incarnation and our relationships with each other.

In societies like ours, where industry, speed, productivity, and self-mastery are supreme values, bodies that are chronically sick, in pain, impaired, fat, and old represent everything we have been taught to disdain: loss of control, inefficiency, dependence on others, and having to slow down. These bodies become repositories for feelings that are difficult to recognize in ourselves: fear, vulnerability, and aversion. They remind us of the gradual decay that all who live long enough will inevitably experience—the very finitude that the culture of physical improvement conditions us to deny, defy, or vanquish. Stepping off the commercially sponsored "better body" treadmill can strengthen our sense of solidarity with and appreciation for the plural and evolving nature of physicality—our own and that of others. Ultimately, taking this step may allow us to give ourselves the same kind of radical acceptance, responsible care, and uncompromising respect that everybody wants, needs, and deserves, while freeing us to devote our time, energy, and attention to address the real sources of human misery. In the end, how we relate to our own bodies—in all their fragility, interdependence, biodiversity, and unpredictability—influences not only how we see and interact with others, but also how we relate to life itself.

PART ONE

1

Deconstructing the "better body" story

Prior to the years when my hip started hurting, my body was, according to dominant standards, both "normal" and "healthy." Not only was I physically well, but I'd come to enjoy a friendly relationship with my body. This was something I'd worked on for years in the aftermath of my adolescent eating disorder. From about the time I was 14 until I was 17, I waged an all-out war against my flesh, alternating between starving, bingeing, and purging, propelled by a ferocious desire to look like the actresses on *Charlie's Angels* or the models in *Seventeen* magazine (never mind that I've never been taller than 5'2"). It was the late 1970s, and terms like "anorexia" and "bulimia" were not yet part of mainstream society's lexicon. I was way too ashamed to tell anyone what I was doing. Ashamed *and scared*. I'd stopped menstruating, developed cavities for the first time in my life, and lived in fear of someone discovering my awful secret. This fear motivated me to stop most of the destructive behavior by the time I went to college. But I would need the skills and perspectives I gained from my undergraduate education to make the longer journey out of the self-negating mentality that made me sick in the first place.

I attended a college run by Benedictine nuns, who introduced me to feminism. This perspective enabled me to see that the real problem wasn't the size of my thighs but the dominant culture's tendency (which I had internalized) to value women based on their appearance. A mature group of friends, similarly empowered by the critical thinking learned in their classes, supported my recovery by affirming my struggle to change harmful thought patterns. During that period of my life, the academy was not just a place for intellectual expansion, but also a context for personal growth and healing. By the time I graduated from college, thinness was no longer my ultimate purpose. I'd found more interesting things to think about than fat grams and calories. An endless array of philosophical conundrums and social problems needed my attention. I wanted to make the world a better place, to improve something larger than my body.

The story of a "better body"

Almost four decades later, I still feel grief and regret when I think back on the years I spent torturing myself. How could I have been so convinced that my happiness depended on being slimmer? Why had I felt such deep hostility and mistrust toward my body? The relevancy of such questions hasn't waned with years. In fact, these questions feel more urgent than ever as I listen to many of my female students describe their struggles with body-image. I'm talking about fiercely beautiful, physically healthy, intelligent young women who, to varying degrees, live in a perpetual state of war with their flesh. Witnessing the pain, their lack of acceptance, creates compels me to keep asking and exploring: Why are so many of us deeply dissatisfied with our bodies? Why are we convinced we need to improve them? And what do we mean by a *better body* anyway?

nan.

At first glance, this question may seem too obvious to ask. What heavy-set person wouldn't want to lose weight? What older person wouldn't want to look and feel younger? Why would anyone who is chronically sick, physically impaired, or suffering from persistent pain not do whatever it takes to be more "normal" and "healthy?" These questions may not seem parallel, but investigating the idea of "improvement" they presume reveals connections we may not have anticipated.

Indeed, the very notion of a "better body" is based on beliefs we would do well to examine. According to the *Merriam-Webster Online Dictionary*, "better" means "higher in quality," "more skillful," "more attractive, appealing, effective, and useful." Similarly, "improve" means "to enhance in value or quality," "to make better."[1] Clearly, "better" and "improve" are comparative terms. They assume and imply inferiority and superiority. When applied to bodies, these terms raise critical questions: How do we know that certain forms of physicality are superior in quality, skill, or appeal? Superior to what? Who decides?

These preliminary questions point to an assumption I make throughout this book: Our expectations of how bodies are *supposed* to look, act, and feel are neither natural nor universal. In fact, the meaning of "physical improvement" is not self-evident, but reflects particular interpretations of somatic traits, processes, and conditions. In other words, the notion of a "better body" is a socially constructed fiction, a contemporary salvation myth. This myth unfolds along a trajectory from "flawed" to "fixed," "undesirable" to "attractive," "sick" to "cured," "defective" to "normal," and, importantly, *unhappy to happy*. But where did this storyline come from? Who is narrating this drama? What are its psychic, social, physical, and spiritual consequences? Are there any alternative narratives? Let's begin exploring these questions by identifying the corporeal ideal in relation to which "improvement" is typically defined.

Commercial fantasies of physical perfection

In developed Western societies today, the salvation myth of physical improvement is constructed in reference to a fantasy of bodily "perfection" that permeates commercial culture. Both the homogeneity of this fantasy and its pervasiveness authorize the "ideal" body to function as a perfect example of how all bodies should look, act, and feel, and this example provides a yardstick—a norm—for measuring the merits (or lack thereof) of every body. By replicating this perfect form *ad nauseam*, mass media images have normalized it. Thus I refer to it as a "normative ideal"—even though it's anything but normal! Ultimately, the ideal body is the standard vision to which people are encouraged to compare themselves as they work to make their bodies "better."

Visual characteristics of exemplary physiques vary between men and women. Whereas the feminine ideal (Figure 1.1) is tall and lithe, soft and hairless, and often postured in ways that appear awkward or unbalanced, the idealized masculine form is unambiguously strong, sturdy, and ready for action (Figure 1.2). Indeed, athleticism is a visual marker of the ideal male form, whose fitness is displayed through sculpted abs and limbs and chiseled chins. For women, of course, the mandate is thinness—with or without well-defined muscles. In addition, youth is an essential feature of female beauty because of its association with women's sexual and reproductive capacities. To a lesser extent, youth is important for the ideal male body as well insofar as it leverages such "manly" qualities as independence and virility—hallmarks of masculine sexuality and success in mainstream popular culture.

Male or female, the physical ideal is defined in association with economic and ethnic privilege. It's typically depicted in affluent settings (e.g. tropical beach) or garnished with expensive clothing and other markers of affluence (e.g. sparkling jewelry). A disproportionate number of perfect bodies are blond and Anglo-Saxon, representing what some have described as an implicitly white Protestant ideal.[2] Those that do have darker skin often have Caucasian-looking features (thin lips and nose) or are posed in sexualized positions or settings that suggest their proximity to nature (e.g. a jungle), thus reinforcing racist stereotypes of people of color as more animalistic and exotic.[3]

FIGURE 1.1 *Women on the beach—"Goddess of Summer"* © *Yuri_Arcurs.*
Source: *Getty Images.*

FIGURE 1.2 *Australian Olympic Swim* © *Ryan Pierse.*
Source: *Getty Images.*

Commercially defined ideal bodies are frequently positioned in ways that suggest heterosexist attraction—often with a male figure gazing at an "attractive" female. The Western artistic-religious trope that John Berger described over 40 years ago—namely, of "woman as sexual object" for the male gaze—still permeates commercial images today:

> Men act and women appear. Men look at women. Women watch themselves being looked at. This determines not only most relations between men and women, but also the relation of women to themselves [and, I would add, *among* themselves].[4]

Whether endowed with the prerogative to look or the power to attract, idealized bodies appear to epitomize good health: free of pain, no trace of disease, and unencumbered by physical impairments, debility, or limits. You don't see many models or actors in wheelchairs selling shampoo, beer, or the latest wireless service. And in a consumer-oriented culture, selling things is the ideal body's primary purpose.[5]

The symbolic hierarchy of bodies and the "normalizing gaze"

Even a cursory glance at this familiar fantasy of physical perfection reveals how the ideal body gains its authority/appeal through its visible association with various forms of social privilege. If we zoom in a little closer, however, we can see that this ideal is designed not only in connection with what is socially *desired*, but also in contrast to what is commonly *feared*: the lack of control, dependence, inefficiency, and unpredictability that certain physical traits or conditions represent. Such dreaded qualities are often associated with bodies that are fat, old, impaired, chronically sick or in pain, or some (or all) of the above—bodies whose irregularities, vulnerabilities, or limits do not properly conform to the normative ideal. These nonconforming bodies may also be dark, gay, poor, or marginalized in other ways. Whatever their particular configuration, such physiques are relegated to the lower ranks of the *symbolic hierarchy of bodies*: the somatic taxonomy that gives the normative ideal its superior status.

This hierarchy permeates the visual landscape of commercial culture. It is a ranking system constructed through what Michel Foucault called the "normalizing gaze"—a way of seeing that measures, classifies, compares, and judges physical differences according to a singular standard.[6] This optic gained prominence during the modern period as medical science pathologized bodies that deviated from the Anglo-Saxon, bourgeois ideal, and as capitalist economies delegated inefficient or "unproductive" bodies (e.g. people who were sick, poor, insane, or disabled) to society's margins.[7] Throughout this process, neither scientific perspectives nor the growing influence of capitalism entirely replaced traditional religion's *moral* interpretations of bodily behaviors and conditions. Rather, modern institutions tacitly incorporated concepts like "sin" and "salvation" into their ideologies of "deviance" and "normalcy," "depravity" and "progress," "sickness" and "health," secularizing religious categories in the name of scientific "objectivity."

Despite its supposed neutrality, the "normalizing gaze" is a shaming gaze. Circulated through commercially manufactured images and the scientifically informed discourses of self-help culture, this way of seeing teaches us to distinguish between "right" and "wrong" bodies, to internalize this distinction, and to evaluate and improve ourselves accordingly. Based on the moral–scientific–aesthetic taxonomy this gaze constructs, some bodies are good, healthy, and beautiful, while others are degenerate, sick, and ugly.[8] The same gaze that generates awe and admiration of figures at the top directs dread, gawking, and pity at those at the bottom. This somatic ranking provides a symbolic backdrop for the salvation myth of physical improvement.

Compared to the singularity of the ideal at the summit of this corporeal hierarchy, the diversity of low-ranking physiques is enormous, as variables such as age, size, chronic pain or illness, and disability interface with differences in race, class, sexuality, religion, and other social variables. Despite their diversity, however, anomalous bodies are connected by their "failure"—or, as I prefer to see it, their *refusal*—to comply with prevailing body norms. Whether involuntary or intended, this refusal has consequences. As disabilities theorist Rosemarie Garland Thomson observes, "Corporeal departures from dominant expectations never go uninterpreted or unpunished, and conformities are almost always rewarded."[9] For nonconforming bodies, punishments come in the form of ostracism, stereotypes, invisiblization, dehumanization, discrimination, self-hatred, and shame. Situated in stark contrast to the flawless form at the hierarchy's apex, representing all that people in Western capitalist societies are conditioned to loathe and fear, these unorthodox bodies are deemed in dire need of improvement. Their corporeal "sins" require forgiveness. They are our culture's *shameful bodies*.

Shameful bodies and body shame

Shameful means "very bad," or "bad enough to be ashamed."[10] This definition seems to suggest that something "shameful" is not only full of shame (shame-full), but somehow deserving of shame, as if its badness were intrinsic to it. Of the various meanings of "shame" *Merriam Webster* offers, the one defining shame as the feeling of "dishonor" or "disgrace" is most illuminating for my purposes, for it aptly conveys how many people experience their bodies, namely, as inadequate, wrong, humiliating.[11] This definition resembles the one shame researcher Brené Brown uses. Brown defines "shame" as "the intensely painful feeling or experience of believing we are flawed and therefore unworthy of love and belonging." Brown distinguishes shame from guilt: whereas guilt involves an internal voice that says "I *did* something bad," the voice of shame says, "I *am* bad." She also differentiates between shame, which has an abiding quality, and embarrassment, which is usually temporary. Her research suggests that the feeling of shame is often manifest in the sense of never being "good enough."[12]

Shame is often thought of as a private emotion. And yet, to paraphrase anthropologist Mary Douglas, where there is shame, there is a system.[13] As Brown points out, shame tends to flourish in cultures that are "steeped in comparison"[14]—cultures such as that of the United States, where ideas like "getting ahead" or "keeping up with the Jones" are as pervasive as the air we breathe. This comparative/competitive ethos is embedded in the symbolic hierarchy of bodies, which mirrors patterns of inequality and privilege within the social order, including well-known disparities in wealth, education, health care, and political representation based on race, gender, class, and physical (dis)ability. In this context of social injustice, the shame people feel about their bodies can be seen as a specific form of internalized oppression: an inner sense of inferiority that reflects the prevailing social/symbolic hierarchies that commercially defined visions of somatic perfection reflect and reinforce. To the extent that we compare ourselves to the normative ideal, our own bodies will never be good enough.

Brown's research also demonstrates a connection between shame and perfectionism, particularly among women, who repeatedly report feeling the need to look, act, and be "perfect" and who consequently feel inadequate. Brown defines "perfectionism" as "a self-destructive and addictive belief system that fuels this primary thought: *If I look perfect and do everything perfectly, I can avoid or minimize the painful feelings of shame, judgment, and blame.*" Oriented by an unattainable ideal, perfectionism not only sets you up for failure; it fosters the potentially addictive, exhausting habit of trying to achieve the impossible. In the end, the cycle of attempting-and-failing-to-be-flawless perpetuates the shame perfectionists are trying to avoid.[15]

The connection between shame and perfection illuminates a painful irony of the culture of physical improvement: the mission to enhance or fix our bodies often leaves us feeling estranged from the very flesh we long to inhabit. This estrangement is reason enough to investigate the external sources of internal feelings of badness. Additionally, we may not realize how the criticisms we direct at our own bodies perpetuate similar judgments of other people's physiques, or how our efforts to normalize our corporeal irregularities may contribute to a society in which certain forms of human physicality are considered wrong, disgusting, pitiable, unworthy. In short, our socially induced habit of shaming our bodies for being "less-than-perfect" trains us to find faults in the flesh of others. All the more reason to investigate the sources and dynamics of body shame and explore ways to transform it.

Throughout this book, I suggest that body shame is not a natural response to our physical vulnerabilities, particularities, and limits, but a culturally/religiously conditioned reaction to our bodies' refusals to comply with the rules that emanate from the normative ideal. This understanding relocates the source of the negativity we frequently direct at our bodies and the bodies of others—from the frailties and peculiarities of our flesh to the symbolic/social systems that idealize certain incarnations while shaming others.

Because of its deep roots in commercial culture, the better body quest may seem like an entirely secular phenomenon. But this is largely because we've learned to see it as such. Indeed, the feelings of shame this quest frequently generates are our first clue that it has quasi-religious, moral dimensions. And when we consider how for many people the mission to create a better body functions as a quest for salvation—a search for happiness, health, and healing—its distinctively secular character is even less clear. Religion's significant (though largely hidden) role in the culture of physical improvement becomes apparent when we investigate

- the religious-like function of the pursuit of physical improvement;
- some traditional Christian narratives embedded in this pursuit;
- the quasi-religious features of the better-body crusade (i.e. beliefs, images, rituals, moral codes); and
- the spiritual or existential needs that attract us to this mission.

We will explore these religious dimensions of the culture of physical improvement in the remaining chapters of Part I.

2

Christianity's hidden contributions to the culture of physical improvement

It's probably no coincidence that my scholarly work has focused on questions relating to religion, gender, and embodiment. Both my parents were medical professionals and thus concerned about physical well-being. My dad is a retired family physician, and my mom kept her RN (registered nurse) license current for over five decades, even though she stopped working outside the home when her five children started arriving. My parents' traditionally gendered division of labor synched well with the teachings of their Catholic faith, which emphasized the "complementary" gifts of men and women (i.e. men as leaders and women as helpers). Although both my mom and dad now heartily reject this gender ideology, there's no denying that traditional Catholicism infused my youth.

Looking back, I now see that my family had another religion, or something akin to "religion," though we never saw it as such. This secondary faith revolved around my brothers' sports activities. All three of them were state champion athletes in high school, having trained diligently to cultivate their somatic skills and talents. The rituals, symbols, rules, and goals surrounding their team practices and competitions fostered a tangible sense of community and purpose—not unlike the sense of belonging and shared values Catholicism instilled—both in my white, middle-class family and in the small, rural Minnesota town where we lived. It was the 1970s and 1980s, and neither my parents, nor my sister, nor I gave any thought to the male preeminence in the Catholic Church or in my family's devotion to boys' sports. When my sister and I were not cheering on our brothers in their athletic contests (literally, we were cheerleaders!), or watching them serve as altar boys at Mass (a role we were not, as females, qualified to perform), we happily spent our free time shopping or searching women's magazines for tips on the latest looks and fashions.

Prior to studying religion in college and later in graduate school, three unexamined assumptions prevented me from noticing the intersections between these crucial facets of my upbringing (i.e. religion, physicality, and gender). First, I saw religion as something separate from the rest of society—something essentially different from "secular" aspects of life. Second, I thought religion was all about what you believed—that it had nothing to do with your body (besides the rule against premarital sex). Third, I believed the gendered practices of my tradition, which placed authority in the hands of men, reflected natural or God-given differences between males and females. These assumptions stopped me from seeing the overlap between religion and culture, the body's central role in spirituality, and religion's power to interpret—not simply reflect—the meaning of humans' physical diversity.

What is "religion?" A fluid, functional definition

Throughout history, people have created and turned to religions in their search for meaning and serenity amid the difficulties, uncertainties, and mysteries of life. Through their various stories, teachings, symbols, and rituals, religious traditions give their members a deeply felt sense of what's most important in life, an ultimate purpose and perspective in relation to which everything else—all problems and possibilities—can be understood.

This short description of "religion" highlights religion's *human* origins and its historic *functions*. In this view, religion is defined not by certain characteristics that make it categorically unique and distinct from the rest of society, but by the role it plays in helping people cultivate a sense of ultimate meaning and providing a set of tools and guidelines for pursuing that sacred truth. This functional definition of religion deconstructs any solid boundaries between "religion" and "culture," "spiritual" and "secular," "sacred" and "profane." This definition illuminates how the beliefs, stories, and behaviors comprising traditions that are commonly described as "religious" (e.g. Hinduism, Buddhism, Judaism, Christianity, Islam) are evolving systems that are constantly being reshaped by "nonreligious" practices and worldviews in the context of specific historical circumstances. A fluid, functional understanding of religion also enables us to recognize the meaning-giving, quasi-religious aspects of secular discourses, images, narratives, and rituals in contemporary society, including those that comprise the quest for a better body.

A changing religious landscape

It's interesting to consider the changing landscape of religion today in light of religion's historical role in fostering people's sense of ultimate meaning and purpose. In contemporary Western societies, traditional religions do not necessarily play a direct role in shaping people's sense of what's most important. In the United States, for example, the fastest growing religious identity is "unaffiliated." This group, which researchers refer to as "nones," comprises an increasing portion of the American population. Thirty-two percent of those under 30 are "nones."[1] Yet the apparent decline in conventional religion's influence in the lives of some is complicated by the fact that many others still strongly identify with institutional forms of faith—not only in the United States, but especially in the global south.

This mixed trend is further complicated by another interesting phenomenon, namely, the religious-like function of many seemingly secular activities and their value systems—from sports, Hip Hop, and Harry Potter, to political ceremonies and even surfing.[2] By highlighting how such phenomena use rituals, symbols, moral codes, and salvation myths to foster quasi-spiritual experiences and provide deep sources of meaning among those who participate in them, a number of scholars of religion share my perception that various forms of "secular" culture can be seen as functionally religious.[3] This perception does not imply that these cultural phenomena are, *in fact*, a religion. But it does raise the fascinating question womanist scholar Monica Miller asks: What is "religious" about religion?[4]

One of my favorite analyses of the religious-like function of a seemingly secular value system is David Loy's "The Religion of the Market." In this essay, Loy illuminates how the system of global capitalism functions as a kind of "world religion" by telling us what's most important in life (i.e. material wealth) and what we need to do to be "saved" (i.e. make and spend lots of money).[5] According to Loy, "the Market is becoming the first truly world religion, binding all corners of the globe more and more tightly to a worldview and set of values whose religious role we overlook only because we insist on seeing them as 'secular.'"[6] Despite the ecological devastation and the extreme wealth disparity this commercially oriented value system fosters, most people in developed societies support the religion of the market because its omnipresence makes it seem natural and because the conversion tactics of its secular theology are incredibly seductive.[7] A multibillion dollar advertising industry manufactures and stimulates desires for products it promises will make us happy.

Commercial underpinnings of our devotion to physical improvement

Loy's analysis of the religion of the market is especially interesting for my purposes because it aptly describes the socioeconomic system that sponsors the quest for physical improvement. The salvation myth of somatic perfection plays a crucial role in keeping this system running smoothly. Deployed to sell everything from underwear to running shoes (Figures 2.1 and 2.2), the ideal body is both a linchpin of consumer capitalism and a commodity in itself. Theologian Sharon Betcher observes, "The Western, idealized self, cosmetically and prosthetically enhanced, has become… the most lucrative item for sale in the global market place."[8] Like the shiny new things it helps to sell, the flawless physique is itself a status symbol that communicates the prestige and authority of its "owner," while tacitly affirming the "truth" of the social/symbolic system that privileges some bodies over others.

Perhaps it's no coincidence that as the authority of traditional religions has shifted, advanced capitalist societies have increasingly promoted the individual body as a source of profound meaning. As psychotherapist and cultural critic Susie Orbach observes, several overlapping social trends have made physical improvement a "project" of utmost value:

> Over the past thirty years, the new grammar of visual culture, the notion of the consumer as empowered, the workings of the diet, pharmaceutical, food, cosmetic surgery and style industries, and the democratization of aspiration have made us view the body we live in as a body we can, must, and should perfect.[9]

Indeed, these developments encourage a kind of *devotion* to a better body as a means for cultivating a sense of identity, worth, and purpose—and for compensating for feelings of inadequacy. Because the ideal form is so strongly associated with the material privilege that consumer culture depicts as a supreme value, the "project" of normalizing or perfecting one's flesh functions as a means for climbing the social ladder to the "good life."

The degree to which people derive meaning from their efforts to improve their bodies varies considerably. While many people in developed Western societies modify their appearance in some way (e.g. combing or styling their

FIGURE 2.1 *David Beckham in Armani underwear © Kevin Sam.*
Source: *Getty Images.*

hair, wearing makeup, shaving), some make physical enhancement a priority, and some go to extreme measures, as is the case with those addicted to cosmetic surgery. Some seek to mitigate physical pain or other debilitating ailments; yet even this goal is pursued with varying magnitudes of fervor. Just as members of historic religions practice their faith with different levels of earnestness, so too people attempt to fix or cure their bodies with varying degrees of intensity. Whatever our relationship to the normative ideal—whether we zealously aspire to embody it, intentionally reject it, unknowingly accept it, or find ourselves simultaneously drawn to and hating it—commercial culture encourages everyone to internalize the salvation myth of a better body,

FIGURE 2.2 *"Kelly Brook Unveils new Reebok Billboard"* © Mike Marsland. *Source: Getty Images.*

to make this story an abiding source of meaning and a decisive guide for self-definition.

Classic Christian narratives and the salvation myth of physical improvement

Whether or not you are religious, you live in a society that has been influenced by the narratives and norms of traditional religion. In the West, the prevalence of Christianity has given it the power to influence many people's worldviews, values, and habits—including those who do not identify with this tradition. Some of Christianity's stories are part of our cultural DNA; they encode the structure and provide instructions for many of the "nonreligious" discourses that shape our collective imagination. Three prominent Christian narratives are especially relevant for examining the culture of physical improvement: 1) the body's "pivotal" role in the quest for salvation; 2) women's association with physicality; and 3) the homogenized perfection of bodies in the heavenly afterlife. Such narratives emerged in the writings of early Christian leaders, whose ideas set the stage for the development of a theological tradition that has been simultaneously preoccupied with and ambivalent about human flesh.

The body as the "pivot of salvation"

Throughout Christian history, a doctrinal affirmation of the intrinsic goodness of human physicality coexisted with repeated warnings about the liabilities of the flesh: its unpredictability and susceptibility to sin, decay, and death—all of which needed to be contained and eventually transcended on the path to spiritual perfection. Though early Christian theologians rejected the Platonic view of the body as a "prison," they nevertheless saw the body as a potential impediment on the path of spiritual progress.

Christianity's earliest texts demonstrate this ambivalence toward physicality. In his letter to the Galatians (54 C.E.), for example, Paul admonishes Jesus' followers to "Live by the Spirit," and not to "gratify the desires of the flesh." According to Paul, "what the flesh desires is opposed to the Spirit, and what the Spirit desires is opposed to the flesh" (Gal. 5:16–17). As oppositional as this rhetoric sounds, New Testament scholars have shown that Paul's attitude toward physicality was complicated. For him, "flesh" was a shorthand way of referring to the whole person (body and soul) in her or his fallen state—a state that anticipated the "spiritual body" of the resurrection. Whereas "flesh" (sarx) represents humans' fallible nature, "the body" (soma) is "the temple of the Holy Spirit" (1 Cor. 6:19).[10]

Early church leaders extend and elaborate Paul's ambivalence toward physicality. The belief that the divine took on human flesh in the person of Jesus led Origen of Alexandria (circa 200) to tell Christians not to despise their bodies, lest in so doing they despise Christ.[11] Around the same time, Tertullian argued against his Gnostic opponents that "the flesh is the pivot of salvation" because it links the soul to God.[12] Two centuries later, Augustine described the body as the "spouse of the soul" and said Christians should be taught "to love their bodies that they may take care of them reasonably and wisely."[13] Such education was necessary because physicality was the primary, tangible instrument for attaining spiritual purity: "When the body is punished, the soul is purified," Origen explained.[14] Somewhat ironically, classic Christian authors were intensely preoccupied with the body, even as they cautioned against giving into its demands for attention.

Despite the body's "pivotal" role in the drama of spiritual perfection, early church leaders understood corporeality to be subordinate to the beauty, intelligence, and will of the soul. Though Augustine described the body as the "spouse" of the soul, he also said, "It is stupid to deny that the soul is better than the body." Elsewhere he referred to the body as humans' "heaviest bond" and urged Christians to "rise above" their carnal urges.[15] Similarly, Jerome characterized the flesh as a "burden" the soul must bear and try to subdue on its earthly pilgrimage,[16] and Basil of Ancrya saw it as weighing down the "wings of the soul," which might otherwise soar to the heights of heavenly holiness.[17] Ultimately, whether the body was a "temple" or "tomb" depended on one's ability to master its cravings.[18]

The body's potential to advance or impede spiritual progress was vividly on display in the ascetic practices of early and medieval Christians. In an attempt to distinguish themselves from ordinary believers, Christian ascetics denied their corporeal cravings (for food, sex, and the company of others) and sometimes mortified their bodies (wearing hair shirts or flagellating themselves). As "spiritual athletes," these Christians disciplined their desires in earnest pursuit of holiness, valiantly battling demons of lust, boredom, pain, sickness, anger, and pride. For them, the virtuously disciplined flesh expressed and anticipated the incorruptible body in the life to come.[19] Ascetic practices may appear to dualistically disparage the flesh in favor of the spirit. But these disciplines affirmed the intimacy between body and soul that Christians of this era took for granted. Paradoxically, ascetic renunciation rigorously and intentionally *engaged* the flesh in the effort to transcend it. As the "pivot of salvation," physicality was not only a problem but an opportunity.

There are obvious differences between the historical practices, beliefs, contexts, and aspirations of Christian ascetics and those of people today who seek happiness, health, and healing through physical improvement. Whereas ascetics' pursuit of self-mastery through controlling the body expressed a profound rejection of prevailing social norms and systems, which they perceived to be corrupt, the commercial quest for a better body is oriented by definitions of health, normalcy, and beauty that reflect the dominant status quo. Whereas ascetics cultivated conformity to a spiritual ideal, rather than the "vainglory" of social approval, today's better body pursuits are based on compliance with a commercial ideal and earn you praise in the eyes of others. These differences are important because, as well shall see, they point to elements in the Christian tradition that can be used to challenge the better body storyline.

Despite such differences, however, the ascetic tradition overlaps with the contemporary quest for a better body in interesting ways. Both cast the body in a leading role in the pursuit of salvation (i.e. happiness, health, healing). Both depict physicality as simultaneously a liability and an opportunity: the body is the site of praise or blame, depending on how well you control it. Both the ascetic and commercial narratives enlist the flesh to construct a worldview characterized by aggressive combat against "demons" such as gluttony, pain, and disease. Both position the body as a potential "enemy" that needs to be conquered, and as an intimate ally in the quest for inner progress.[20] And both promote the paradoxical pursuit of transcendence *from* and *through* the flesh.

Women and the body: The patriarchal legacy

The story of the body's pivotal role in Christian spirituality intersects with another narrative that shapes the quest for physical improvement today: women's association with physicality. Throughout Christian history, the fiction that women are more carnal than men—that they are more naturally susceptible to (and preoccupied with) the corporeal side of existence—overlapped with the story of the body's inferiority and corruptibility and its corresponding need for supervision, regulation, and redemption. Woven together, these narratives define women through the very flesh they must monitor and master in order to be virtuous. The lingering influence of this legacy is apparent in the multiple ways women today are conditioned to distinguish their worth and pursue happiness, power, and fulfillment through physical improvement.

In traditional Christian theology, the woman/body association takes its cue from patriarchal interpretations of the second creation myth. Ignoring the ambiguity of the Hebrew meaning of *'adham*—the term refers generically to humankind, and not simply to a man named Adam[21]—early church leaders pointed to Eve's derivation from Adam's flesh as proof that females represent the inferior/corporeal side of human existence. In their eyes, Eve's designation as Adam's "helper" indicated women's primary role in caring for the body's needs via domestic labor and childcare, and Eve's lack of restraint in eating the forbidden fruit revealed females' susceptibility to bodily cravings. The narrative linking women's subordination with the inferiority of the flesh is recycled in New Testament texts like 1 Timothy 2.11–15, where women are ordered to be silent and submissive because of Eve's shameful transgression.

The church fathers repeatedly pointed to Eve's disobedience as evidence of women's susceptibility to sin and temptation and the subsequent need for their control and supervision. In the fourth century, for example, the bishop Ambrose pointed out that "the woman was the first to be deceived and she deceived the man."[22] In Augustine's view, this fateful act was the result of woman's "small intelligence" and her corresponding tendency to live "more in accordance with the promptings of the inferior flesh."[23] Ambrose explained this tendency by reminding us of Eve's derivation from Adam's body: she was made from his rib, not his soul.[24] While these fathers' interpretations of the Fall symbolically linked females and flesh, their commentaries implicitly equated males with the superior realm of mind and spirit.[25]

The woman/body nexus contributed to a view of females as sexual temptresses who threatened men's spiritual progress by inciting their lust. Thus, Jerome warned male virgins to wrap their hands in their robes before giving the sign of peace, lest the touch of a woman ignite their passion.[26] For Augustine, the agonizing conflict between love for God and attraction to women is resolved only when he commits to celibacy. Interestingly, Basil of Ancrya interpreted women's innate sexual desirability as compensation for their inferior rank in the divine scheme of things: the Creator bestowed female bodies with the power of sexual attraction so women would not be completely helpless in their subordination to men.[27] Women's ability to seduce and even imprison men was not, however, a proactive power; rather, it revealed their passive "nature." Disobeying this "nature" was tantamount to defying God: was it not Eve's self-willed audacity that led to humanity's downfall? For centuries, male Christian leaders argued that the damning consequences of Eve's agency "proved" women were not suited for leadership but should be confined to the domestic sphere, where they could pursue a career of consecrated virginity, or fulfill their divinely sanctioned duty of procreating children and serving their husbands.[28]

The slippage between Eve and the generic "woman" in these writings implied that all women are blameworthy, untrustworthy, and deserving of shame. Throughout Christian history, Eve's disobedience is repeatedly invoked to vilify women in general. Though men's bodies were also seen as suspect among the church fathers, the most serious contempt was reserved for unruly female flesh. Feminist theologians Elizabeth Stuart and Lisa Isherwood note that what disturbed male theologians most about women's bodies "was their state of flux and change . . . which was taken to symbolize the disorder and chaos that constantly threatened to engulf and destroy the patriarchal, sacred order."[29] Perhaps not surprisingly, the carnal, insubordinate, vilified image of Eve was frequently juxtaposed with the virginal, obedient, redeeming image of Mary, creating a bad woman/good woman moral typology that is not unfamiliar today.

The patriarchal association of women with the inferior, evolving, vulnerable, and finite realm of the flesh was reinvented throughout Christian history. Though the characters, backdrop, and details of this story have varied over time, the master narrative repeatedly emphasized women's susceptibility to sin, their dangerous powers of seduction, their bodies' unruliness, and their need for control and supervision. However antiquated it seems, this narrative still influences how many women feel about their bodies. Today, however, the story is communicated not primarily by church authorities but by the beliefs, images, codes, and rituals of the culture of physical improvement. From an early age, this culture teaches girls two things: 1) that how they look matters (a lot!) and 2) that there is always room for improvement. These crucial lessons set girls up to be eager consumers of products and programs designed to enhance their beauty, cover their flaws, and make them worthy. Without question, women today seek to control and correct their bodies for reasons that differ dramatically from those of their historical sisters. Yet their efforts are similarly guided by a storyline that makes physicality pivotal to female identity, worth, and power.

Heavenly (eschatological) perfection

Both the story of the body's pivotal role in the quest for salvation and women's precarious situation in this drama overlap with a third Christian narrative that echoes in today's culture of physical improvement: the anticipated redemption/perfection of the flesh at the end of time. A vision of resurrected bodies as flawless is central to classic Christian eschatology (the part of theology that deals with the final judgment and the afterlife). In the eschatological storyline, virtuous believers will enjoy the rewards of eternal life in flesh that is fit for paradise. Freed from the stains of sin, corruption, and death that hamper life on earth, resurrected bodies represent an angelic/perfected state—relieved of (and redeemed from) the burdens, needs, changes, and limits of embodied life.

In her essay, "Heavenly Bodies," historian Candida Moss describes how early church leaders envisioned bodies in the resurrection as having been "cleansed" of their imperfections and afflictions—their deformities and diseases erased in a manner prefigured by the miraculous healings of Jesus.[30] In Moss' analysis, the removal of bodily "defects" in paradise was part of the narrative of salvation history, whose storyline moved in a direction away from physical diversity/adversity, which signified humanity's sinful condition, toward a celestial future in which the sick are healed, the lame can walk, the crooked are made straight—in short, all physical maladies are cured. In this heavenly scenario, "salvation" is synonymous with "healing," which is synonymous with "curing," and God plays the role of cosmic/cosmetic surgeon, "augmenting, extracting, and appending in order to produce aesthetically pleasing, harmonious bodies."[31] By equating bodily redemption with physical perfection, early church leaders systematically removed somatic impairments, afflictions, and irregularities from God's kingdom. In so doing, they implicitly conflated disease, deformity, and disability with sin, impurity, and punishment. Ultimately, this eschatological cleansing interpreted bodily anomalies and ailments as signs of corruption in God's perfect creation.[32]

In historical Christianity, the heavenly narrative of somatic perfection looked backward as well as forward. Images of perfected/resurrected bodies mirrored the corporeal wholeness and shamelessness envisioned prior to humanity's fall into sin. This eschatological nostalgia for wholeness echoes in the longing to "get back to normal" described by some people living with chronic illness or pain, disability, or the processes of aging. Whether the ideal body that orients this thinking is located in the past (e.g. "before I got sick") or future (e.g. "when I'm cured"), the mentality itself diverts our attention away from the present and makes it very difficult to feel at peace in a body that refuses to be cured or improved.

The vision of "heavenly bodies" in Christian eschatology has several features in common with the salvation myth of physical improvement. The other-worldly character of these immortal bodies—they exist beyond the limits, sufferings, desires, and perishability of somatic life on earth—resembles the unattainable perfection commercial images construct with the help of various technologies and technicians. Moreover, even as they signal a return to paradise (i.e. prior to shame, disease, entropy, and death), resurrected bodies represent a utopic future, pursued through a forward-looking trajectory of "corrective transformation" that resembles the progress-oriented plot of the better body story.[33] Marketers of this story frequently solicit our attention with promises of anticipated improvement: "**10 MINUTES TO A BEAUTIFUL BUTT**," the April 2015 cover of *Health* magazine reads. Explicitly or not, most advertisements for better body products employ a before-and-after logic that mirrors the born-again thinking of eschatological improvement. That "improvement" is code for "normalizing" becomes apparent when we consider how—in both commercial culture and Christianity's classic vision of celestial perfection—preferable/superior bodies are created through the elimination of anatomical anomalies.

Historians may cringe at the connections I'm suggesting between early Christian visions of "heavenly bodies" and contemporary fantasies of the normative ideal that orients the pursuit of physical improvement. To be sure, the contexts and meanings surrounding these two visions of bodily perfection are very different. And yet, they share a common template: *a corporeal ideal whose abnormalities and afflictions have been erased*. Both embody a fantasy of flesh redeemed—a body whose flaws/sins have been fixed/forgiven. Both perpetuate what Sharon Betcher refers to as the "hallucination of wholeness"[34] that fosters judgment and aggression toward physiques that refuse to conform to the ideal. Both encourage every body to become devoted to the never-ending project of improvement.

The storylines described above reappear (in modified form) throughout my analysis of body issues in Part II of *Shameful Bodies*. Though not the only perspectives on embodiment traditional Christianity offers, these narratives have influenced Western attitudes toward physicality for centuries. In varying ways and degrees, they represent the controlling paradigm of religion, in which the body's unpredictable nature poses a problem, human biodiversity is judged and ranked, the mysteries surrounding embodiment are resolved with definitive rules, and the individual sin associated with bodily imperfections is overcome in other-worldly salvation. The influence of the values and beliefs these narratives convey need not be direct or uniform for it to be worthy of investigation. My analysis in the chapters that follow is more interested in intersections than causes.

The multiple and implicit ways some traditional Christian narratives are embedded in the culture of physical improvement become more apparent when we examine this culture's religious-like features: the beliefs, images, rituals, and moral codes that encourage us (especially women) to make our bodies "the pivot of salvation," and that define salvation in reference to an other-worldly fantasy of bodily perfection.

3

Religious-like features of the culture of physical improvement

Several months before I finally went through with hip surgery, I attended a semiformal, work-related dinner. I'd had misgivings about going to the event. My pain had been particularly aggravating that whole week, and I worried that being sedentary for an extended period would only make it worse. As it turned out, my worries were well founded. The dinner featured two-and-a-half hours of speakers, during which my discomfort escalated by the minute. Unluckily, my table was located just beneath the podium, which made inconspicuous trips to the bathroom (where I could do some pain-reducing impromptu yoga) impossible. I fidgeted in my seat the entire evening, trying to find a comfortable position, adjusting my dress and shifting my legs under the table in an effort to stretch, trying not to bump the knees or feet of my colleagues. All the while, I couldn't help but be amused by my own writings encouraging women to cultivate a sense of connection with their bodies as a strategy for empowerment and healing. I'd never felt so "connected" to my body, and nothing about this connection felt empowering or healing.

As the speakers droned on, my mind drifted to a line from the seventeenth-century French philosopher René Descartes who, just after pronouncing his famous dictum—"I think, therefore I am"—observed, "I could imagine that I had no body." Descartes could envision himself without a body because he had just identified the essence of a person—the human soul or self—with the process of thinking, which, he argued, did not require a body.[1] For Descartes, "me" and "my body" are two separate entities. As I hobbled out of the auditorium after the dinner, I found myself wishing he were right, even though my aching hip told me he was dead wrong.

Religious-like features of the culture of physical improvement

Descartes' beliefs about the self and body provide the philosophical foundation of the salvation myth of physical improvement. In this chapter, I discuss these beliefs and the better body images, rituals, and moral codes they support. As we shall see, modern Cartesian (i.e. Descartes-inspired) views melded with and modified classic Christian narratives about physicality. In particular, Descartes' view of the body as separate from and subject to an autonomous, individual "self" merged with Christian notions of the soul's moral superiority over the flesh and the body's pivotal role in the pursuit of salvation. This merger created the expectation that you can/should control your body, and that your body ought to obey.

Beliefs

Unlike Christian authors before him, who saw soul and body as intimately connected, Descartes believed the "self" (or "soul") was categorically distinct from physicality. For him, the body was a container for the self (the "I" of a person), which he identified with the mind (the process of thinking). This mind/body separation fostered a view of a person as composed of a rational, autonomous, individual will, housed inside an unintelligent, involuntary biodegradable structure (i.e. the body).[2] Although Descartes believed women were endowed with reason, the long-standing association between masculinity, rationality, and agency suggested that the ideal/normative self is male.[3]

Descartes' understanding of selfhood differed from Christian conceptions of the soul. Christianity teaches that a soul depends on God for its life, which means it is neither sovereign nor self-sufficient. Nor is the Christian soul identical with the rational, controlling power of the will. Rather, one's mind/reason is limited in its capacity to determine behavior. St. Paul sounds exasperated when he observes: "I do not understand my own actions. For I do not do what I want, but I do the very thing I hate" (Romans 7:15). Perhaps the most important distinction between the Cartesian self and traditional Christianity's view of the soul is that the latter is embodied—different yet inseparable from physicality.[4] In Christian theology, spirit is enfleshed.

The difference between the modern Cartesian view of mind and body as separate entities and the classic Christian view of body and soul as distinct-but-connected may seem subtle, but it has profound implications. Descartes' view of a person as a "ghost in the machine" implies that an individual (the "ghost") ought to be able to control her or his body (the "machine"). Perhaps a more familiar analogy for people today is that of a person driving a car. Not only are the driver ("me") and the car ("my body") distinct entities in Descartes' view, but the driver's decisions directly determine the vehicle's movement. If the driver wants to go right, she turns the steering wheel in that direction and the car turns accordingly. If she opts to go backward, she puts the vehicle in reverse, and it complies. The car's automatic, obedient response to the driver's agency represents the body's (presumably) compliant response to the self's commands. This Cartesian view of the body as inert, unintelligent, and subject to the will of the sovereign self (the "driver") represents the mechanistic picture of humans that became prominent during the industrial, political, and scientific revolutions of the modern era—revolutions whose principles of efficiency, self-governance, and progress still dominate Western societies.

It's hard to overstate the ongoing impact of this mechanical view of persons on contemporary attitudes toward human physicality. Although Descartes' mind/body dualism has been widely discredited by scholars in various fields—neuroscientists have identified the biochemical basis of thoughts and emotions, and sociologists and psychologists recognize the powerful influence of social, familial, and unconscious patterns on the development of the supposedly rational, individual self—many people today still have a mental image of a distinct little person living inside them: the "I" who is driving the "car" of their bodies and who is totally free to determine his or her destiny.

It's easy to see why a Cartesian view of human beings would have such lasting appeal. There's no denying that, at least to some extent, our decisions *do* impact our physical well-being. For example, a sedentary lifestyle combined with a diet of processed foods that are high in fat, sugar, and salt typically leads to weight gain and increases one's risk for certain diseases. Smoking is a well-known carcinogen that accelerates the process of aging; alcohol abuse contributes to liver problems; stress compromises the immune system, and so on. Conversely, certain behaviors can lead to positive physical outcomes. The benefits of regular exercise, sufficient sleep, and a diet rich in whole grains, fruits, and vegetables are too numerous and familiar to mention.

Nevertheless, sometimes you can do everything "right," and *still* your body doesn't cooperate with your/society's plans for how it's supposed to look, feel, or function. You can work your butt off at the gym, eat loads of leafy greens, take vitamins and flaxseed oil, get plenty of sleep, see your doctor regularly—but there's no guarantee your flesh will do what you want it to do, look how you want it to look, or feel how you want it to feel. The fact that our choices affect our physical condition doesn't mean our decisions will automatically create a desired outcome. These decisions *influence* our health; but we can't totally *control* their results. This lack of complete sovereignty "over" our flesh leaves many of us feeling ambivalent about our corporeal experience, particularly when it seems like our bodies have betrayed us (e.g. by getting sick, gaining weight, becoming old or disabled). That this lack of absolute control over our bodies not only surprises but frustrates us indicates just how deeply Descartes' legacy is embedded in our thinking.

Certain ideas become believable and gain authority not because they are true but because they are continually repeated, to the point where alternative viewpoints become eclipsed. The belief that we can control our bodies is one such idea. This idea seems all the more believable because it synchs with some of Western society's most cherished values: self-sufficiency, upward mobility, productivity, efficiency, and progress. Ultimately, the Cartesian dream of self-mastery supports commercial culture's view of bodies not just as objects we can work on and work out, monitor and manipulate, defy, compel, transfigure, and fix, but as advertisements for who we are as a person. Paradoxically, the improvable body is both *subject to* the will of the self and a *visible manifestation* of that self.

The iconography of the culture of physical improvement

In contemporary society, the presumed correspondence between the ideal (internal) self and the perfect (external) body is constructed through commercial culture's iconography. In terms of content, mass media images differ dramatically from those of traditional Christianity. Consider the contrast, for example, between the female models and celebrities on the electronic billboards in Times Square, like those featuring Jessica Simpson (Figure 3.1), and the holy women portrayed in stained glass windows of the Catholic Church in the small town where I grew up—wearing layers of long, loosely fitted robes, with downcast eyes, somber faces, in postures that suggest modesty and humility (Figure 3.2). Despite their obvious differences, the educational and inspirational *functions* of these images are similar. Just as historical Christians were inspired by saintly role models (i.e. holy women and men depicted in stained glass windows, sculptures, icons, and paintings), so people today look to the paragons of commercial culture (i.e. rock stars, athletes, models, and movie stars on TV and in films, advertisements, the internet, and magazines) to guide their self-definition.

Unlike historical Christians, however, who consulted the visual role models of their faith with the *conscious intention* of being educated by them, today's consumers of media images are largely unaware of the lessons these images instill.[5] Most of the time, we view popular pictures and personalities as a source of entertainment. Together with advertising, the entertainment industry comprises a central artery in commercial culture, providing a pantheon of

FIGURE 3.1 *Jessica Simpson on Times Square Billboards © Walter McBride.*
Source: Getty Images.

iconic figures and dramas that capture our imaginations. For many celebrities, bodily perfection is a *fait accompli*, a precondition of their prominence in the visual galaxy of popular culture. Increasingly, however, ordinary people are recruited to participate in the drama of physical improvement. "Reality" TV shows like *Extreme Makeover* and *Biggest Loser* invite us to identify with contestants' struggles and aspirations—their sense of shame over perceived somatic deficiencies and their corresponding desire and strivings to be "born again."

In *Empire of Illusion*, Chris Hedges notes the quasi-religious dimensions of celebrity culture. "We all have our gods," he says, paraphrasing Martin Luther, "it is just a question of which ones."[6] Hedges argues that ordinary people gravitate toward the deities of commercial culture as a way of escaping a pervasive sense of chaos, monotony, insignificance, or inadequacy in their lives. We are drawn to images of idealized humans and seek to live vicariously through them because "[t]hey do what we cannot": they defy anonymity and inhabit a sphere of seemingly supernatural affluence and power. Celebrities are the 1 percent who "control more wealth than the bottom 90 percent combined…[They] live and play in multimillion-dollar beach houses…marry professional athletes and are chauffeured in stretch limos to spa appointments. They rush from fashion shows to movie premieres, flaunting their surgically enhanced perfect bodies."[7]

FIGURE 3.2 *Window(s) in the Sacred Heart Church in Staples, MN (USA).* © *Photo by Marge Lelwica.*

Besides the supernatural powers associated with their socioeconomic privilege, the cosmetically perfected people Hedges describes display something else ordinary humans often crave but don't possess: bodies that transcend the liabilities and limits of the flesh—i.e. the possibility of getting sick or injured, feeling pain or hunger, slowing down, growing old, and eventually dying. In the iconography of commercial culture, this aura of transcendence is created not only via surgical "enhancement," but also through digital manipulation that renders some icons all the more surreal.

It's interesting to encounter undeniable evidence that the bodies we are taught to admire are more fabricated than real. Several years ago, Dove (a company that makes "personal products") produced a short video that showed an apparently ordinary white woman being transformed into a glamorous model with the help of makeup artists, hair stylists, and digital manipulations. As part of its "Campaign for Real Beauty," this film brought the behind-the-scenes commercial process of manufacturing beauty into full view. (To watch this film, google "Dove Evolution"). While many appreciated seeing this process exposed, others questioned the company's intentions. Given that its parent company (Unilever) sells skin-whitening creams to women in developing nations, and given that Dove products are often marketed as improving women's appearance, it's hard not to wonder whether the film's apparent aim of raising consciousness harbored an even bigger motive of raising profits.[8]

These days, many of us know that commercial images of idealized bodies have been Photoshopped to increase their appeal and thereby the earnings of companies that produce them. We may, as Orbach suggests, think ourselves too smart to buy into such artificial visions and "reject the idea of being under 'assault' from the beauty industry as offensive to our intelligence."[9] Yet even those of us who recognize both the fabricated quality of the unattainable ideal and its commercial function may nonetheless find ourselves involuntarily wishing we looked more like it. You might know *intellectually* that images of perfect bodies are designed to make you feel bad so you'll buy things you don't need, but you might still *feel* like a failure compared to such visions of perfection. This is because the mythical truths the perfect body conveys—its superiority, goodness, health, happiness, affluence, and beauty—are not just cerebral ideas. These messages get under our skin through the repetitious prescriptions we are encouraged to follow: the rituals we are advised to perform to make our bodies better.

Better body rituals

Rituals are the most embodied part of any religious or cultural system. As symbolic actions performed in formulaic and repetitious ways, they create a sense of order and stability by linking our physical selves to our personal convictions and to the values, beliefs, and structures within our communities and the wider society. Just as a culture's visual images of somatic perfection remind us of its body norms, so its recommended rituals enable us to internalize these norms, absorbing, assimilating, incorporating them into our flesh to the point where they become second nature, beyond the level of conscious awareness.

Anthropologist Talal Asad studied the changing role of rituals in Western history. In the medieval Christian era, ritual behavior involved *disciplined activity* based on instructions that reflected "a pre-defined model of excellence" (i.e. saints and holy people). Such prescribed behavior aimed to cultivate moral virtues in service to a higher authority (i.e. God). By contrast, rituals in the modern era functioned primarily as *symbolic actions* that required decoding and served a strategic purpose of crafting a self well-suited to the conventions and organization of an emerging industrial capitalist society.[10] Aspects of both medieval and modern ritual activity—prescribed disciplined conduct with a moral aim, and symbolic behavior with a practical end—can be seen in the contemporary culture of physical improvement: bodies are regulated, trained, and corrected according to a "pre-defined model of excellence" (the ideal body), with the twofold goal of cultivating the virtue of self-mastery and pursuing/communicating a privileged status within society.

Both of these ritual functions are evident in practices prescribed by commercial texts devoted to physical improvement. Consider, for example, some of the recommendations on the cover of the March 2015 issue of *Health* magazine:

"**BANISH BELLY FAT** YOU CAN DO THIS!"
"**Erase Years Off Your Face** Skin Docs' New Tricks"
"**KICK SUGAR CRAVINGS** And Drop Pounds"

The repetitious, formulaic character of such imperatives becomes apparent when we compare them to the better body strategies promoted on the June 2015 cover of the same magazine:

"**LOSE EVERY BULGE**
*FLAT BELLY
*TONED LEGS
*GREAT BUTT"
"**Sexy Skin All Over**"
"**22** FOODS FOR A LONG LIFE Bread is Back"

In case the rhetorical redundancy is not yet obvious, consider the following sampling of enticements from the covers of *Health* in preceding years— all situated on the upper left side of the cover page in large, dark font, all promoting weight loss rituals:

"**LOSE YOUR BELLY! MELT 4 LBS in 7 DAYS**" (June 2011)
"**LOSE 10 * 25 * 35 LBS! THE NO-DIET WAY**" (July/August 2011)
"**MELT 12 LBS IN 28 DAYS! WITHOUT HUNGER**" (September 2011)
"**LOSE 6 LBS IN 7 DAYS All New CarbLovers Diet**" (January/February 2012)
"**LOSE YOUR BELLY: Melt Stubborn Fat in 5 Days**" (March 2012)
"**LOSE 5, 10, 20 LBS! Drop Your First Pound Today**" (May 2012)

The repetitive, formulaic quality of these enticements is reinforced by the homogeneous images accompanying them—all of which feature slender, fashionably dressed young women, most of whom are white with long blond or light brown hair. In fact, some of the "cover girls" look so similar, one might guess they were sisters.

I seriously doubt that most readers see these images and the prescriptions surrounding them as in any way related to the symbols and rituals of traditional religion. But this may be because they assume an overly narrow and disembodied view of "religion." In Western societies today, religion is often seen as operating in a separate sphere—apart from "secular" society. Moreover, religion is often assumed to be primarily a matter of *belief* (narrowly defined as cognitive agreement with certain doctrines or faith statements), while flesh-and-blood experiences are thought to be either antithetical or peripheral to "spiritual" concerns.[11] But both the history of Christianity and the contemporary pursuit of physical improvement suggest that through ritual activities, bodies participate in the construction of metaphysical meanings, and that the line dividing sacred/secular truths is far from clear.

In her studies of symbols and rituals, Mary Douglas noted both the constitutive role of the body in the creation of religious meanings and the fluidity of the distinction between religious and nonreligious behavior.[12] Building on Douglas' insights, Catherine Bell highlighted the role of the "ritualized body"—a body that has been socialized to look, feel, and act in culturally and religiously sanctioned ways—in the creation of such distinctions. The significance of ritual practices rests not in their essential difference from more instrumental or practical behavior, Bell suggested, but in their capacity to constitute themselves as *holier than* more mundane ways of acting by referencing both the dominant social order and "realities thought to transcend the power of human actors."[13] Ultimately, this theory of ritual helps explain how activities as ostensibly mundane as applying age-fighting cream every morning to minimize wrinkles (Figure 3.3) or exercising to burn calories (Figure 3.4) can foster a sense of transcendent meaning insofar as such activities reconnect you to the larger goal of physical improvement and generate feelings of virtue (self-mastery) and coherency (i.e. "normalcy") within the dominant social order.

In a culture devoted to somatic enhancement, the social approval that comes from successfully renovating or repairing a wayward body can bolster self-confidence. Indeed, the language of self-worth is ubiquitous in commercial culture. For example, L'OREAL markets its "antiaging" skin cream with the assurance: "Because you're worth it.™" But the self-esteem such rhetoric promises comes with a price: the daily rituals we perform to improve our bodies and social status require obedience to the very norms that render us docile. As Foucault and others have shown, contemporary body

FIGURE 3.3 *Woman applying face cream in front of mirror* © *Hero Images.* *Source: Getty Images.*

norms function as a means of social control. Whereas in premodern Western societies, social order was preserved through the threat of public torture or execution (e.g. crucifixion, hanging, beheading, burning), today such order is maintained through individual self-surveillance: we police our bodies and strive to comply with prevailing medical, aesthetic, and moral standards in exchange for others' approval. By ritually monitoring, regulating, and normalizing our flesh according to the normative ideal, we not only avoid public derision, we help sustain the dominant culture's social/symbolic hierarchy of bodies.[14]

The analyses of Asad, Douglas, Bell, and Foucault illuminate how rituals we perform to improve our bodies "empower" us by linking our personal practices and preferences to the system of commercial values and social hierarchies that congeal in the fantasy of physical perfection. Our complicity with this system can be difficult to see. For one thing, our collusion may be hidden in our well-intended efforts to get healthy and feel more confident. For another, it's hard to admit that our good intentions may unwittingly entangle us in a web of superiority/inferiority complexes we consciously reject. Most of us don't like to think that our private efforts to "age-proof" our faces, "blast" belly fat, or "conquer" disease and disability may inadvertently perpetuate prejudice against bodies that are old, fat, sick, or disabled. But can we critique, feel ashamed of, and wage war on the alleged defects in our own bodies without at least implicitly judging similar flaws in the flesh of others?

FIGURE 3.4 *"Contour Style-Punch Shot, Madame Figaro"* © *Alexandre Weinberger/Figarophoto.*
Source: Getty Images.

Moral codes

Body shame—the feeling that there's something *wrong* with your body—is a common consequence of participating in this system. This feeling is not morally neutral. Consciously or not, body shame is ensconced in judgments (e.g. good/bad, worthy/unworthy, desirable/undesirable). We may not think of physical conditions like being fat, old, disabled, or chronically sick as "sinful," but the shame many people experience in relation to these conditions suggests that this language is not too far-fetched.

Body shame is no stranger to Christianity. Indeed, this tradition has a reputation for fostering aversion and antagonism toward physicality through its moral disciplines and rules to regulate carnal desire. This reputation is at least partially deserved, given Christianity's traditional emphasis on controlling the body to mitigate the effects of humanity's sinful nature. This emphasis was developed by early church leaders like Augustine, whose theory of "original sin" pointed to the guilt inherent in the human condition: our inborn propensity to act contrary to God's will. Augustine didn't blame the body for being the original source of sin (he traced sin's origins back to the Fall); but his own tortured experience of sexual desire prior to his conversion to Christianity led him to view physical craving as the fundamental *symptom* of humanity's fallen state. For him, undivided devotion to God was the only remedy for this shameful affliction.

By conceptualizing the body's disorderly desire as the primary symptom of humans' propensity to sin, Augustine crystallized a theological tradition that associated physicality with shame. Yet the role of shame in Christianity is more complex than this classic association suggests. Historian Virginia Burrus notes that while early Christians adopted the shame/honor dichotomy that permeated the Roman Empire, they revised this dualism in ways that enabled them to distinguish themselves as members of a movement whose highest authority was God—not the emperor. Through the public humiliation of martyrdom, the self-abnegation of asceticism, and the confessional practices of church leaders like Augustine, early Christians simultaneously embraced and defied shame, thereby inverting and transforming its destructive potential. By deliberately transgressing ancient Roman imperial norms, they defiantly cultivated and welcomed the public stigma of shame. In so doing, they contested and inverted it, exposing, rejecting, and critiquing the shameful/shaming values of the society around them. Ultimately, the early Christians that Burrus describes became shameless about their shame, embracing rather than avoiding its destructive power as a means for resisting a sinfully corrupt, unjust society.[15]

Contesting shame by embracing and converting it into self-acceptance and social critique is not a common dynamic in the culture of physical improvement. While there is no shortage of commercially sponsored calls to "love your body," this message is consistently contradicted and overshadowed by body-perfecting prescriptions, products, and programs that implicitly suggest that the *un*improved body is *un*worthy of such love. Indeed, the value system of consumer capitalism cannot afford for consumers to unconditionally love their bodies. Multiple industries depend on us feeling bad about some part of our anatomy, which is why marketers spend billions trying to trigger the very shame they promise to cure.

This shame-triggering business strategy is evident in the never-ending list of "shoulds" and "shouldn'ts" embedded between the lines of better body instructions. A women's magazine article entitled "**So Long, Cellulite**," implies that we should try to get rid of our adipose tissue. Another article, "**STOP PAIN**," suggests that you shouldn't have to live with chronic hurt.

Yet another, entitled "***Erase Years Off Your Face***," insinuates that you shouldn't have wrinkles.[16] But what if your body breaks these laws? And who defines them anyway? In the end, the same corporeal rules that make us feel virtuous when we adhere to them make us vulnerable to shame when we don't.

According to Brené Brown, feeling physically inadequate or unattractive is the number-one "shame trigger" for women, in terms of both its intensity and universality.[17] This is not surprising, given long-standing religious/cultural narratives that (de)value women based on their bodies. But many men feel bad about their bodies as well, not only in relation to appearance but also in connection with performance—especially sexual performance. Ever wonder why there are so many ads for Viagra (and similar remedies for "erectile dysfunction") on commercial television, particularly on channels catering to men (e.g. ESPN)? In posts filed on the MedHelp Website under "The Shame of ED," several men—some in their teens—share their fears of disappointing their partners and describe their condition as "extremely embarrassing."[18]

Throughout Christian history, too much sexual attraction and activity have been associated with immorality. But in commercial culture today, insufficient sexual desire and underperformance are cause for alarm. Historian Joan Jacob Brumberg observes, "the media and popular culture...push the idea that sexuality is the ultimate form of self-expression."[19] Thus companies like Victoria's Secret teach girls in their teens and tweens to sexualize their bodies with its "Pink" line of underwear, which includes thongs that say "Call Me" and "Feeling Lucky?"[20] In striking contrast to the Christian ideal, the commercial archetype is hypersexualized: able, ready, and willing to probe the depths of carnal pleasure. This somatic fantasy converts the historic iniquity of lust into a badge of glory. But the ideal body's liberation from shame is far from complete. For rather than abolish the body's propensity for moral failure, the normative ideal relocates it: from the hazards of unfettered sexual desire to the dangers of unimproved flesh. Thus the nonconforming bodies of those who are disabled, fat, sick, or old are seen as shamefully *un*-sexy.

The assumption that a "good" body represents inner virtue is seen in the stereotypical association between beauty and virtue that social psychologists have investigated for decades. A classic 1972 study of this stereotype showed that "attractive" people were perceived to possess more desirable personality traits than their "unattractive" peers, and these "good-looking" people were assumed to be more successful and happy.[21] More recently, Doris Bazzini et al., found the beauty–virtue cliché to be prevalent in animated Disney films, most of which positively correlated "beautiful" characters with traits like intelligence, friendliness, higher socioeconomic status, romantic appeal, and moral character. This study revealed that children as young as 6 associate "attractive" people with virtuous qualities.[22]

It's been well over a century since the heyday of modern physiognomy— a racist-motivated pseudoscience that deduced the invisible quality of a person's soul based on her or his body's visible attributes (e.g. facial features, body shape, complexion).[23] In the Victorian era, female complexion was seen as an index of moral character, and young middle-class women were taught that the face was a "window to the soul." If a girl's skin was clear, her soul was pure. Conversely, facial blemishes were seen as evidence of immoral behavior, including masturbation.[24] Over a hundred years later, the dominant optic and discourses of commercial culture depict and interpret bodies in a similar manner—as if an individual's physical condition or outward appearance manifests her or his inner qualities. In this moral universe, the well-crafted physique expresses a virtuous self, which in developed Western societies means rational, independent, and "in control."

The flip side of the association between the good body and the well-ordered self is seen in stereotypes surrounding those whose bodies don't conform to the normative ideal. People who are fat, old, disabled, chronically sick, or in pain are frequently perceived to be feeble-minded, needy, undisciplined. Heavy-set individuals are assumed to be lazy. The elderly are seen as dependent. People with physical disabilities are frequently treated like children. Those living with chronic illnesses are often blamed for causing their conditions by unhealthy choices. It's no coincidence that these *un*desirable, *un*virtuous qualities (laziness, dependency, immaturity, irresponsibility) are also stereotypically applied to people who are poor. If the commercially defined good body represents a self who's mentally and economically "on top of things," then the unimproved, unconventional body is an expression of someone who has morally failed: someone whose lack of self-determination makes her unable to pull herself up by her bootstraps.

Ultimately, the same moral codes through which the good body is defined, pursued, and praised foster judgment and shame toward bodies that violate these rules. This moral ambiguity adds suspense to the drama of physical improvement: whether our flesh is a source of pride or shame, accomplishment or failure, praise or blame depends on our ability to make it obey and conform to the ideal.

The web of beliefs, images, rituals, and moral codes that support the better body narrative is so familiar that it's hard to see—much less challenge. Indeed, the salvation myth of physical improvement may seem "too big to fail." Deconstructing it would require us to rethink not just our relationship with our own bodies, and not just our perceptions of other people's bodies, but our understanding of what health, happiness, and healing really mean. In the next chapter, I explore some possibilities for such rethinking by outlining an alternative perspective on physical improvement that honors the truths of embodied life.

4

An alternative approach to embodied life

A few years before I started writing this book, I bought a subscription to *Health* magazine as part of a fund-raiser for my niece's volleyball team. I wasn't familiar with this popular periodical, but my choice turned out to be fortuitous for my research. *Health* is what you might call a "primary text" of the culture of physical improvement. It's dedicated to helping women achieve a better body by proffering articles, ads, images, editorials, and readers' input relating to topics like weight, disease prevention, healthy eating, exercise, pain remedies, beauty tips, and aging. Its overall message captures a cornerstone belief in the culture of physical improvement: that building a better body is key to a happier life. Indeed, the top of the cover of each issue reads: "Happy Begins Here." To see examples of these covers, please visit http://www.bloomsbury.com/uk/shameful-bodies-9781472594945/ and look under "Chapter Four."

One summer, I decided to read all eight issues of *Health* that came with that year's subscription. Previously, I hadn't so much as opened a page, so I was curious to see what I'd find. As I studied the magazine's images, rhetoric, and worldview, I was struck by its curious mix of superficial and serious content. On the one hand, many of its pages tell us exactly what we want to hear: that you can drop 5 pounds in a week eating what you love, make wrinkles disappear in an "instant," prevent cancer, cure allergies, beat back pain, get toned in just 10 minutes, and so on. On the other hand, some of the articles are more substantive, advocating the importance of stress reduction, self-care, and integrating mental and physical health. No doubt, such rhetoric resonates with readers' struggles to stay balanced and feel whole amid the multiple pressures, relentless speed, and nonstop busyness of contemporary life. Nonetheless, the potentially helpful messages in some articles are undercut by the texts' overall inconsistencies: admonishments to care for, love, and enjoy your body are surrounded by instructions on how to regulate, renovate, or fix it.

Beneath the quest for physical improvement

The more we study the better body story as exemplified in this primary text, the more we might see its mixed messages as an insult to our intelligence, or perhaps just the product of clever marketing. But we may also wonder why so many people find the prospect of physical improvement to be so enticing. Are those of us who seek to enhance, correct, or cure our bodies so shallow-minded that we are easily duped by this prospect's superficial veneer? Or is something deeper, more complex, and significant at stake?

Perhaps what makes the salvation myth of physical improvement so compelling is that it appeals to some fundamental human needs. Perhaps this myth's images, beliefs, rituals, and moral codes hook us by addressing these needs, at least temporarily. For example, if we look carefully, we might see in our efforts to lose weight or look younger a need for unconditional acceptance, and in our attempts to conquer pain or fight disease a need to feel both psychically empowered and physically well. Maybe the energy we devote to enhancing our bodies reveals a need for creativity and self-definition. Perhaps our attempts to rehabilitate somatic impairments and increase mobility indicate a need for equal access to any number of social opportunities. These needs for acceptance, empowerment, creativity, agency, well-being, and justice could be characterized as "spiritual." In different ways, they involve the process of creating meaning, transforming suffering, and seeking "salvation" (i.e. happiness, health, and healing)—all functions of traditional religion. Such needs could also be described as "existential," as they seem to be part of the human condition, whether or not one identifies as "spiritual" or "religious."

Whatever we call these basic needs, the better body story shortchanges them. The sense of belonging this story fosters is conditional: you're accepted/acceptable as long as you're committed to assimilating to the normative ideal. Moreover, the empowerment generated by pursuing this ideal depends on obedience to a symbolic/social system that perpetuates prejudice and shame. The self-definition this pursuit encourages is based on the other-ing and subordination of nonconforming/"not-me" bodies. The picture of health the ideal body promotes conceals an aggressive, adversarial attitude toward the flesh that to me seems decidedly *un*healthy. Finally, better body story's definition of healing is highly individualistic, even though (ironically) it effaces the peculiarities of individual bodies—their history, culture, heredity, and social circumstances.

An alternative approach to health and healing

I thought a lot about the better body story as I considered getting a prosthetic hip. My deliberations brought into focus some questions I'd been struggling with as I developed my critique of the culture of physical improvement: does this critique imply that we should abandon all efforts to enhance or repair our bodies? Should people living with chronic pain or illness stop looking for a cure? What about persons with physical impairments—should they stop trying to increase their mobility and functioning? Should the elderly give up on trying to look or feel younger? Should people who are fat stop trying to lose weight? While each of these questions needs to be explored in light of the particular body issue involved, my decision to finally go through with the surgery was based on my conclusion that rather than abandon the quest for physical improvement, *we need to reframe it*.

More specifically, we need alternative ways of thinking about and pursuing physical, mental, and spiritual well-being—ways that aren't tethered to a profit-driven ideal, and that don't put us at war with our flesh and make us complicit with a social/symbolic system that shames unorthodox physiques. A more sane approach to embodiment would understand health and healing as processes in which we work to accept, learn from, and live responsibly in the finite bodies we have—the particular bodies we *are*—in relation to others. This understanding does not imply a universal formula for what physical improvement should look or feel like. What it means to work with, learn from, and responsibly care for our bodies will vary as much as people and their circumstances. Nonetheless, there are some principles that can guide our efforts in this endeavor.

The alternative approach to health and healing I outline below and develop throughout this book is based on the principles of biodiversity, vulnerability, impermanence, and interdependence—all of which the better body story suppresses or denies. I engage these principles to construct an approach to embodied life that challenges the shaming gaze and controlling strategies the culture of physical improvement encourages. This approach is the product of decades of formal study of feminist perspectives on religion, and just as many years of informal exploration of Buddhist ideas and practices. Because I'm a feminist scholar of religion, it makes sense that work in this area deeply impacts my thinking about somatic well-being. But since I'm neither a scholar of Buddhism nor a Buddhist, my engagement with resources from this tradition merits some explanation.

Why Buddhism?

Almost 30 years ago, a friend introduced me to the work of Thich Nhat Hanh, a Vietnamese Zen master, peace activist, and poet whose writings have found a receptive audience among Westerners of diverse religious and nonreligious persuasions. Since then, I've informally studied Nhat Hanh's teachings, as well as those of other mostly North American Buddhists, and have found their ideas, practices, and perspectives to be fruitful for my thinking about (and experiences with) various body issues. So the simple answer to the question—*why Buddhism?*—is that some of the resources within this tradition have been intellectually illuminating and personally helpful to me.

In particular, Buddhism's teaching on *nonduality* (what Nhat Hanh refers to as "interbeing"[1]) encourages us to recognize the interrelated nature of life beneath our mental separations. Nonduality implies that conceptual divisions like soul/body, religious/secular, normal/abnormal, inferior/superior, life/death, me/not-me (and so on) are products of our minds and the cultural, religious, and philosophical traditions that shape our thinking. In Buddhist psychology, our habit of dividing and ranking reality is a mental strategy for protecting ourselves from feeling vulnerable and avoiding uncertainty. When we treat such divisions as if they were absolutely real, they create a sense of alienation—what Bernie Glassman refers to as "an illness called separation"[2]—both within and among us. Healing this sickness requires us to appreciate the interdependence of life: its unity and diversity.[3]

Buddhism's emphasis on the interconnected nature of life implies an approach to physical improvement based neither on combating or conquering disease and defects, nor on universal prescriptions of "right" and "wrong" behavior, but on practical considerations of *what's helpful* (*upaya*, or "skillful"), given one's specific incarnation and circumstances, and given the needs of the social body. "What's helpful" means whatever *alleviates suffering*—both mental and physical anguish, both in oneself and in the world. Although the diversity of human bodies and their histories precludes a one-size-fits-all approach to reducing suffering, the Sanskrit term *ahimsa*—usually translated as "nonviolence" or "nonharming"—suggests a beneficial method and direction. We practice nonviolence toward bodies (our own and others') when, instead of berating ourselves for not resembling the normative ideal, we listen to and honor the actual needs of our flesh. We practice *ahimsa* when, instead of treating the noncompliant parts of our bodies as if they were "enemies" that needed to be vanquished or punished, we embrace and, if necessary, wrestle with our physical challenges in the spirit of reconciliation. As Nhat Hanh suggests, no one can practice *ahimsa* completely. Luckily, the goal is not perfection, but to "go in the direction of nonviolence" by making choices that reduce the harm we inflict on ourselves and our fellow inhabitants on Earth.[4]

On the path of cultivating a more friendly relationship with our flesh and with the bodies of others, the Buddhist teaching on *impermanence* is another valuable resource. This teaching affirms the ever-evolving and thus unpredictable nature of life. As Pema Chödrön points out, resistance to change and uncertainty is a primary source of human suffering.[5] Typically, this resistance/suffering involves both a refusal to accept things *as they are* and an attachment to a view of how things are *supposed to be*. Resisting the evolving, unpredictable nature of embodied life is painful because this effort puts us at odds with the truths of our flesh. The alternative to fighting the uncertainty and impermanence our bodies manifest is not passive resignation, but proactive acceptance: the deliberate decision to stop making our happiness and well-being contingent on our bodies looking, feeling, of functioning in a certain way. This approach implies that sometimes the healthiest thing we can do is let go of the relentless drive to be "healthy."

Buddhists cultivate the ability to let go through the practice of staying present. This requires a basic willingness to not run away from difficulties or cling to attractive illusions. Buddhists refer to the intentional effort to stay present to the truth/reality of "what is" as mindfulness. As a strategy for reducing suffering, this practice entails giving your undivided attention to what's happening within or around you in this very moment, without imposing a judgment on it (e.g. "this is good," "this is bad") or getting caught up in stories about it (e.g. "this shouldn't be happening…" "I should be…", "When I…", "What if…"). Though its origins are Buddhist, practicing mindfulness doesn't require assent to a specific set of beliefs and thus can be done by persons of all spiritual (or nonspiritual) backgrounds and commitments.

You can be mindful in any situation simply by giving your full, nonjudgmental attention to what's happening in the present moment. Many Buddhists cultivate this capacity through formal meditation. A basic meditation practice involves focusing on the sensation of breathing. Typically done in a seated position (in a chair or on the floor, with an upright posture), you bring your full attention to the feeling of air entering and leaving your body. When you notice that thoughts, sensations, or emotions have interrupted your concentration (as they inevitably do), you don't judge or engage them, but simply return your attention to the sensations of inhaling and exhaling. In traditional Buddhism, the purpose of meditation practice is not self-improvement because there is no "self" to improve[6]—at least not the rational, autonomous, individual housed in a machine-like body. The purpose is to alleviate suffering through the practice of staying present and letting go of mental, physical, and emotional attachments.

Along with a growing number of academics in various fields,[7] I teach mindful breathing to my students. We meditate for a minute or two at the beginning of class. I find that many college students are, like me, often stressed and preoccupied—if not about their bodies then about something. So I invite them to take some calming breaths and, for a few moments, let go of whatever internal storylines are occupying their minds. Most students tell me they're grateful for this practice because it gives them a break from the relentless demands and hurried pace of their lives and helps them remember their deeper values.

I recognize the hazards of appropriating ideas and practices from a spiritual heritage that's not my own, not the least of which is Orientalism: the creation of a homogenized snapshot of "Buddhism," flattened and sanitized for Western consumption. In drawing on some aspects of Buddhism, I make no pretense to present this tradition's main teachings in all their complexity and diversity. My aim is more *practical*: I seek to apply certain Buddhist principles and practices to challenge the better body story and to construct an alternative approach to overall well-being. Engaging resources from Buddhism that I find helpful does not imply that this tradition is problem-free—either historically or currently. Like Christianity, Buddhism has no shortage of misogynist, body-transcending, and other-worldly narratives.[8] And some forms of Buddhism that are popular today, especially among Westerners, appear to support rather than question an individualistic, commercially oriented, self-help culture.

These problems notwithstanding, the Buddhist authors I engage with link personal growth to social transformation. In various ways, they proffer practical methods for pursuing self-understanding and cultural critique, while affirming the fragility, plurality, transience, and interdependence of embodied life. Generally speaking, their approach to health and healing is process oriented, integrative, this-worldly, nonviolent, and pragmatic. In this regard, their insights, practices, and perspectives complement and overlap with those of various feminist scholars of religion.

Insights from the field of feminist studies in religion

Appreciation for the diverse, interconnected, and evolving nature of embodied life has been central to the work of various kinds of feminist scholars of religion (e.g. womanists, mujeristas, third world, indigenous, Asian, white, lesbian). These scholars critique the denigration of women and the flesh in religion and culture and insist on the intrinsic goodness of every body. Their analyses expose the psychic, spiritual, social, and physical damages caused by patriarchal religion, including both the blatant and the subtle/internalized violence against women it perpetuates. Feminist scholars of religion challenge the idolatrous web of superiority complexes that makes some lives seem more important than others. Those working out of biblical traditions expand individualized notions of "sin" and "salvation" to illuminate the concrete/social dimensions of harm and healing in which religious faith is implicated. Their studies highlight how variances in race, class, ability, age, sexuality, religion, and culture influence women's experiences of oppression and liberation in the global context of capitalist patriarchy.

The work of feminist scholars of religion who have influenced my thinking on embodiment is far too rich and diverse to do justice to here. Yet even a cursory glance at some of its major ideas and methods illustrates its potential as a resource for crafting a new narrative of physical improvement that promotes self-examination and social critique based on the principles of interdependence, fragility, impermanence, and biodiversity. Key to this potential is feminists' emphasis on diverse women's embodied experiences as sources of spiritual insight and sacred truth. Understood critically, such experiences generate fresh interpretations of traditional religious teachings that can serve as resources for an alternative understanding of health and healing.[*]

Imago Dei *and (re)imagining the divine*

Within the biblical tradition, one such resource is the first creation myth. In contrast to the story of the Fall, in which Eve's transgression symbolically links women, physicality, and sin, *Genesis* 1–2.3 depicts male and female as created simultaneously in God's image. Indeed, every created form is good, and there's no occasion for shame. As feminist theologians point out, the doctrine of *imago dei* (i.e. humans are created "in God's image") implies the *equal* dignity and worth of every person. There's no suggestion that some people more closely resemble God, no hint that some bodies are superior to others.

Yet the meaning of *imago dei* is not self-evident. For what it means to be created "in God's image" depends on your understanding of "God." This point is crucial for exploring body issues since how we think about God influences

---

[*] Since my critique throughout this book highlights Christianity's complicity with the culture of physical improvement, I draw most heavily (though not exclusively) on the works of Christian feminist scholars of religion to identify principles, practices, and perspectives that are useful for constructing an alternative narrative of physical improvement.

how we feel about our own bodies and how diverse bodies are valued in society. For theists in particular, God images and body image are intricately related. For example, exclusively male depictions of the divine (e.g. as a loving father or almighty king) suggest there is something less spiritual about women's bodies—as if God could not be well represented in female flesh. As Carol Christ argued decades ago, masculine images of divinity require women to deny their physical experience (consciously or not) in order to see themselves as created "in God's image." Moreover, by envisioning the ultimate power of the universe as male, traditional images of God tacitly associate authority with masculinity, thereby devaluing female agency.[9] As a result, many women learn to distrust the truths of our own embodied experiences and look instead to external (often male) authorities and man-made norms to define our worth.

Images of the divine also impact how we think about/experience the relationship between body and spirit. The classic image of God as a totally transcendent, all-powerful Being—a sovereign Lord who resides above the material world, which "He" judges and controls—mirrors the Cartesian view of the self/mind as separate from and ruling over the inferior, unintelligent body. Not only does this view of God promote the perception of the body as subject to the commands of the will, but it encourages us to relate to ourselves/bodies and to others through judgment, conquest, and constant supervision. What's more, if we cling to this ossified view of God—or even to its softer, Sunday school version of a grandfatherly figure dwelling in the clouds—we may miss the opportunity to experience the divine presence/power right in our midst.

Catholic nun and ecofeminist theologian, Elizabeth Johnson, refers to this sacred presence/power as "the living God." This is her biblically derived way of naming the life-generating force that permeates creation, including human bodies. Johnson envisions the divine as the source of life, the mysterious, dynamic, bounteous, liberating, and sustaining Spirit that calls us into loving relationships with each other and all of Earth's creatures. Far from being a distant, almighty, judgmental king—an image that has historically been used to justify the exploitation of certain groups of people and the natural world—this God is the creative power of life itself, the fertile, nurturing, disruptive, and empowering Spirit that's variously manifest in rocks, squirrels, trees, whales, and insects; in the blood, bones, and tissue of human bodies; in our suffering and our capacity for compassion; and in our struggles for peace and justice.[10]

Ivone Gebara is another Catholic ecofeminist scholar/nun who affirms the divine presence/power within (not above or ruling over) embodied life. Writing from the southern hemisphere, where she lives among the poorest of the poor, Gebara revitalizes traditional theological concepts by asking Christians to consider what these concepts mean on an experiential level. For example: What does it mean to experience salvation or redemption in your life, in your body, and in the world? Challenging both androcentric (male-centered) and anthropocentric (human-centered) theologies, Gebara understands the divine to be the Sacred Mystery that is both beyond and within us, a mystery that destabilizes our certainties and calls us to live in ways that honor and care for the diverse, fragile, unfolding, and interrelated manifestations of life.[11]

If, with scholars like Johnson and Gebara, we envision the divine as the mysterious, mothering power of life, then to be created "in God's image" means that each person has the innate capacity to live creatively and responsibly in relation to the infinite variety of configurations of life on planet Earth, including one's own body. Precisely this creative potential—this divine life within, beyond, and among us—enables us to make choices that promote growth, acceptance, and justice in our pursuit of physical, mental, and spiritual well-being.

The story of the incarnation

From an ecofeminist perspective, the power and presence of divine life is "unrepentingly incarnational" (Johnson's term).[12] This view offers an alternative to the anti-body, other-worldly, normalizing narratives that make Christianity complicit with the culture of physical improvement. Though the doctrine of the Incarnation is often narrowly understood—i.e. God became human once and for all 2,000 years ago in the person of Jesus (a view that has fueled claims of Christian supremacy)—feminists interpret the Incarnation more broadly, both *symbolically* and *politically*. Symbolically, the story of divine life incarnated in human flesh represents the inextricable connection between spirit and matter, a link that affirms the sacredness of every kind of body—including flesh in disrepair. Politically, the divine presence/power incarnated in the life of Jesus is manifest in the challenge his teachings present to social hierarchies and cultural norms that privilege some bodies at the expense of others. Feminist scholars remind us that Jesus' death was a *political execution* carried out by the Roman Empire for his opposition to an oppressive social system.

The symbolic and political implications of the incarnation are relevant for anyone seeking a noncommercial definition of physical improvement. What if we embraced the intrinsic goodness of our one-of-a-kind bodies and relinquished the shame we are conditioned to feel when we gain weight, grow old, get sick, feel pain, or experience disability? What if we stopped judging our somatic irregularities and started appreciating the ingenious ways our bodies refuse to conform to mainstream society's monotonously narrow and damaging definitions of health, virtue, and beauty? What if we reversed the shame such definitions generate and directed it back at a culture that encourages us to feel bad about our bodies? What if human biodiversity were seen as an expression of the creative/sacred/mysterious power of life? As a resource for fostering appreciation and care for embodied life, as well as social critique, the story of the incarnation is not just something to believe in; it is something to experience, cultivate, and put into practice.

This retelling of the incarnation narrative implies a fresh understanding of Jesus' resurrection that has implications for reimagining health, happiness, and healing. Instead of being a tale about "conquering" death and "overcoming" bodily losses and limits, the resurrection becomes a metaphor for interdependence of death and life. Understood metaphorically, this story calls our attention to the transient, composting character of life—the metamorphosis that makes growth, healing, liberation, and social change possible. This interpretation suggests that salvation is an ongoing, messy, transformative process of healing that happens in *this* life, rather than a blissful state of perfection in the *after* life.

Prophetic critique and critical thinking

Such a this-worldly understanding of redemption is part of the Bible's prophetic tradition. Rooted in the Hebrew prophets' critiques of social injustice, renewed in the ministry and message of Jesus, and expressed in the lives of countless women and men representing different cultures, classes, ages, sizes, colors, sexualities, and abilities, who use their ingenuity and wit to build a world in which every body can flourish, this tradition promotes *critical thinking* about dominant cultural norms, narratives, and perspectives. Thinking critically revolves around two key questions: What is being assumed? and What do these assumptions imply for the diverse inhabitants of our planet? Critical thinking exposes the idolatries of a social/symbolic system that treats some human incarnations as superior to others, and highlights the social dimensions of sin: the harm caused by intersecting forms and systems of injustice, e.g. racism, sexism, economic exploitation, heteronormativity, ableism, ageism, weight discrimination, and so on. Seeing sin as a social phenomenon—to be sure, one that individuals all-too-often collude with—can help alleviate body shame by revealing it to be symptomatic of larger societal dysfunctions.

To illustrate this point, I'd like to share a story about a milestone on my own journey out of an adolescent eating disorder. By the time I entered college in 1982, I was no longer starving and bingeing and purging, but I still thought about food and weight far more than I wanted to, and I felt a lot of shame— both about my "imperfect" body and my history of disordered eating. One night, I attended a screening of Jean Kilbourne's film, *Killing Us Softly*, which critiques how diet and beauty industries teach women to feel bad about their bodies. That movie changed my life. Simply put, it helped me understand that my preoccupation with thinness wasn't just a personal weakness; it was conditioned into me by a culture that rewarded me for obsessing about being skinny. What I'd thought of as my *personal* failure was actually part of a larger *social* pathology that permeated mainstream society. This new perspective not only increased my compassion for myself and those with similar struggles, but, with time and practice, it guided me to stop worrying about the size of my thighs and start thinking critically about oppressive beauty norms.

Critical/prophetic thinking is crucial for the alternative vision of health and healing I'm proposing because it exposes the commercial quest for physical improvement for what it is: a socially sanctioned idolatry. Relinquishing devotion to the false goddesses and gods of somatic perfection requires us to find new strategies for identifying and addressing the existential needs that draw us to them. Critical thinking is one such strategy. Such thinking helps us remember that none of us came out of the womb feeling bad about our cellulite, wrinkles, or physical limits. Body shame is a *learned* experience, and it can be *unlearned*. With practice, critical thinking fosters an atypical perspective that redirects our scrutiny away from our somatic peculiarities toward the narratives, images, rituals, and beliefs that encourage us to feel inadequate and unworthy. In this sense, critical thinking is a kind of spiritual practice: a means for fostering an alternative consciousness and sense of purpose and for transforming suffering in oneself and in the world.

"What is a body?"

Several years ago, I attended a session at the annual American Academy of Religion Conference that was sponsored by the Religion and the Body Group. One of this group's cochairs, Rebecca Sachs Norris, started the session by asking: "What is a body?" Before I had time to wrap my mind around this question, she posed another query: "What is *not* a body?" Norris' ruminations on these questions were fascinating. "Even our thoughts are produced by biochemical, physical processes," she pointed out, echoing what I'd learned from my excursions into the field of neuroscience. "And whose body are we talking about anyway?" Norris continued with her line of questions, reminding us that attention to gender, race, (dis)ability, sexuality, class, and cultural diversity complicates our perspectives on embodiment. She encouraged us to think about our own physicality: the bodies of scholars who think and write about bodies. We are, she noted, both "knowing subjects" and "the objects of our knowing": bodies writing about bodies, flesh thinking about flesh. How do our own physical experiences shape what we know and perceive to be true about embodied life?[33] Sachs Norris posed and ruminated on such marvelous questions without providing definitive answers, which challenged me to keep thinking about them long after the session had ended.

What is a body? More specifically, what's the relationship between human bones, blood, organs, muscles, and tissue and the part of us that's capable of thinking about bodies, the part that seeks to *improve* them? Is there something more to humans than our physicality and this capacity to think? If so, what is this "something more," and how does it relate to our irreducibly diverse, biodegradable flesh?

Just as human bodies have evolved to maximize our survival and thereby help us achieve our creative potential, so they are destined to disintegrate, die, and decay. This is the paradox of embodiment. Hamlet's depiction of the body as "Food for worms" is either downright depressing or totally fascinating, depending on how you look at it. This book opts for the latter perspective, privileging curiosity over despair, investigation over denial. In the chapters in Part II, we will see that it's easier to project our fear of impermanence, biodiversity, vulnerability, and limits onto bodies that seem to incarnate these qualities more than others than it is to own and explore these qualities in ourselves. We will also see how this projection—and the shame it fosters—deprives us of the opportunities to experience the mystery of our own physicality, and to participate in creating a world that honors and respects the mystery and beauty of all bodies.

PART TWO

5

Disability shame

In an interview with Guy Raz for the TED Radio Hour, Amy Purdy recalls her struggles to accept her new life after losing her feet to an illness caused by a vaccine-preventable meningitis bacteria. She was 19 at the time. This same illness resulted in the loss of her kidneys, spleen, and hearing in her left ear. In talking with Raz, Purdy is clearly grateful for how incredibly rich her life now feels. With the help of prosthetics, she's a Paralympic snowboard champion, a finalist on *Dancing with the Stars*, a model, actress, motivational speaker, clothing designer, product spokesperson, founder of a nonprofit organization, and author of *On My Own Two Feet*. Purdy's ability to thrive becomes all the more poignant when she recalls her feelings about disability prior to her amputations: "I remember hearing about a kid who had lost his legs when I was in high school and thinking, oh, if I lost my legs, I would get myself in a wheelchair, and I'd wheel myself off a cliff."[1]

Purdy's celebrity status makes her an unusual representative of people with disabilities. Nonetheless, the thought she describes—that death is preferable to disability—reflects widespread attitudes and beliefs about physical impairment within mainstream Western societies. For many nondisabled people, it's difficult to imagine a meaningful, fulfilling, happy life in a body that lacks "normal" form or functioning.

This difficulty raises a broad, existential question—what does make life worth living?—along with more specific queries: What about disability is so dreadful that some people imagine they would rather be dead than disabled? How does this dread, and the shame surrounding it, shape cultural attitudes toward physicality not just among those who are disabled but among able-bodied people as well? How do certain religious narratives, philosophical ideals, and cultural discourses contribute to this dread? How does it quietly inform our collective definitions of the "good," "desirable," "healthy" body? And what alternative perspectives might we consider? These are some of the questions we will explore in this chapter. But first, a confession.

Discovering disability studies

I'm embarrassed to tell you how little I knew—or even thought—about physical disabilities prior to my experience with chronic hip pain. My infrequent interactions with people with bodily impairments made disability a "problem" others had to deal with. Intellectually, it was a minor bleep on my radar—a topic I imagined some highly specialized scholars studied. It wasn't until the hurt in my hip became debilitating that I started wondering what it would be like to have permanent limitations in anatomical functioning in a world designed for able-bodied people. And it wasn't until I examined my reluctance to use a cane that I started questioning the extent to which I'd internalized disparaging views of disabled bodies.

Around that time, a peer reviewer of an article I'd submitted for an academic journal suggested I take a look at Sharon Betcher's *Spirit and the Politics of Disablement.*[2] Reading this book, I was surprised to discover what now seem like obvious intersections between the work of disability studies scholars and my previous writings on body image problems. Both Betcher and I critiqued commercial culture's glorification of the "perfect body" as a linchpin in the mechanisms of global capitalism and a key factor in the self-loathing many people, especially women, experience in the shadow of that ideal. But Betcher's book revealed a major gap in my previous work. Although I had interrogated dominant ideologies of race, class, sexuality, culture, and religion through which the slender feminine ideal is constructed, I'd failed to seriously scrutinize a crucial feature of this ideal: its nondisabled status.

Since my introduction to disability studies through Betcher's book, I've explored the field more broadly. Still, it's not my area of expertise. Nor am I disabled. Rather than try to speak for or to people living with disabilities, my aim in this chapter is to use what I've learned from my readings in this area to critically examine how prevailing definitions of somatic "improvement" are constructed through disparaging views of disability. By exposing the confluence of religious, philosophical, and cultural discourses that support these views, I hope to encourage nondisabled people like myself to recognize our possible, albeit unwitting, complicity with the shaming of impaired bodies that the able-bodied ideal promotes, and to challenge the internalized shame this collusion encourages among every body. While the term "disability" covers a wide range of issues, including various psychological and cognitive conditions, this chapter focuses primarily on attitudes toward conspicuous corporeal disabilities against the backdrop of the culture of physical improvement. As we shall see, however, perceptions about disabled bodies are intimately related to idealized understandings of the "self."

Becoming disabled in an able-bodied society

Rosemarie Garland Thomson captures some of the most important lessons I've learned through my studies in this field when she "challenge[s] the persistent assumption that disability is a self-evident condition of physical inadequacy and private misfortune whose politics concern only a limited minority."[3] To break this down a bit, Garland Thomson contends that a physically impaired body is not an intrinsically flawed or inferior form of embodiment, and that it need not be interpreted as defective or pitiable. In fact, as the title of her book—*Extraordinary Bodies*—suggests, Garland Thomson sees disabled bodies as exceptional, rather than deformed or dreadful.

This perception reflects an important distinction many disability scholars and activists make between "impairment," which refers to a limit or loss in anatomical form or function, and "disability," which describes the negative consequences of having an impairment that are shaped by dominant/able-bodied cultural expectations and social structures.[4] Whereas impairment is a corporeal condition that is basically neutral, prevailing ideologies interpret this condition disparagingly and social structures marginalize it, thereby "disabling" someone with an impairment. Alison Kafer characterizes this view when she writes: "People with impairments are disabled by their environments... impairments aren't disabling, social and architectural barriers are."[5] In the words of Robert Murphy, "disability is a social malady," rooted not in physical deficits but in "deficiencies of perspective."[6] Ultimately, whether we see anatomical impairments as defective—or simply as unusual—depends on our vantage point, though an ableist culture conditions us to perceive such "difference" in belittling terms.

Simi Linton elaborates the distinction between impairment and disability throughout *My Body Politic*. Describing her experience of losing use of her legs as the result of a car accident in 1971, she writes: "The injury was a sudden cataclysmic event, and the paralysis in my legs was instant. Becoming disabled took much longer."[7] For Linton, "becoming disabled" was a process of encountering architectural, social, and psychic obstacles—e.g. needing to ask two male students to carry her up a flight of stairs everyday so she could attend a college class in an inaccessible building; wondering whether she would be able to fit her wheelchair through a doorway, or use the bathroom of a private home or public establishment; (initially) struggling with feelings of shame during sexual intimacy; and having to endure public gawking and condescension: "There were so many times, entering a party, a restaurant, or a grocery store, when people startled at the sight of me...someone was bound to come up and utter a long sigh, or tell me I was brave, or start pushing my chair across the room, uninvited."[8]

Many of the difficulties Linton experienced as a newly disabled person in the 1970s were directly caused or exacerbated by demeaning attitudes toward disability and structural barriers to access. The landmark Americans with Disabilities Act, which outlawed discrimination against people with disabilities, was not passed until 1990—and only after decades of organizing among activists in the disability community to challenge such systemic exclusion and the prejudices that fuel it. Initially, Linton was reluctant to identify with other disabled people, fearing she would become "tainted by disability's ugliness and shame." But the more involved she became in the movement, the more she understood that the problem wasn't her inability to walk, "it was that the society was configured for those who do walk, see, hear, etc."[9]

Reflecting on his experiences growing up queer with cerebral palsy, poet and activist Eli Clare cautions against absolutizing the difference between "impaired" and "disabled" for two reasons. First, disabling ideologies and social conditions are easily internalized. "To neatly divide disability from impairment doesn't feel right. My experience of living with CP has been so shaped by ableism…that I have trouble separating the two."[10] Second, both "impairment" and "disability" are deeply embodied experiences. Thus, for example, the difficulties Clare experienced when teachers refused to give him enough time to complete answers on a test—despite muscle spasms and hand tremors that made writing difficult—could have been rectified by access to alternative technologies for recording answers. But his unsuccessful attempt to summit Mount Adams, which was too steep and slippery for his unstable feet, was more of a physical limitation than a socially constructed one. Clare concludes that while it can be theoretically helpful to distinguish between a physical impairment and hardships layered onto that impairment by an ableist society, the emotional realities that sometimes accompany involuntary bodily restrictions, including frustration and disappointment, obscure any neat and tidy distinction.[11]

The relevance of disability for every body

Although the emotional/physical difficulties surrounding somatic loss or limitations suggest that "disability is not solely a constructed reality,"[12] there is little question that widespread cultural attitudes and conditions exacerbate these difficulties. Many nondisabled people overlook the social dimensions of disability because our culture's individualistic orientation conditions us to perceive body issues as personal concerns. The same cultural narratives that teach us to view our own body as a project—something each of us can and ought to improve based on the normative ideal—construct disability as a private tragedy that affects a few unlucky individuals. This perception implies that able-bodied people don't need to examine how our beliefs about (dis)ability shape our self-perceptions, social status, and life opportunities. An ideology of individualism allows us to say, "if it's not my problem, I don't have to worry about it." But this mindset overlooks the extent to which our "personal" relationship with our own bodies is linked to our perception of other people's physiques, and how able-bodied privilege is tied to disability discrimination. Ultimately, just as sexism is not just a woman's issue, and racism is not only a problem for people of color, so disability is everyone's issue.

Connected by the better body story

One of the most pervasive yet hidden ways attitudes toward disability shape the perceptions of nondisabled people is through commercial culture's story of a better body. This connection may seem surprising at first. After all, the somatic ideal that guides the quest for physical improvement seems to have nothing to do with disability. But that's precisely the point: the ideal body is *assumed* to be nondisabled. It goes without saying that the physique we are encouraged to want and create has no visible losses or limits. The normative ideal we see virtually 24/7 is not only ready for action; it is achieved through action. Its movements are strong, swift, and unencumbered, capable of shaping a lean, fit, and flawless form (Figures 5.1 & 5.2), male or female. As Alison Kafer points out, "norms of gendered behavior and appearance—i.e., 'proper masculinity and femininity'—are based on nondisabled bodies."[13] Both the rugged, aggressive, muscular body of the "manly" man, and the svelte, graceful, "lovely" figure of feminine perfection assume a completely intact, fully functioning physique.

What this assumption hides, however, is how the presumed normalcy and desirability of the nondisabled ideal are defined in silent contrast to the supposed abnormality, imperfection, and undesirability of the disabled figure. Perceptions of impaired forms as defective or ugly play a hidden role in constructing the somatic ideal everybody is encouraged to want. Largely banished from the iconography of commercial culture, disabled bodies become receptacles of fear and pity. Indirectly, these "refused" bodies support the fantasy of somatic perfection by providing its quintessential "other": the ultimate not-me figure.[14]

Nondisabled people may not recognize the extent to which able-bodied assumptions about "normalcy" shape our ideas about the kind of body we want to have—and the kind of body we *don't* want to have. By defining "improvement" as conformity to the nondisabled ideal, the better body story encourages us to collude with a disabling system of invisible prejudices and privileges. In this system, nondisabled people enjoy the psychic ease that

FIGURE 5.1 *"Model Released Weight Training"* © *Zoran Milich.*
Source: Getty Images.

comes from being considered normal, along with social access to buildings, jobs, leadership positions, educational and recreational opportunities that perceived normalcy bestows. This same system deprives people with bodily losses or limitations the internal comfort of being seen as normal, while excluding them from full and equal participation in society.

A continuum model

The relevance of disability for nondisabled people becomes even more apparent if we consider the tenuous and evolving nature of human

FIGURE 5.2 *"Model Penny Lancaster Launches New Fitness DVD 'Ultimate Body Workout'" © Mike Marsland.*
Source: Getty Images.

physiology. As disability scholars and activists point out, people without physical impairments are "temporarily able-bodied."[15] Anyone who lives long enough will eventually lose some of her or his "normal" somatic abilities. Matthew Sanford, who became paralyzed from the chest down at age 13 as the result of a car accident, reflects on this point: "In principle, my experience is not different from yours. It is only more extreme....My mind-body relationship changed in an instant—the time it took for my back to break. But the changing relationship between mind and body is a defining feature in everyone's life."[16]

Instead of thinking in binary terms (i.e. either you have a disability or you don't), it makes more sense to envision a continuum of disability. The continuities between disabled and nondisabled people are especially pronounced among those advanced in years. In the United States, for example, nearly two-thirds of the noninstitutionalized population aged 65 and older experience difficulty or limitation when performing at least one basic action.[17] Significantly, a disproportionate number of persons with disabilities are people of color. To give just one example, study of Medicare claims found that "blacks with diabetes or vascular disease are nearly five times more likely than whites to have a leg amputated."[18] Moreover, nearly a third of people with disabilities live below the poverty line.[19] These numbers illustrate how the symbolic hierarchy of bodies that governs the culture of physical improvement reflects and reinforces a social system in which various forms of injustice (e.g. ableism, ageism, racism, poverty) intersect.

The prevalence of physical impairments among a diversity of people indicates the relevance of disability studies for a broad range of "body issues." While scholars in this field focus critical attention on the "deviance" assigned to impaired bodies, their analyses yield insights for examining how other nonconforming figures are stigmatized and targeted for correcting, controlling, and curing. In some regards, all of the body issues discussed in this book can be seen to fall somewhere on a continuum of "disabilities." Aging, chronic pain and illness, and being "overweight" are sometimes seen or experienced as disabling conditions. Moreover, anxieties surrounding these experiences may be symptomatic of "compulsory able-bodiedness," a term Alison Kafer uses to describe the assumption that every body *should* be nondisabled.[20] Additionally, each of these body issues represents a form of physicality whose "difference" is commonly seen as undesirable and therefore needing "improvement." These continuities do not imply that aging, chronic illness, or being fat are *in fact* disabilities.[21] But they underscore both the broad relevance of disability studies and the need for a fluid understanding of "disability."[22]

Recognizing a continuum of disabling conditions raises interesting questions: How is "disability" defined and by whom? Given the distinction between bodily "impairment" and "disability"—with the implication that "disability" is a social issue, rather than a physical pathology or private tragedy—to what extent should people with disabilities seek to be rehabilitated or "cured"? These questions are complicated by the wide variety of disabling impairments people experience. Paralysis, multiple sclerosis, cerebral palsy, amputation, and blindness (to give just a few examples) involve vastly different functional limits, even as they are likely to create similar experiences of stigma and exclusion in an ableist society. And while Deaf people frequently experience discrimination, many of them do not regard deafness as a disability; rather, they understand themselves to be a linguistic minority with its own subculture.[23] The varying extent of a particular impairment and complications surrounding it further confound attempts to define disability. Some conditions are progressive; others are unchanging. Some are congenital, but most are acquired.[24] Some are painful, but many are not.[25] Needless to say, the broad spectrum of disabling conditions and their irreducible variety makes the category "disability" unstable and generalizations about "people with disabilities" problematic. Thus when you see these terms throughout this chapter, it's best to imagine quotes around them. Doing so enables us to approach "disability as a site of questions,"[26] as Kafer recommends, rather than a self-evident condition.

A legacy of shame: Some biblical views on physical impairment

Among the many questions disability raises, one of the most important is: Why are physically impaired bodies the targets of so much dread and shame? Why do many able-bodied people imagine disability to be "a fate worse than death?"[27] Although there is no single or causal explanation, some long-standing Christian narratives have contributed to Western culture's disparaging perceptions of somatic impairments. These narratives draw on the broader storylines about physicality we saw in Chapter 2 (i.e. the body as the "pivot" of salvation; the eschatological vision of somatic perfection; the association between women and physicality), and they fall into three interrelated categories:

1) **A shaming narrative** interprets bodily impairment as a visible manifestation of sin, a kind of blemish on God's perfect creation that represents a fall from wholeness. In this storyline, the visible body is an index of the state of the invisible soul—a tangible reflection of the inner self

2) **An eschatological narrative** equates salvation (i.e. healing) with curing, correcting, or eliminating anatomical abnormalities. In this storyline, "defects" in form or functioning are "overcome" as an expression of God's saving power

3) **A spiritualizing narrative** views disability as an opportunity for cultivating virtue. In this storyline, disabled individuals become inspiring role models by demonstrating personal courage in the face of adversity, while those who care for them demonstrate the charity disabled people presumably need

Many people, including many Christians, are unaware of the extent to which these ancient narratives have influenced our assumptions about the kind of body we want to have and the kind we want to avoid. Learning to recognize these storylines is a crucial step in challenging their legacy's lingering influence.

The shaming narrative: Disability as a sign of sin

In her groundbreaking work, *The Disabled God*, Nancy Eiesland identified Christianity's long-standing association between physical impairment and moral impurity.[28] This sin/disability nexus is exemplified in New Testament texts like John 5:14, in which Jesus heals a man who was unable to walk, then tells him: "Do not sin anymore, so that nothing worse happens to you." Throughout Christian history, this text (and similar passages) fostered a symbolic connection between disability and sin: bodily impairment was viewed as a visible punishment for immorality and unbelief.

The symbolic link between disability and sin supported other demeaning beliefs about somatic impairment that became prominent in Western culture.[29] Within the biblical tradition, blind, deaf, or lame bodies are seen to besmirch the image of God, who is envisioned as fully intact and unencumbered. As John Hull points out in *The Tactile Heart*, "God walks in the Garden of Eden; God does not limp" (Gen. 3.8).[30] If the God of the Bible is imagined to be able-bodied, it's not surprising that both the Hebrew Bible and the New Testament indicate that those representing God ought to embody that holy perfection. People with physical impairments were prohibited from serving as leaders or even entering the temple.[31] And up until quite recently, some denominations banned them from serving as ministers, with one church stating that "pastors are expected to be sufficiently able-bodied, ambulatory, and mobile" in order to fulfill ordinary parish duties.[32] Throughout Christian history, visibly flawless bodies were seen to manifest inner states of holiness, while somatic imperfections were seen to express internal states of sin.[33] Thus a disabling theology construed impaired bodies as shameful and needing redemption.

The eschatological narrative: Healing/overcoming disability

The association between disability and sin assumes that the body is the "pivot" of salvation—the site of salvation/damnation—since it is the visible barometer of one's moral state. This connection is illustrated in the gospel text, John 9.1-3, when Jesus' disciples ask him: "Rabbi, who sinned, this man or his parents, that he was born blind?" Jesus responds: "Neither this man nor his parents sinned; he was born blind so that God's works might be revealed in him." Although some scholars read this passage as evidence that Jesus refuted the sin/disability conflation,[34] others point out that Jesus' repeatedly used disparaging images of blindness as a metaphor for sin, unbelief, ignorance, or disobedience. Moreover, Jesus' response in this passage implies that "God's works" are "revealed" when the blind person is "healed," but not in a blind person that remains unsighted. Salvation thus pivots on divine healing—on the disabled body being "cured." In Hull's view, the story itself functions more to create a kind of "photo opportunity" for God's power than to challenge the undesirability of blindness.[35]

Biblical representations of physical impairments as manifesting moral deficiencies are the flip side of theological visions of "wholeness" envisioned in the fully intact and functional form. Such visions assume a normative/ idealized human body that "falls" into various kinds of "imperfections"— moral/physical defects that will be overcome in the resurrection.[36] Just as disabled bodies are regarded as evidence of the Fall, so classic Christian eschatology anticipates the removal of physical deformities at the end of time. Formulated in the writings of early church fathers and developed throughout the centuries, this homogenizing vision draws on the words of Isaiah: "Then the eyes of the blind shall be opened, and the ears of the deaf unstopped; then the lame shall leap like a deer, and the tongue of the speechless sing for joy" (Isa. 35.3–6).[37] Many Christians are familiar with this narrative through hymns that associate physical impairment with moral wretchedness and construct salvation as overcoming this miserable condition. Here's one example of the many hymns Hull cites to illustrate this association:

> Jesus is the Name exalted
> Over every other name;
> In his Name, whene'er assaulted,
> We can put our foes to shame;
> Strength to them who else had halted
> Eyes to blind, and feet to lame.[38]

The eschatological vision this hymn constructs uses the rhetoric of religious supremacy (i.e. "Over every other name…") to reinforce a disparaging view of disability. Blindness and lameness are akin to religious "foes" that need to need to be conquered. Employing a brokenness/wholeness binary that defines healing as the elimination of disability, this song's eschatology assumes a "convergent model" in which salvation depends on conformity to an able-bodied ideal.[39] Such equations lead Betcher to observe that "Theologies of healing…can be unwitting agents of imperial ideals."[40]

Spiritualizing narratives: Disability as an opportunity for virtue

Whereas some biblical narratives depict disability as a sign of moral fault in need of redemption, others connect it with virtuous suffering.[41] In this storyline, the difficulties surrounding bodily impairment are a kind of divine test through which one is purified. Drawing on the sin/disability association, this narrative makes the body the pivot of salvation: disability is not just a burden but an opportunity to develop spiritually, i.e. to cultivate exceptional faith by enduring somatic limitations with grace and courage. Seeing disability as a "cross to bear" suggests that people with disabilities need not (and thus ought not) fall into despair and can even be grateful for their condition. Trusting that God can use an unwanted situation for redemptive purposes, this logic suggests, disabled persons can and should bravely and obediently accept and adjust to their conditions.[42]

The story of Bethany Hamilton, the 13-year-old surfer who lost her arm in a shark attack in 2003, illustrates the ambiguities surrounding this narrative. On the one hand, Hamilton's unrelenting trust in God empowers her to accept her loss. Both her book (*Soul Surfer*) and the movie about her (*Heart of a Soul Surfer*) illustrate how religious faith enables her to reject the normalizing expectations of an able-bodied society. Hamilton opts not to wear a prosthetic, which she finds cumbersome; and she makes no attempt to conceal her amputation, fondly referring to what's left of her arm as "stumpy." On the other hand, her understanding of the loss of her arm as part of "God's plan" reinforces a view of the divine as using disability to test and purify the spirit—a view that makes God cruel, while leaving an ableist culture unchallenged.[43]

Within the biblical tradition, disability is not only an opportunity for an impaired individual to develop moral fortitude; it's also a chance for others to cultivate virtue by extending healing, charity, and inclusion. The story of a disabled man at the Beautiful Gate (Acts 3.1–10) illustrates this dynamic.[44] In it, Peter and John are on their way to the temple when they pass a beggar who is "lame from birth." In lieu of giving the disabled man alms, Peter performs a healing miracle that restores his ability to walk and enables him to accompany them to the temple, where he leaps and praises God while others look on in amazement. This narrative of miraculous curing and inclusion recalls the healing stories of Jesus, who enabled the lame to walk, the blind to see, and the deaf to hear as gestures of forgiveness and inclusion in God's kingdom. While such miracles and hospitality may be favorable to those who are cured, they raise questions about the spiritual status of those who are not. As Eiesland reminds us, the classic sin/disability nexus implies that disabled people who remain "uncured" must be harboring some moral transgression.[45] In addition, the assumption that disability *needs* to be cured reinforces its status as an inferior state. Hull goes so far as to ask Jesus: "why was there not a blind person among your followers?" His answer: Jesus would have restored a blind follower's sight since an uncured blind person would have shocked those who believed in their savior's power, and, Hull speculates, may well have been an embarrassment to Jesus.[46]

The same narrative that makes inclusion contingent on healing/curing also supports the Christian ethic of charity toward disabled persons. This ethic still guides many institutions today—e.g. hospitals, nursing homes, and rehabilitation centers—that aim to help those with "special needs."

FIGURE 5.3 *Bethany Hamilton at the 2004 Teen Choice Awards © Gregg DeGuire.*
Source: Getty Images.

Without question, many people with disabilities have benefited from these establishments. At the same time, the charity ethic positions "the disabled" as "objects of pity" on which benevolent caretakers can cultivate their virtue.[47] This patronizing model is epitomized by Jerry Lewis's television fund-raising charity, which understandably infuriates many disabilities rights activists by depicting disabled "kids"—many of whom are adults—as tragic victims who make nondisabled viewers grateful for their normalcy.[48] Somewhat ironically, the charity ethic offers a "suffocating surplus of compassion" to people with disabilities,[49] even as it distances "the disabled" from those in (superior) helping positions, who ostensibly have no need for healing. In the end, this ethic exacerbates the separation between "normal" and "not-me" bodies by treating disability as a private tragedy without challenging the social/symbolic systems that view differently abled bodies as dreadful.

Traditional Christian narratives are neither the cause of, nor the sole contributors to, stereotypical views of people with disabilities as unattractive, pitiful but potentially brave victims of personal adversity. Nonetheless, they lend conceptual support to these views by depicting disability, in Thomas Reynolds words, "as something to be healed or gotten rid of—a fault, a lesson in lack of faith, a helpless object of pity for the non-disabled faithful to display their charity, a vehicle of redemptive suffering, a cross to bear, or fuel for the inspiration of others."[50] Becoming familiar with these narratives prepares us to recognize—and challenge—their harmful effects beyond the realm of traditional religion.

(De)constructing normalcy and disability

These days, disparaging perceptions of bodily impairments are not typically couched in explicitly religious terms. Of course, there are exceptions to this general rule. Buddhist author Joan Tollifson, who was born without a right hand, recalls that when she was a toddler, people would stop her mother on the street to inform her that God was punishing them.[51] Most often, however, theologically sanctioned fear and shame of bodily impairment hides in pointed fingers, hushed questions, gawking stares or averted glances, in "feeling sorry" for "those poor, unfortunate people," turning them into heroes, or segregating or striving to "rehabilitate" their bodies. In *Too Late to Die Young*, the late Harriet McBryde Johnson describes some common reactions to her unconventional body, which she describes as frail and withered as the result of a wasting disease, and which used a wheelchair for mobility:

> "I admire you for being out; most people would give up."
> "God bless you! I'll pray for you" [note: McBryde Johnson was an atheist].
> "You don't let the pain hold you back, do you?"
> "If I had to live like you, I think I'd kill myself."[52]

In different ways, these comments reflect the undesirability of disability that Christian narratives convey. "In high school," Tollifson recalls, "I was not a hot item with the boys. Growing up, the only cultural images I saw of disabled people were negative: Captain Hook or the Easter Seal poster seemed to be my choices." Understandably, Tollifson resisted thinking of herself as disabled, even as she unwittingly internalized these images.[53]

In an ableist society, the undesirability of disability seems obvious. But humans are not born believing that bodies without certain parts or functions are inherently inferior. We *learn* to see bodies this way. Tollifson observes that when babies (and animals) approach her arm, "the one that ends just below the elbow...they aren't frightened or repulsed by it. They don't feel sorry for me. They don't think I'm heroic or amazing. They see the actual shape of what's in front of them without concepts or labels."[54] The same social conditioning that teaches us to view impaired bodies as shameful and needing redemption (i.e. curing) encourages us to perceive nondisability as normal and therefore better. For nondisabled people in particular, the belief that a better body = a normal body = an able body is difficult to question in part because dominant religious/cultural narratives constantly reinforce these equations, and in part because we regularly benefit from them.

Despite such benefits, many able-bodied people struggle with feelings of disgust and shame in relation to their bodies, and these feelings suggest that *every*body has a stake in dismantling the able-bodied/normative ideal that *no*body can achieve. This deconstruction is not something nondisabled people should do as a favor to people with disabilities; it is something we can do as we explore our own relationship with physicality, and examine what "health," "healing," or "improvement" might mean for our particular body. Deconstructing the able-bodied dream of normalcy requires nondisabled people to wrestle with a question Betcher poses: "What do we hide from or reject about ourselves in that classification of physiological variations known as disablement?"[55] Investigating the insecurities we feel and judgments we direct toward our own tentatively able bodies may help nondisabled people stop projecting them onto the nonconforming anatomies of others and start cultivating a more friendly relationship to our own uniquely vulnerable flesh.

This investigation requires us to examine various beliefs about bodies we've internalized, often without our conscious consent. Such beliefs reflect a confluence of cultural discourses—commercial, medical, aesthetic— that gained momentum during nineteenth and early twentieth centuries, as the authority of Christian narratives became increasingly contested and dispersed. Rather than simply replace traditional Christian views of disability as a morally inferior, pitiable condition that proffers opportunities for virtue, modern commercial, aesthetic, and scientific discourses reinvented them, incorporating and modifying beliefs about somatic variation in ways that expanded and deepened the undesirability of disability.

The spectacle of "otherness" and the production of the ideal "self"

As a child, I was taught that "it's not polite to stare" at someone whose body is visibly disabled. However well-intended, this instruction already assumed the "otherness" of disability, as if there were something wrong or shameful about it. On the surface, my socialization contrasts sharply with the culturally sanctioned gazing at disabled (and other anomalous) bodies encouraged in the "freak" shows of nineteenth- and early twentieth-century America. In *Extraordinary Bodies*, Garland Thomson examines how these commercial exhibitions—spectators paid an entrance fee to see the "freaks"—contributed to the construction of somatic normalcy and otherness in that historical context. Her analysis reveals how these public spectacles deployed racist, sexist, and colonial ideologies to transform the "raw materials" of atypical bodies into "human curiosities" whose "monstrosities" assuaged their viewers' anxieties about their own normality.[56]

Whereas biblical narratives interpreted anatomical abnormality as a sign of sin that created a moral opportunity, modern freak shows cultivated audiences' lurid fascination with notable physical eccentricities, tapping the commercial potential of "prodigious bodies" by presenting them as the antithesis of the able-bodied, ideal American. The spectacular "otherness" of figures like the "Armless Wonder" (a man born without arms), the "Hottentot Venus" (a dark-skinned woman with unusually large buttocks), and "The Ugliest Woman in the World" (a hirsute Mexican-Indian woman, also dubbed "Ape woman") earned their exhibitors considerable profits. At the same time, these alien bodies reassured paying spectators of their superior position on the prevailing somatic/cultural hierarchy of the time. The figure of the freak offered onlookers the relief of fitting into a society where standing out made one vulnerable to the perception of deviancy. As Garland Thomson observes "Admissions fees were good investments for those who could walk away from the freak show with their normalcy affirmed."[57]

Not every body on exhibit was noticeably impaired. Unusual size (e.g. fat or thin), hair in the "wrong" places, or visible signs of ethnic "difference" were sufficient qualifications for freakdom. Just being a colonized person of color was a disability in this context.[58] In some cases, a mix of cultural/corporeal otherness increased a freak's allure. Dark-skinned, disabled, female bodies provided an especially powerful spectacle of otherness for privileged, Anglo-Saxon Americans. Consider, for example, the first "freak" P. T. Barnum exhibited in Philadelphia in 1835: an elderly, toothless, blind, partially paralyzed black woman named Joice Heth. The poster advertising this "marvelous relic of antiquity" declared her "THE GREATEST *Natural and National* **CURIOSITY**

IN THE WORLD."[59] The polar opposite of both the Victorian "White Lady" ideal and the autonomous, self-sufficient man of reason, Heth's body simultaneously displayed and domesticated the threat of corporeal diversity and frailty from which the privileged sought to psychically protect themselves. Safely contained by the freak shows' ritual codes and conventions, anomalous figures like Heth visibly affirmed the desirability of the nondisabled/ideal American self by embodying, in Garland Thomson's phrasing, its "ultimate not-me."[60]

The freak shows illustrate not just how perceptions of able-bodied normalcy and disabled otherness mutually define each other, but also how the ancient practice of reading the visible flesh as an index of the soul's status continued into the modern era. Just as Christian narratives assigned transcendent meaning to physical impairment (i.e. as manifesting sin), so the freak shows associated nonconforming bodies with such "un-American" vices as passivity, inefficiency, dependency, and lack of control. Unlike the traditional Christian view of a person, however, who (at least in theory) depends on the power of God, the ideal modern self is seen to operate through its own sovereign will. This Cartesian self is defined not by faith but by reason. Its personhood resides in its power of self-definition—precisely the power the freaks seemed to lack.[61] What made disabled bodies so fascinating and so awful—so abnormal and so obviously inferior in the eyes of their viewers—was the perceived absence of self-controlled agency and their corresponding impossibility of improvement.

Refusing to be an object of pity or fascinating spectacle

From today's perspective, the freak shows of the nineteenth and early twentieth centuries are a case study in distasteful, offensive commercial entertainment. Nonetheless, the beliefs about "normalcy" and "otherness" these shows supported continue to inform the culture of somatic improvement. What makes the able-bodied ideal that orients this culture *ideal* is its association with self-mastery. The flawless form is perceived to represent a self that is "in control"—a self presumably capable of overcoming the limits, irregularities, and vulnerabilities of the flesh.

In *Too Late to Die Young*, the late Harriet McBryde Johnson tells tales of her resistance to such (mis)perceptions and the fantasy of normalcy embedded in them. A lawyer and disabilities rights activist, McBryde Johnson was born with a muscle-wasting disease that left her adult body, in her words, "a jumble of bones in a floppy bag of skin." At age 15, she threw away a cumbersome back brace designed to keep her spine straight. For decades after that, she lived comfortably in her S-shaped frame, resting her rib cage on her lap, propping her elbows with rolled towels, maneuvering about in her power wheelchair, seeking adventures, challenging assumptions, telling stories.[62]

One day she received an invitation from *The New York Times Magazine* to publish one of her stories: an account of her conversations with Princeton philosopher Peter Singer, who advocates killing disabled fetuses because of their allegedly dismal prospects for a happy life. As McBryde Johnson put it, "he regards lives like mine as avoidable mistakes."[63] Singer also supports physician-assisted suicide for people with disabilities, a position that, McBryde Johnson points out, does little to challenge the common causes of suicidality among disabled people: "dependence, institutional confinement, and being a burden." Countering Singer's assumption that disability is a one-way ticket to a life of misery, McBryde Johnson argues that "the presence or absence of a disability doesn't predict quality of life," that much of the difficulty disabled people experience stems from societal prejudice and injustice, and that nondisabled people are not the best judges of the happiness (or lack thereof) of people with disabilities.[64]

As part of its plan to publish her account of this lively exchange, the *New York Times Magazine* wanted to include "a big photodocumentary spread" depicting details of a typical day in McBryde Johnson's life. The photography department assured McBryde Johnson that the pictures would be done tastefully, but she wasn't convinced. She imagined the story of her debates with Singer being eclipsed by "a distracting visual narrative about the Amazing Crippled Attorney!" In lieu of a series of photos, she agreed to a single cover portrait and promised to discuss other possibilities with the *Times* photographer assigned to shoot the portrait. Despite good intentions to be respectful, however, the photographer failed to grasp the wider context of ableism that led McBryde Johnson to suspect that even the most artful images of her extraordinary body would likely reinforce—rather than challenge—a perception of her as an alien other. Such images "would draw readers out of the story, make them distance themselves from my experience, and invite them to stare at me the way they usually do."[65] She refused to cooperate with the photographer's ideas and insisted that all photos be taken and featured on *her* terms. You can view some of these images by visiting http://www. bloomsbury.com/uk/shameful-bodies-9781472594945/ and looking under "Chapter Five."

McBryde Johnson's unwillingness to be turned into a freakish spectacle or an object of pity expresses the very agency people with disabilities are not supposed to have, according to dominant stereotypes of disabled people as tragic victims. Her agency brings into focus questions about the relationship between human physicality and our more-than-physical selves.

What (if anything) does your one-of-a-kind body express about who you are as a person? What is the relationship between your particular corporeal configuration and your inner life-process—that part of you Christians traditionally refer to as your "soul?" The questions themselves may be more valuable than any definitive answers. But the mystery surrounding them is obscured by a cultural/religious optic that views disability as a sign of misery and weakness. On the symbolic hierarchy of bodies, McBryde Johnson's unusual form is not just the antithesis of able-bodied perfection, it's the opposite of the ideal self such perfection presumably displays. Her nonconforming body/self epitomizes the dependency, unpredictability, and fragility for which there is no cure.

Medicalization, normalization, and invisiblization

The lack of a cure for exceptional bodies like McBryde Johnson's has not stopped scientific authorities from making them its business. In fact, a "medical model" provides the dominant paradigm for understanding disability today. In *Vulnerable Communion*, theologian Thomas Reynolds describes how this model tends to "reduce disability to a problem requiring diagnosis and treatment, a broken object to be fixed, made better, or overcome." This approach constructs the relationship between the medical expert and the disabled patient primarily as a one-way street in which "the healer has the knowledge to define illness and the power to rehabilitate, the advantages of which are passively received by a beneficiary regarded as someone with nothing to offer."[66] The medical paradigm secularizes notions of disability as a sign of sin in need of redemption, viewing it as an illness that needs to be corrected, supervised, or cured.

Historically, the medical model emerged in tandem with the freak shows. In fact, some of the freaks' bodies became "medical specimens" after their deaths, as men of science used them to create taxonomies that classified and ranked corporeal variations, identifying certain bodies as aesthetically, morally, and medically superior, and others as ugly, degenerate, and sick.[67] Ironically, scientists' accounts of anatomical diversity recycled the religious ideas they claimed to surpass—including the belief that a body's external contours, abilities, and features manifest a person's internal moral character.

These accounts were shaped by economic developments of the nineteenth and early twentieth centuries. The factories and markets of the industrial revolution required able-bodied workers to assure smooth functioning and expansion. This system reinforced the mechanistic view of human physiology that had come to dominate the field of science. In *Enforcing Normalcy*, Lennard Davis notes that "the increasing reciprocity between humans and machines led to the conception of the human bodies as machines...and of the mechanical perfection of the human body."[68] Implicitly, people with physical impairments challenged the modern view of the self as an autonomous agent capable of controlling and perfecting a machine-like body. Explicitly, disabled people made for less-than-ideal workers in an economic system that prioritized productivity, efficiency, uniformity, and speed. Increasingly, this system defined the American Dream in terms of one's capacity to earn and spend money. Within this system, impaired bodies posed another problem: they refused to support the myth of progress—the belief in perpetual improvement—that the industrial and scientific revolutions took for granted.

This was also the era in which the idea of "normalcy" gained prominence in Euro-American culture, thanks largely to the growing influence of the field of Statistics. With concepts like "the average man"—a supposedly generic though obviously idealized white male human being—nineteenth-century scientists set standards by which moral and physical deviations were measured. Davis points out that nearly all the founders of Statistics were eugenicists: "scientists" who advocated improving humanity by eradicating undesirable characteristics (e.g. disability) from the population, usually by encouraging (or forcing) people with those characteristics not to reproduce. Eugenicists lumped together "undesirable traits" and the people who had them, so that "criminals, the poor, and people with disabilities would be mentioned in the same breath."[69]

Perceptions of poverty, disablement, and criminality as shameful coalesced in the "ugly laws" cities across the United States instituted during the later decades of the nineteenth century. One of the most famous of these laws (a 1881 Chicago ordinance) stipulated that "Any person who is diseased, maimed, mutilated, or in any way deformed, so as to be an unsightly or disgusting object...shall not therein or thereon expose himself to public view, under the penalty of a fine of $1 [about $20 today] for each offense." As historian Susan Schweik points out, municipal leaders aimed such laws specifically at those who "exposed" their diseased or disabled bodies "for the purpose of begging."[70] Thus "unsightly beggar" laws used aesthetic judgments to link somatic impairment and economic dependency in ways that reflected the eugenicists' agenda of eliminating various forms of "degeneracy," while affirming the capitalist imperative for a society of "productive" workers and consumers.[71] Not coincidentally, the same aesthetics that underwrote the "ugly laws" found its way into modern literature and early films, which frequently depicted villains and delinquents as physically disabled.[72]

In its various articulations, the pseudo-scientific link between disability and various kinds of depravity (moral, economic, and aesthetic) recalls the biblical association between sin and disability and the need for eschatological "healing." In the modern retelling of this narrative, however, human variations from the ideal were seen not as blemishing God's good creation, but as contaminating the Nation. Hitler's agenda was a logical extension of a eugenics mentality that was widely shared among cultural elites of his time. In 1933, for example, the prestigious scientific publication *Nature* endorsed a Nazi proposal for "the controlled and deliberate improvement of the human stock" by sterilizing people with disabilities.[73] In disturbing ways, the eugenicists' utopic dream of "improving" society by eradicating "deviant" and "defective" people resembles the eschatological vision of heaven as a place only flawless bodies/souls inhabit. Both visions are connected by a colonialist logic that damns difference and seeks to save it by converting it to a singular ideal.

In the early decades of the twentieth century, this mentality increasingly led to the institutionalization of people with disabilities. During this era, the "freak" was reconfigured "from its earlier visible, public position as strange, awful, and lurid spectacle to its later, private position as sick, hidden, and shameful."[74] By mid-century, people with atypical anatomies were largely invisiblized, relegated by a "powerful medical industrial complex" to a separate sphere—e.g. nursing homes, hospitals, schools, rehabilitation centers—where they could be treated by doctors, therapists, and teachers who specialized in "helping" them minimize, correct, or overcome their corporeal abnormalities and limits.[75]

Eli Clare describes how the prospect of institutionalized seclusion exacerbated his desire for normalcy. As a child, he was determined not to be seen as a "special ed" kid. At school, he tried to "pass" as "normal," even though cerebral palsy slurred his speech, made writing difficult, and prompted classmates to call him "retard," "monkey," and "defect."[76] As he grew up, these words and "all the lies contained in [them]" fostered feelings of self-loathing: "For too long, I hated my trembling hand, my precarious balance, my spastic muscles so repeatedly overtaken by tension and tremor, tried to hide them at all costs. More than once, I wished to amputate my right arm so it wouldn't shake. My shame was that bald." Looking back on these experiences, Clare notices the parallels between queer and disabled bodies. Both have been labeled by religious institutions as defective and disordered. Both are encouraged to internalize the dread others project on their flesh. Both have been seen as "freaks of nature," medicalized and pathologized according to a symbolic/social hierarchy of bodies. And too often, both live in shame and isolation because they don't fit society's definition of normal.[77]

The dream of normalcy and the myth of overcoming

What links the institutionalization/invisiblization of disabled bodies with the commercial spectacles of the freak shows, the disabling discourses of science, statistics, nationalism, and eugenics, and the "ugly laws" is a colonial impulse to contain or control human diversity. In *Waking*, Mathew Sanford describes the damage this homogenizing tendency inflicted as he sought to make sense of his reconfigured 13-year-old body after a car accident left him paralyzed from the chest down. In the hospital following the crash, doctors inform him that he won't experience any sensation in the lower two-thirds of his body and that he should plan on never walking again. As Sanford tries to digest this information, he can't help but notice the presence of something as he tunes into the absence of sensation in his legs. "It's not like normal sensation, like what I feel in my arms…all the same, it is noticeable: tingles, surges, sometimes even mild burning." He mentions what he notices to the doctors, who worry that he's in denial. Apologetically, they assure him that whatever he feels, it "isn't real." To prove their point, they set up an experiment that involves poking Sanford's feet with needles, to the point where they bleed. Sanford is humiliated. "Now I am an object of pity…Stupid boy, what were you thinking?" Shamed into accepting the medical/master narrative, he stops listening to the "silence" of his paralysis, and spends the next decade moving further away from his body.[78]

Sanford's experience illustrates the mixed messages the medical model conveys. On the one hand, the doctors discourage him from any delusion that his body is normal. On the other hand, his rehabilitation plan is guided by the dream of normalcy this model presumes: the salvation myth of "overcoming" disability by becoming as nondisabled as possible. At the rehabilitation center, this dream is introduced to Sanford through series of hypermasculine role models: men in wheelchairs who have triumphed over their disabilities by creating ultra-ripped upper bodies. There's Dwight, who is paralyzed from the chest down but who can bench press 190 pounds—without stomach muscles; and Dennis, a paraplegic businessman who brags about hunting, killing, gutting, and dragging a deer from the woods all by himself (using an ATV four wheeler); and Steve, an award-winning wheelchair athlete whose biceps bulge without even being flexed. And there's Rick, the physical therapist who, frustrated with Sanford's slow recovery, challenges him to "be a man." Though the promise of normalcy these men represent brings Sanford temporary relief, in the end it leaves him feeling more dissociated than ever from his internal/physical experience. Intuitively, he questions the narrative the doctors and rehab specialists script for him: that his paralysis and its accompanying silence are obstacles to overcome, and that if he succeeds in defeating them, he can regain his masculinity and become an inspiration to others.[79] But he finds no support for his questions—not to mention any genuine healing—until he begins studying yoga over a dozen years later.

The "myth of overcoming"[80] is a salvation story that permeates the culture of physical improvement. It shapes our attitudes toward health and illness, pain, size, aging, and various other body issues as well. Combining a Cartesian notion of the "self" as an individual, autonomous, rational will with Christianity's moral imperative to master the "flesh," this myth fuels the perception that we can and should improve our bodies, and that such improvement makes us "good." In relation to disability, this myth says that with enough fortitude and courage, a person can "defeat" (i.e. control or transcend) the limits that a physical impairment imposes and become a role model for others.

The myth of overcoming seems to challenge stereotypes of disabled people as helpless, unhappy victims. But, as Eli Clare suggests, it is precisely these stereotypes that make the "believe-it-or-not" stories of conquering disability so titillating for able-bodied audiences. "A boy without hands bats .486 on his Little League team. A blind man hikes the Appalachian Trail from end to end. An adolescent girl with Down syndrome learns to drive and has a boyfriend." As Clare observes, what makes these "supercrip" dramas so riveting for nondisabled people is the widespread, if unspoken, assumption "that disability and achievement contradict each other." The view of disabled persons as tragic victims is what makes the story of a one-legged runner "amazing." Like the biblical accounts of miraculous healings, such tales of transcendence depend on, rather than question, a disparaging view of disability. They celebrate, rather than challenge, the dream of normalcy that shapes able-bodied expectations of how a body should perform. Meanwhile, Clare points out, the disabling attitudes and social conditions that make it difficult for kids with disabilities to play sports, for people who are blind to have outdoor adventures, or for a girl with Down syndrome to be romantically involved, go unquestioned.[81]

When people with disabilities are visible at all in popular culture, it's often because their presence in some way supports the myth of overcoming. The pull-yourself-up-by-your-bootstraps philosophy this myth assumes boldly affirms: "you can do anything you want, you just have to want it badly enough."[82] This mentality ignores not only the various kinds and degrees of limitations people with disabilities experience, but also the way these limitations frequently intersect with various forms of systemic discrimination (e.g. sexism, racism, classism, homophobia, ageism).

Kafer examines the effects of this self-help mentality in her analysis of an American public service campaign that used billboards featuring disabled people to promote "community values" and "character development."

Sponsored by the Foundation for a Better Life (FBL), a self-described nonpartisan philanthropic organization, the billboards depicted people with disabilities who have overcome their somatic restrictions by cultivating personal/moral qualities. Kafer describes some of these images:

> Adam Bender, who lost a leg to cancer, stands one-legged in his baseball uniform as a symbol of *overcoming* ("Threw cancer a curve ball"); Brook Ellison, smiling as she poses in her wheelchair and wearing a graduation gown, was able to graduate from Harvard ("Quadriplegic. A-. Harvard") because of her *determination*...Eric Weihenmayer, a blind hiker photographed in profile on a snowy mountaintop, succeeded ("Climbed Everest. Blind") thanks to his *vision*.[83]

As Kafer points out, the billboards' focus on individual achievement downplays the systemic barriers (social and internalized) that people with physical impairments routinely confront. By depoliticizing disability, their images efface the complex realities of those "who haven't managed to graduate from Harvard, or climb Mount Everest, or sport high-tech prosthetic limbs." As Kafer observes, disabled people who haven't triumphed over their anatomical losses or limits cannot represent (and are denied access to) the vision of a "better life" the FBL promises. Meanwhile, responses to the billboards posted on the FBL's website express able-bodied viewers' "not-me" relationship with disability in their reassuring acknowledgement that "things could be much worse"[84]—an acknowledgement that seems to say: "at least I'm not disabled."

Negotiating normalizing gender narratives

The ableist imperative to overcome disability is linked to normalizing narratives about gender. As Clare points out, "To be female and disabled is to be seen as not quite a woman; to be male and disabled, as not quite a man."[85] For men, the undesirability of disability is exacerbated by the expectation that being "manly" means being in charge and self-reliant. Thus the hypermasculine role models Sanford is encouraged to emulate are designed to help him reclaim his "manhood." By building a beefy upper body, he can "look strong" enough to communicate manly authority and project an image capable of attracting women's attention.[86] The cultural imperative to regain masculinity by defeating disability is similarly seen in the iconic figure of Christopher Reeve, whose Campaign to Cure Paralysis inspires millions of nondisabled people with its defiant, rationally scripted message: "We don't have to accept—as though it is a fact—that after a spinal cord injury you have lost mobility and function forever. We know this is not true. Scientists and researchers know it is not true."[87] An earlier version of the masculinized myth of overcoming is evident in Franklin D. Roosevelt's refusal to be photographed in his wheelchair or seen being carried up stairs, lest his disability reveal weakness—evidence that he was less than a man powerful enough to lead the free world. According to Lennard Davis, Roosevelt wanted to be seen as a "cured cripple," and his alleged ability to triumph over adversity was scripted to parallel the United States' recovery from the great depression.[88]

"Overcoming" disability presents particular challenges for women, given their ancient designation as "deformed males" (Aristotle), their long-standing association with carnal craving, and their ongoing cultural conditioning to establish their worth by creating a desirable appearance. The assumption that feminine beauty is incompatible with disability is evident in comments Simi Linton sometimes heard after becoming paralyzed in her lower body: "what a shame," people would tell her, "and you're so pretty too"—as if being disabled somehow compromised her good looks.[89]

Commercial culture's sexual objectification of able-bodied women complicates disabled women's efforts to challenge stereotypes of them as unattractive and asexual. This has been the case for decades, as illustrated by the controversy Ellen Stohl stirred back in 1987 when she posed for *Playboy* magazine. The normalization of Stohl's quadriplegic body in the explicitly sexualized images (her wheelchair was conspicuously absent from these photos) angered some disabilities advocates, who saw *Playboy* as perpetuating the stereotype that only able-bodied women can be sexually appealing. But others praised the magazine for depicting a disabled woman as sexually alluring, even if her impairment was effaced in the soft porn pictures.[90] These mixed responses reflect the conundrums women with disabilities face as they navigate the mutual stereotypes of nondisabled women as sexual objects and disabled female bodies as asexual.

Decades later, we can still appreciate these difficulties as we heed Clare's words of caution about "the dangers of accepting beauty and sexuality as defined exclusively by nondisabled people, by straight people, by white people, by rich people, by men."[91] The normalizing trajectory of the "myth of overcoming" makes it easy to forget that disabled bodies, like all bodies, come in diverse abilities, colors, classes, ages, and sizes. Removed from its wheelchair and seductively posed on a bed, Stohl's body achieves the normative femininity required to gain entrance into pages of *Playboy*. But would McBryde Johnson's self-described twisted and skeletal body pass the same test? How much does "overcoming disability" for women hinge on conformity to a hyper-feminine ideal?

Embracing/reforming normalizing visions of femininity

These questions return us to the story of Amy Purdy, the woman quoted at the beginning of this chapter who said that prior to having her legs amputated, she imagined she'd rather be dead than disabled. When I first heard Purdy's interview with Guy Raz in spring of 2015, I didn't realize she was (and is) a celebrity. At dinner one night, I was telling my then 14-year-old son about Purdy's TED Talk. "Oh, I know who you're talking about," he said. "I saw her on a Superbowl commercial."

The ad features Purdy using prosthetic legs to run, mountain bike, snowboard, ballroom dance, pose as a fashion model, and drive a Toyota Camry. A clip from Muhammad Ali's well-known speech, in which he chants about "wrestling with the alligator" (an allusion to his 1974 fight with George Foreman), plays in the background. Purdy's story of grappling with "the alligator" is interesting to examine in the context of the culture of physical improvement not only because it defies the unspoken rule that only nondisabled bodies are commercially viable, but also because it simultaneously relies on and resists normalizing visions of femininity.

Purdy's interest in maintaining a "feminine" figure is evident throughout her memoir, *On My Own Two Feet*. Before her illness, she says her only worries in life were "whether I shaved my legs or gained any weight." After her amputations, she continues to enjoy doing her hair and makeup and getting "all dolled up." Her descriptions of significant women in her life (e.g. her mother, sister, a high school friend, a post-high school roommate, and Madonna) are peppered with praise for their attractive features (i.e. "tiny waist," "gorgeous green eyes," "amazing skin," "long blond hair," "awesome body," "petite").[92] Looking feminine seems central to Purdy's self-definition. In fact, one of the most difficult moments of her post-amputation recovery happens when she gets her first pair of prosthetic legs, which are big and bulky, and which she describes as "ugly as hell...as indelicate as anything I'd ever laid eyes on." Purdy understands that these legs are designed to help her learn to walk on prosthetics—they are "100% about function" rather than "fashion or femininity." Nonetheless, their unattractive clunkiness triggers a serious episode of depression that leaves her feeling "completely out of control." Later on, Purdy realizes that "when I lost my legs, I also felt like I lost part of what made me a woman."[93]

Purdy's embrace of normative definitions of femininity stands in tension with her wholehearted acceptance of her reconfigured body. Once she's able to use legs that look sleek and elegant, she begins to experience them as "extensions" of herself: "I decided that my legs...were going to be part of me. Rather than resenting the legs or seeing them as a daily chore I had to tolerate, I learned to actually embrace them."[94] Beyond her book, Purdy's appreciation for her extraordinary body seems evident in the myriad images of her available on the internet. If you google "Amy Purdy Images," you'll see a few pictures showing her in everyday situations (e.g. sitting on a couch, opening a car door), along with many more glamorous images that resemble those commonly found in women's fashion and fitness magazines. Some show her wearing nothing but prosthetics, posed in ways that are simultaneously athletic and sexy by popular cultural standards. In these images, Purdy seems uninterested in hiding her body's nonconformity, suggesting that she's moved beyond the shame of disability and is challenging able-body norms for femininity (Figure 5.4).

FIGURE 5.4 *Amy Purdy "10th Anniversary of 'Dancing with the Stars' "* © *Steve Granitz.*
Source: Getty Images.

Nonetheless, elements of conventional femininity remain central to Purdy's image. Admittedly, my own history of struggle with this ideal—especially its mandatory thinness—along with my awareness of the pain this ideal triggers in so many girls and women, make me suspicious of its capacity to serve as a basis for self-acceptance. My skepticism is directed not at Purdy's experience but at the narrow norms for femininity that leave many females feeling hopelessly flawed. I find myself wondering, to what extent, and in what ways, do disabled women's bodies need to be normalized to merit inclusion in the iconography of popular culture? Do efforts to look or function more like the standard feminine ideal soften the challenge someone like Purdy presents to disabling stereotypes?

That Purdy rejects such stereotypes is clear. "I am not a victim," she explains, elaborating her goal to never feel sorry for herself. When the nurses objectify her amputated body by asking her how her "stumps" are doing, Purdy pushes back: "*My stumps? What am I, a tree?*"—and tells the nurses, "My *legs* are fine." Her resistance to being labeled an "amputee" is the flip side of her desire to be seen as a whole person—one who uses prosthetic legs, but whose legs do not define her. At the same time, this resistance involves a desire "to feel as normal as I possibly could," as if "wholeness" and "normalcy" were synonymous—which, of course, they are, in an able-bodied worldview. Perhaps it's Purdy's desire to feel normal that makes her reluctant to identify with more politicized groups within the disability community. In contrast to many self-described disability scholars and activists, some of whom affectionately and unashamedly refer to themselves as "crips" (short for "cripples"), Purdy is "turned off" by what she sees as restrictive labels, preferring "to focus on capabilities, not disabilities."[95]

In fact, a primary message of Purdy's TED Talk and her book is that "each of us is far more capable than we could ever know," and that with enough heart, grit, and dedication, we can "[d]efy expectations" and rise above "our so-called limitations." In just three months, for instance, she went from lying on a surgery table for a kidney transplant, to snowboarding down a snowy mountain: "If that was possibile," she reflects, "anything was—and is." Purdy's "anything is possible" philosophy is not purely individualist. She's determined to use her experiences to "help others."[96] Together with her boyfriend, she launched a nonprofit that enables people with disabilities get involved in action sports.

Moreover, Purdy recognizes the ironies and intersections of different forms of loss and injustice—i.e. that the kids she encounters on a trip to South Africa have feet but no shoes, while she has more than enough shoes but no feet; that a pair of prosthetic legs costs 30,000 dollars; and that her amputated body resembles that of the wounded Vietnam vet she once saw holding a sign that said "will work for food." On the whole, however, her story plays to a nondisabled audience's preference for tales of personal triumph rather than social critique of ableism. Her primary aim is to encourage individuals to "Dream bigger." She wants disabled and able-bodied people alike to see that by shifting our perspective, "an overwhelming challenge can start looking like a beautiful blessing."[97] This shift leads her to view her own story as a "spiritual journey."

Purdy's account of this journey taps popular interest in spirituality today. For example, her narrative feeds Americans' appetite for stories about near death experiences, their New Age fascination with native traditions, and their "everything happens for a reason" theodicy.[98] Throughout the memoir, however, these spiritual clichés are mixed with more thoughtful reflections— i.e. about the limits of reason to explain everything, and the benefits of letting go of what we can't control.[99] Purdy also explicitly rejects traditional views of disability as a sign of divine punishment, speculating that "God" is "bigger" than a "Heavenly Father" who sits in the clouds casting judgment, and that what religion calls "God" is "really a creative life force that connects everything."[100] She sees this force at work in her own capacity to convert her loss into an opportunity for personal growth.

Unresolved dilemmas in an ableist culture

Purdy's story illustrates the multiple challenges people with disabilities must navigate in an ableist culture: How to resist this culture's construction of disability as shameful without conforming to able-bodied norms and ideals? How to live as fully, comfortably, and freely as possible with physical impairments without buying into disabling definitions of "improvement"? How to visually represent disability without feeding an ableist hunger for "not-me" spectacles? How to tell the stories of people living with disabilities without sensationalizing them? How to counteract stereotypes of disabled people as tragic victims without denying the difficulties that anatomical losses and limits create in society designed for the nondisabled? How to embrace such losses and limits as opportunities for personal growth without ignoring the systemic barriers that make "overcoming" an impossible dream for many disabled people? How to view nonconforming bodies as extraordinary in the context of a culture devoted to a singular, nondisabled ideal?

The documentary film, *Fixed: The Science/Fiction of Human Enhancement*, explores many of these quandries by representing a diversity of views on physical improvement among people with disabilities. Some advocate for creating technologies designed to "enhance" the functioning of impaired bodies. For example, Hugh Herr, an engineer who runs the Biomechatronics

Lab at MIT, designs bionic legs that enable people like himself (a double amputee) to run, rock climb, play tennis, and lead a relatively normal life. Others, like Gregor Wolbring, a biochemist and ability studies scholar who "walks" without legs by using his partially formed arms to maneuver his torso, challenges ableist definitions of normalcy and advocates for greater appreciation for physical variation. These varied responses to the technological "enhancement" of impaired bodies reveal that diversity within the disability community is not just physical but also philosophical.

Amid this diversity, disability scholars and activists who refuse to repent for the "sin" of their nonconforming flesh provide an especially valuable perspective for challenging the culture of physical improvement. Their unapologetically "unproselytized"[101] bodies challenge everybody to critically examine the disabling narratives around and within us, and to explore what we might be avoiding when we judge and recoil from anatomical configurations that confound the dream of normalcy.

What are we avoiding?

The day I was beginning to organize my thoughts for the final section of this chapter, two local teens—brothers—were killed in a car accident. I didn't know the family personally, but I knew who the younger boy was because his basketball team had played my son's team for several years in area tournaments. He was small for a basketball player, even more so because he usually played up, meaning he was good enough to play with kids who were older (and bigger) than him. He had a brilliant three point shot, amazingly reliable and utterly maddening for the opposing team. The night before the accident he played in the same 3-on-3 league as my son. By 9:10 the next morning, he was dead.

Even when death doesn't take us by surprise, its reality can seem painfully unreal. Perhaps this is because we spend most of our lives avoiding death, consciously or not. Sanford reminds us of the futility of this avoidance: "We are all living a death sentence of sorts, it is delivered to us through the disintegration of our bodies." The truth of this disintegration—the reality that "Death cannot be avoided"—becomes increasingly difficult to deny as we age. But death, and the mystery surrounding it, is present throughout the course of our ordinary lives—in our disappointments, dissatisfactions, losses, and limits, whether or not we notice it, whether or not we accept it. "In some ways," Sanford reflects, "I was lucky to be exposed to this truth so early" (he was 13 when he became paralyzed). The "death of [his] life as a walking person" generated an awareness that living and dying are part of the same continuum: "You are living and dying simultaneously…Life and death, silence and action, emptiness and fullness at the same time—these are inward features of everyone's life."[102]

McBryde Johnson also felt the presence of death in life early on. Having been sick a lot as a child, she knew her body was both alive and dying. When she was 8, she dreamed she was in a courtroom. Looking up from the defendant's table, she hears a judge sentence her to death. "A gasp rises from a faceless crowd. They're shocked, astonished. I'm not. I've known all along." In fact, what surprises McBryde Johnson as she gets older is that "others seem oblivious. They seem to think that dying is only for the terminally ill, only for people like me."[103]

What the world needs: An atypical vantage point

As disability scholars and activists point out, disabled bodies are often the target of fear and shame because they remind the nondisabled majority of the very things we find intolerable in our lives: the presence of loss, suffering, and death.[104] Theologian Mary Lowe suggests that the dread of disability "can be framed in theological terms as the failure of the temporarily able-bodied to accept their limits as mortal, fragile, embodied and vulnerable creatures of God."[105] Whether or not we envision ourselves as "creatures of God," anyone who suffers under our culture's "tyranny of normalcy" can benefit from the alternative perspective religions at their best have historically provided. Scholar of religion and rabbi Julia Watts Belser captures this perspective when she marvels at the holy mystery that permeates her disabled flesh: "Muscle, heart, body, and bone testify to the One who made me, to the Source of wind and rain and soil who cobbled my elements into form and breathed soul into my veins. Who had the brilliant audacity to call it good and know it whole."[106] This same prophetic perspective prompts theologian Deborah Craemer to ask: What if we viewed the losses and limitations of disabled bodies as unsurprising manifesations of humanity's irreducible diversity—a diversity that is *good*?[107]

Able-bodied people need this atypical vantage point. We need the unorthodox vision of those with disabilities who challenge the assumptions that some bodies are better than others and that happiness depends on converting/conforming our flesh to a rigidly defined ideal. In making this suggestion, I don't mean to romanticize disability. Nor do I wish to turn disabled people into "inspiring heroes," gloss over the diversity of their somatic conditions and life situations, or downplay the multiple exclusions they experience in an ableist society. Rather, I seek to explore what tentatively able-bodied people like myself might learn by not averting our gaze from, or gawking at, or feeling pity for, or assuming the misery or valor of people with disabilities. In the final section of this chapter, I aim to unpack and endorse McBryde Johnson's suggestion that "We [people with disabilities] have something the world needs."[108]

Deconstructing idealized views of "body" and "self"

The world needs people who challenge a religious/cultural/commercial optic that encourages us to judge each other based on physical appearances. After years of living with a disability, Kafer still marvels at the assumptions nondisabled people make about her based on the sight of her body: "my wheelchair, burn scars, and gnarled hands apparently tell them all they need to know" about how miserable, frustrating, and isolated her life supposedly is and will be.[109] They do not see a woman whose atypical perspective and solidarity with other unconventional bodies enables her enjoy her life, think critically, love passionately, and contribute to a more just society. Similarly, McBryde Johnson says most people she encounters "think they know everything there is to know just by looking at me." Mostly, she says, they see a life of suffering.[110] Were they to read her book, they would discover a woman who is quick-witted, sharp-thinking, fiesty, assertive, adventurous, adacious, playful, and extremely funny.

The stories of women like Kafer and McBryde Johnson interrupt our habitual assumptions about the relationship between our "bodies" and our "selves." On the one hand, their experiences challenge the belief that "who I am" is transparently communicated through "my body"; on the other hand, they resist the notion that "self" and "body" are separate entities. For example, throughout McBryde Johnson's life, nondisabled people encouraged her to view her frail and twisted body as "unimportant" and to focus on her mind instead. But rather than dissociate from her unusually configured flesh, she embraced it as a fundamental aspect of herself: "the body I live in doesn't only affect me. It is me."[111]

The paradox of embodiment McBryde Johnson experiences—her sense of her "self" and "body" as neither identical nor separate—reminds me of Kafer's suggestion that we approach disability as "a site of questions" rather than a self-evident condition. As a site of questions, disability invites us to ask: what do we really know about a person based on anatomical functioning or appearance? How should we think about the relationship between the blood, bones, organs, and tissue that comprise our "flesh" and the thinking/feeling/conscious part of us typically referred to as "self," "soul," or "spirit"? Which cultural and religious norms and narratives shape our thinking about this relationship? We need to spend more time with the questions disability raises in order to remember just how much we *don't* know—not just about the relationship between human physicality and consciousness, but about the larger mystery that envelops our existence.

Scholar of religion Karen Armstrong observes: "Religion is at its best when it helps us to ask questions and holds us in a state of wonder— and arguably at its worst when it tries to answer them authoritatively and dogmatically."[112] Some of us might find it helpful to perceive the mystery surrounding our lives in traditional religious terms, i.e. as holy or divine. Ecofeminist Ivone Gebara envisions God as "the Greatest of Mysteries," a power both within us and beyond us, a "sacred energy [that] pervades all beings." To devote oneself to this mystery is to remain open to that which we do not comprehend and cannot control, even as we draw on this sacred energy/power in our efforts to heal ourselves and the world.[113] It's not necessary to perceive the mystery of our lives theologically. What's important is that we have strategies for questioning our assumptions and letting go of "fixed ideas." Zen teacher Bernie Glassman recommends the practice of "unknowing," the repeated effort to "give up our certainties" in order to "see things as they are" and be present to reality as it is.[114] Armstrong encourages a similar process of learning to recognize and appreciate "the unknown and unknowable," to question "overconfident assertions of certainty," and to become "aware of the numinous mystery of each human being we encounter during the day."[115]

The repetitious and formulaic commercial images of flawless bodies we are exposed to day in and day out make it difficult to see and appreciate the mysterious biodiversity of human incarnations. Such images and the better body instructions surrounding them flatten the relationship between flesh and spirit into a linear trajectory, with a supposedly autonomous, rational self driving the obedient "car" of our bodies toward the ultimate goal of somatic improvement. Against the grain of this trajectory, disabled bodies expose "the illusion of autonomy, self-government, and self-determination that underpins the fantasy of absolute able-bodiedness."[116] Sanford's experience illustrates this point: "After twenty-five years of paralysis and thirteen years of yoga my muscles below my chest remain unresponsive to my direct command."[117] Ultimately, his disobedient flesh reveals a rather obvious flaw in the eschatological myth of overcoming: some physical impairments refuse to be conquered/cured/saved.

Refusing to be conformed/converted

What's more, many disabilities scholars and activists are not preoccupied with defeating their noncompliant bodies. Some, like Kafer, identify as "crip" to express their opposition to "compulsory able-bodiedness," to resist the shame assigned to their transgressive flesh, and to eschew the obsession with being "cured."[118] These scholars/activists are not so much rejecting a cure as they are opting not to spend their lives anticipating, striving, or longing for one. This choice opens the door for a different kind of healing. A few years after her accident, for example, Linton's mother told her about a television program that described new research on treatments for spinal cord injuries. Though not opposed to such remedies, Linton found herself largely uninterested. She knew her condition had no cure, at least "[n]ot a get-up-out-of-bed, stand, get-dressed, walk-to-the-supermarket kind of cure. Not a Christopher Reeve kind of cure, which he told the public would be right around the corner if we just donated enough money." But Linton wasn't troubled by the absence of a cure. She didn't pine for legs that could hold her up. Having "let go of [her] walking self," she focused her energies on living well in the body she had, while working to create a world with greater access for people with disabilities and fewer prejudices about them.[119]

By embracing her body/her life as it is, Linton reverses the shaming gaze of ableism, directing it back at a society that classifies and judges people based on physical abilities and appearance. Eli Clare expresses a similar reversal: "it is ableism that needs the cure, not our bodies." Instead of a medical cure,

> ...we want civil rights, equal access, gainful employment, the opportunity to live independently, good and respectful health care, desegregated education. We want to be part of the world, not isolated and shunned. We want a redefinition of values that places disability not on the margins as a dreaded and hated human condition but in the center as a challenge to the dominant culture.[120]

Although neither Linton nor Clare self-identify as "religious," their atypical perspective resembles the prophetic critique of systemic injustice within the biblical tradition. This critique relocates the "sin" of disability from individual bodies to social/symbolic systems that punish nonconformity with shame, discrimination, and exclusion. This critique shifts the paradigm from charity toward disabled people, to solidarity among those seeking to transform disabling stereotypes and structures.[121]

The world needs people who recognize that human dignity, pleasure, power, health, and beauty stem not from conforming to a normative ideal, but from the kind of agency that can "make a way out of no way." Womanist Monica Coleman uses this black folk expression to affirm the creative and ingenious ways African-American women have collectively navigated the harsh realities of a racist-sexist-classist society.[122] The spirited agency of the black women she describes resembles the audacious self-determination of disability activists like McBryde Johnson: "We take constraints that no one would choose and build rich and satisfying lives within them."[123] In a society where some people imagine they would rather die than be disabled, McBryde Johnson's decision to live "openly and without shame"[124] in/as her unconventional body, her insistence on enjoying the many pleasures of her life, and her commitment to collaborating with others to expose the ignorance of ableist stereotypes suggest a different kind of salvation—not as a future state of perfection when "the lame shall walk and the blind shall see," but as diversly incarnated wholeness, health, and liberation in the here/now. Salvation, as Eiesland suggests, is the healing and freedom that comes from "the revolutionary act of accepting our bodies."[125] Salvation, as womanists affirm, involves the capacity to love oneself—"*Regardless*."[126]

Isn't this the kind of salvation most of us want: an unconditionally accepting, shamefree relationship with our bodies and with each other? Isn't this radical acceptance of "imperfection" a fundamental aspect of health, happiness, and healing? In a letter to Jesus, John Hull, a blind New Testament scholar, tells his Savior he is confused and disappointed that He did not seem to encourage acceptance of disability, but offered only the remedy of curing: "blind people had to become sighted before they could follow you." Since Hull's condition has no miraculous cure, he's interested in a different kind of healing: "What I want is...the healing that comes from acceptance." Hull means both his own acceptance of his blindness, and sighted people's "acceptance of the different world" his condition creates. In the end, Hull forgives Jesus for not comprehending his situation and acknowledges that his soul-searching has made their relationship "more mutual." Ultimately, he embraces the prophetic potential of his blindness and calls on nondisabled people to recognize, respect, and appreciate the diverse worlds people with disabilities construct and inhabit.[127]

Without using religious terms, Clare envisions a similar kind of healing/salvation, namely, as the capacity to accept our bodies' inescapable eccentricities, histories, and limits. Clare suggests that beneath the desire to be "normal," there is an even deeper, existential longing to feel at home in our flesh and in the world. "Home starts here in my body." Not an idealized body, he clarifies, but flesh that for him carries the marks of white privilege, queer desire, cerebral palsy, and a rural and working-class upbringing, as well as the wounds of sexual violence and the lies, stereotypes, and other poisons of an ableist society. For Clare, it's not his body's carefree or manicured perfection that makes "home" possible, but "a deeply honest multi-issue politics"[128] that enables him to identify, interrogate, and challenge external sources of body shame.

Resisting eschatological perfection

The world needs people like Clare who show us how to decolonize our imaginations, to liberate them from norms that keep us fixated on fixing our bodies. "Disability is a problem if we want to fix it, if we think we should be other than we are."[129] From Joan Tollifson's Buddhist perspective, many of the body issues with which we struggle would cease to be problems if we perceived them as babies do: free of preconceptions. This is what mindfulness practice aims to cultivate: the capacity to perceive what is real in the present moment, without narratives, comparisons, expectations, or evaluations. By slowing down and becoming conscious of what's happening in our bodies in the moment (i.e. sensations), while nonjudgmentally observing the contents of our minds (i.e. thoughts and feelings), we can reduce the suffering that comes from constantly wanting things to be different.[130] In many ways, mindfulness practice is training in the art of acceptance—i.e. accepting your body as it is. "Training" suggests that, paradoxically, cultivating acceptance requires repeated effort: the intentional, continual, countercultural decision to feel at home in the idiosyncrasies of your own flesh. From Tollifson's perspective, to experience the body as home is to enjoy "the perfection of imperfection," opting to embrace "life as it actually is from moment to moment. Asymmetrical. Messy. Unresolved. Out of control. Imperfect. Terrible. And miraculous."[131]

Betcher echoes Tollifson's resistance to eschatological perfection/wholeness by replacing idealized notions of "the body" with an affirmation of flesh as "the locus of flux." For her, flesh represents "that which we know to be true of lives—pain, difficulty, disease, transience, aging, error, and corporeal limit," as well as the "epiphanies and critical insights that come with those experiences." Betcher calls on Christians to develop those insights by "renovat[ing] Christian theology's own commitment to the flesh"—not its traditional obsession with mortification and mastery of the body in the pursuit of virtue, but its insistence on the intermingling of matter and spirit and the multiple ways the incarnation continues to unfold in our diversely configured bodies.[132] Historically, the Catholic tradition has affirmed the nonseparation of matter/spirit with its sacramental view of the presence of God *within* the physical world. Since the sixteenth century, Protestant traditions have emphasized the notion of divine grace: the idea of God's unconditional acceptance of humans in spite of sin—a notion Martin Luther (d. 1546) reinvigorated partly in response to Christianity's excessive focus on punishing the body to gain divine approval. Taken together, the ideas of divine incarnation and grace illuminate the embodied experience, attitude, and practice Betcher recommends: "'keeping trust' with the Spirit of life."[133]

Embracing the "corruption" of interconnection

By trusting the diverse, changing, and imperfectly perfect Spirit of life in the flesh, disabilities scholars and activists challenge the myth of self-sufficiency that the able-bodied ideal supports—a myth that says relying on others is a sign of weakness. "Throughout my life," McBryde Johnson explains, "I have needed help from other people to bathe, dress, and get out of bed in the morning." While the prospect of having to depend so heavily on others would horrify many nondisabled people, McBryde Johnson ponders "how strange it would be to do these morning things in solitude as nondisabled people do…it is so natural to feel the touch of washcloth-covered hands on the flesh that is glad to be flesh, to rejoice that other hands are here to do what I'd do for myself if I could."[134] As Betcher points out, for people living with disabilities, "human interdependence names the infrastructure of our freedom."[135] Thus rather than view her life as "dreadful and unnatural," as she knows many nondisabled people do, McBryde Johnson welcomes "the corruption that comes from interconnectedness," honoring "the muck and mess and undeniable reality of disabled lives well lived."[136]

Nondisabled people need "the corruption of interconnection" to liberate us from the ideology of individualism and its creeds of progress, productivity, and speed—all of which coalesce in the cultural imperative to create a body that is streamlined, mobile, and quick. Through their noncompliance with able-bodied notions of time and movement, disabled bodies resist how "capitalism privileges efficiency of time, space, and money." In Betcher's words, "I get in the way, slow the pace, presume too large a buffering presence."[137] Kafer supports this resistance with the notion of "crip time," an idea that captures the flexible schedules with which people with bodily impairments often operate—not only because some of them move more slowly than their nondisabled peers, but also because the ableist obstacles they regularly encounter impede their mobility. By recognizing that "expectations of 'how long things take' are based on very particular minds and bodies," and that "disabled people might need more time to accomplish something or to arrive somewhere,"[138] the flexibility of crip time offers an alternative to the rigidity of "clock time," which encourages us to ignore our bodies' actual needs (e.g. for food, rest, play, fresh air, exercise, sleep) and leaves many of us feeling perpetually dissatisfied and exhausted.

The world needs people who unsettle our assumptions not only about how our bodies should be, but also about how our lives are supposed to go. Just as the culture of physical improvement trains us to believe that our bodies should be better, so it conditions us to imagine that our lives should be more perfect. The belief that we shouldn't have to suffer—that every problem has a solution, that we can rise above pain, loss, weakness—may well be one of commercial culture's most pervasive and persuasive deceptions. Those of us who enjoy first world, white, middle-to-upper-class, able-bodied privilege may be especially susceptible to this happily-ever-after chimera. And our privilege may make us prone to projecting the suffering we think we're not supposed to have onto the irregular flesh of others. By contrast, people with disabilities do not have the luxury of denying life's difficulties; nor can they easily displace their troubles onto other unwanted bodies. In Betcher's words, "the socially abject bodies of the disabled" are "bodies that admit suffering."[149] Amid a culture dedicated to the denial of finitude and death, their conspicuous losses and limits bear witness to pain that cannot be overcome, pain that doesn't "happen for a reason." By "reconciling [them]selves with the contours of corporeality,"[140] disabled bodies show tentatively nondisabled people how we might begin to alleviate suffering—in ourselves and in the world—by refusing to look away from it.

It's precisely this possibility of reconciliation and the reduction of suffering that draws me to the perspectives and stories of the people with disabilities discussed in this chapter. I long to trust the Spirit of embodied life, to make peace with its multiple permutations, its frailties and limits. I crave this reconciliation for myself and for all who struggle to feel at home their flesh, regardless of ability, color, age, size, gender, sexuality, class, culture, or creed. *Regardless.* But for reconciliation to happen, temporarily able-bodied people like myself need to own and examine the dread and shame we project onto disability, critically investigate the cultural, religious, and existential sources of our fear and disapproval, and transform them into energy to create a world in which every body is appreciated and nurtured. This task is similar to the work we need to do in relation to other kinds of nonconforming bodies, including those that are unconventionally big.

6

Fat shame

In the spring of 2015, controversy erupted over an advertising campaign in the London Underground (the city's subway system). Sponsored by Protein World, a company that sells weight-loss supplements, the ads featured a young, white, blonde-haired, able-bodied, tightly toned woman with sizable breasts, sporting a yellow bikini. Next to this image, the copy asked: "**ARE YOU BEACH BODY READY?**"[1] To view this and other beach-body-ready images discussed below, go to http://www.bloomsbury.com/uk/shameful-bodies-9781472594945/ and look under "Chapter Six."

Social activists who believed the ad demeaned women and promoted body shame responded with a variety of tactics. Some vandalized the subway billboards, either by editing the poster's message to affirm that "#EACH BODY'S READY," or by writing disapproving commentary—ranging from "NOT OKAY" to "Fuck Your Sexist Shit"—over the model's cleavage and torso. A Change.Org petition calling on Protein World to remove the ad received over 71,000 supporters. Protesters tweeted and wrote blogs that elicited countless responses. Some participated in a "Take Back the Beach" rally in Hyde Park.[1] Still others challenged the ad's message by donning swimsuits and posing in front of the billboards, shamelessly flaunting their self-described beach-ready physiques.

As Britain's Advertising Standards Authority deliberated whether the ad was harmful, offensive, or socially irresponsible, sales for Protein World products jumped considerably, presumably boosted by the publicity the ad received.[2] Before long, other companies sought to capitalize on the debate by producing ads with a decidedly alternative viewpoint. Dove seized the opportunity to promote its Campaign for Real Beauty and created a billboard featuring three curvaceous women, backs to the camera, wearing only swimsuit bottoms, with the message: **BEACH BODY READY**. Navabi, a fashion retailer for females' sizes 10 to 30, produced a similar ad with two voluptuous women in swimsuits (albeit not bikinis), enjoying themselves and each other next to the copy: "**100% BEACH BODY READY.**" These counter-ads hint that weight is a diversity issue: in addition to the models' unconventional sizes, they are racially varied, and their mutual embrace conveys the absence of homophobia. Still, it's hard to know whether these images' celebration of physical variation will raise consciousness, or simply profits.

As some companies sought to capitalize on the original ad's fallout, Protein World staunchly defended its billboards. The company insisted that the model (Renee Somerfield) is healthy, and Somerfield herself echoed this claim: "I work very hard and live a healthy and active lifestyle which is why Protein World chose me for their campaign."[3] The company's CEO called the ad's critics "crazy," and its global marketing director argued that Protein World couldn't possibly be sexist since women comprise the vast majority of its 300,000 customers. A blogger who defended the billboards called them "tedious, familiar fantasies that we can ignore or indulge in as we wish," adding that such images "shouldn't be a source of shame to those who didn't win the genetic lottery." In her view, the solution is simple: "We need to grow up."[4] Protein World echoed this sentiment by using the hashtag #getagrip to retweet remarks by former Apprentice contestant, Katie Hopkins, who wrote: "Chubsters, quit vandalizing Protein World ads and get your arse running on the road. Feminism isn't an excuse for being fat. Eat less, move more."[5] When comedian Juliette Burton, who has struggled with body dysmorphia and eating disorders, tweeted her reason for critiquing the billboards—"I spent life believing I'm not good enough"—Protein World responded by asking: "Why make your insecurities our problem?"[6]

Disdain for fat bodies

Few corporeal configurations generate as much admiration, anxiety, and yearning as the thinly sculpted figure, and few produce as much animosity, loathing, and aversion as the fat physique. In developed Western societies, the praise and desire surrounding slender bodies are so common that it would be easy to assume they are inborn responses. The disgust directed at ample-bodied people may seem similarly instinctive and thus acceptable and even necessary. In mainstream medical, self-help, and commercial perspectives, weight-loss epitomizes physical improvement. Through various social institutions and media, the belief that heavy is bad and thin is good has become part of our cultural catechism. Questioning such dogma is not just heresy; it's tantamount to lunacy, or even treason. Indeed, the necessity of downsizing big bodies may be the one thing upon which people from every walk of life and political and religious persuasion largely agree.

But why are fat people the target of so much collective contempt? This chapter explores that question by examining a confluence of historical trends, scientific, political, and commercial discourses, along with traditional religious and philosophical narratives, and the first-hand experiences of people who identify as *fat* or who have struggled with weight issues.

Of all the body issues I explore in this book, conundrums surrounding weight and size are the most familiar to me. For decades, I've been reading, writing, thinking, and talking about our culture's obsession with thinness, particularly as it pertains to women.[7] You'd think that after all these years, I'd be ready to give the topic a rest. But the suffering I witness in so many people, including many of my students who are tormented by a longing to be thinner, motivates me to continue exploring weight issues. Besides, I still have a lot to learn. Right about the time that my last book on the subject was going to press in 2009, an academic field I'd yet to investigate was gaining momentum.

Introducing fat studies

Fat studies is an interdisciplinary field whose scholars critically analyze the meanings cultures assign to variously sized bodies, and the personal and social consequences of those meanings for diversely shaped human beings. By investigating common assumptions about people whose bodies are heavier than average, fat studies scholars seek to create a world in which persons of every proportion can live peacefully in the forms they have.

These scholars' analyses challenge beliefs many Westerners take for granted: that fat people *can* and *should* lose weight; that being fat is a disease that needs to be cured; that corpulence is unattractive and symptomatic of moral laxity (e.g. laziness, immaturity) or some underlying emotional disturbance.[8] In lieu of such beliefs, fat studies scholars affirm a continuum of healthy body sizes on which some physiques are naturally heftier than others. Just as some folks are unusually tall or short, so some are unconventionally plump or thin, even as most fall somewhere in between. While fat studies scholars acknowledge that *mathematically average* weights exist in any population, they challenge the categories of "normal" and "abnormal" to describe size variations since it may be normal for a person to be heavier than average, just as it may be normal for someone to be skinnier than average.[9]

Generally speaking, scholars in the field of fat studies have paid little attention to the religious underpinnings of the dominant culture's disdain for fat people, and scholars of religion are only beginning to explore the terrain of fat studies.[10] Working at the intersections of queer, fat, Jewish, and Christian communities, Mycroft Masada is a faith leader who is ahead of the curve in recognizing how traditional religion is both part of the problem and, potentially, part of the solution when it comes to fat shame. Precisely because of traditional religions' powerful influence on cultural attitudes toward bodily appetites, Masada believes people of faith have a crucial role to play in challenging fat-phobia and promoting fat-positive messages and actions. Drawing on the resources of her Jewish and Christian heritages, she affirms that "all people are made *b'tzelem Elohim*, in the image of God," that "our infinite diversity of bodies, our physical transitions over our lifetimes, and our capacity to love people of all embodiments are gifts, blessings, lessons; meant to be realized, expressed, and enjoyed." Echoing a key claim from the field of fat studies, Masada asserts, "Fatness and fat people are *bashert*, meant to be."[11]

The power of words and numbers

What was your initial reaction to my use of the word *fat*? Were you surprised? Uncomfortable? It's understandable if you were because "fat" is typically a pejorative term when used to describe someone's body. In using the f-word, I join scholars and activists who are reclaiming *fat* both as an adjective that accurately describes people with corpulent figures, and as an unapologetic political identity. As fat activist Marilyn Wann points out, "There is nothing negative or rude in the word fat unless someone makes the effort to put it there; using the word *fat* as a descriptor (not a discriminator) can help dispel prejudice."[12] In addition to *fat*, I use other adjectives to describe larger-than-statistically-average physiques (e.g. "ample-bodied," "heavy-set," "curvaceous," "voluptuous," "big"). In so doing, I'm not trying to euphemistically avoid negative associations with fatness. On the contrary, by using an expanded vocabulary for describing fat bodies, I aim to interrupt the culturally induced habit of assuming they are bad.

The negativity associated with the f-word leads many people to use the "O-words"—"overweight" and "obesity"—to describe people of size. These terms may seem more polite, but they're far from innocent. "Overweight" and "obese" are medical designations based on standardized Body Mass Index (BMI) scores, which are calculated using a weight-to-height ratio and correlated with physical well-being (e.g. a "normal" BMI is considered "healthy"). The power of such numbers and classifications to generate long-lasting anxiety is evident in the story of a college woman named Annemarie, who recalled the trauma of being weighed-and-measured in front of her sixth-grade peers in gym class. When the nurse sternly informed her that she was "overweight" and thus "unhealthy," her previously carefree relationship with her body was suddenly flooded with self-consciousness. Despite being a successful, four-sport athlete with a "solid" body, Annemarie's belief "that BMI was the word of God" made weight a source of constant worry.[13]

As Annemarie's example suggests, neither BMI calculations nor the categories they generate are reliable indicators of fitness. The BMI formula ignores racial, ethnic, gender, and hereditary diversity; it also disregards variances in somatic composition (muscle, bone, fat), which explains why even accomplished athletes are sometimes diagnosed as "overweight." Besides ignoring biodiversity, the terms "overweight" and "obesity" assume and imply judgments that reveal the fine line between science and morality. If you are classified as "overweight," the assumption is that you weigh more than you *should*, and the implication is that you *ought* to shed a few kilos. The "obesity" label makes an even stronger scientific/moral claim—that you *really need to* lose—since being "obese" is worse than being "overweight."

Noticing the problems with the BMI and the ambiguities surrounding "overweight" and "obesity" designations reminds us that these categories are socially constructed. They are based on criteria that are culturally specific, historically shifting, morally charged, and influenced by political and economic interests. For example, seven of the nine scientists who decided in 1998 to lower the BMI cutoff points for defining "overweight" and "obese"—a decision that recategorized millions of people as fat and presumably unhealthy—had financial ties to the diet industry.[14] Ultimately, the various "authorities" who determine who is/isn't "overweight" or "obese"—e.g. medical researchers, government officials, insurance companies, popular media, family members, friends, and even strangers—have their own standards and reasons for making such judgments. The shifting and arbitrary basis for such designations explains why many fat studies scholars keep scare quotes around such terms.[15]

The burden of weight discrimination

How we talk about fat people matters because our language shapes our perceptions, and our perceptions influence cultural norms, social arrangements, and ultimately individuals' experiences of their bodies. Unfavorable views of corpulent physiques foster a society in which weight prejudice and internalized fat-phobia are serious problems.

In *Fat-Talk Nation*, anthropologist Susan Greenhalgh asks: "How do heavy people feel being the object of…visceral hatred, verbal abuse, and outright discrimination?" To get at this question, she examines her college students' responses to the prompt: How have weight issues played out in your life or the lives of people you know?[16] Most of these students grew up in southern California ("SoCal"), whose beach body scene, materialistic values, and Hollywood influence make it the "epicenter" of the culture of physical improvement and the myth that "perfect bodies bring perfect lives."[17] In response to Greenhalgh's prompt, fat students tell of parents warning them that they'll never find love, success, or happiness unless they lose weight. Fat students also describe episodes of vicious bullying at school—e.g. a young woman has trash hurled at her as she walks through the schoolyard. Withdrawal is a common survival strategy among those seeking refuge from such brutality; anxiety and depression are familiar consequences of withdrawal; and binging on fattening foods is sometimes a means for soothing such feelings. Heavy students of various colors, classes, and cultural backgrounds also describe: failed attempts to overcome fat shame by dangerous weight-reducing methods; efforts to "get healthy" by dieting that escalate into eating disorders; agonizing preoccupation with body size; and a profound, pervasive sense of unworthiness. We can hear the painful burden of internalized fat shame in the remarks of a female student: "It was hard for me to communicate effectively with boys or prettier girls, since I felt I was too ugly to speak to them...Overall, I felt that I was inferior to everyone and that I would disgust people because I was fat."[18]

Greenhalgh's students' narratives bear witness to the psychic/spiritual damage that animosity toward fat bodies inflicts on young people who are heavy or who live in fear of gaining weight. While this hostility tells us more about our cultural conditioning than it does about people of size, it underscores the importance of fat studies for anybody who seeks to create a more just, compassionate society. By challenging prevailing assumptions about what having a better body means, this academic field has the potential to significantly revamp our thinking about human biodiversity.

The relevance of fat studies for every body

The implications of such rethinking are profound since fear of fat infects people of all sizes, including those who enjoy thin privilege. My own story illustrates this dynamic. Having lived the majority of my life in the middle of the bell curve of weight distribution for my height, I have escaped the dehumanizing cruelty and systemic discrimination fat people endure every day. But as my adolescent history of anorexia and bulimia suggest, I am no stranger to the internalized oppression and self-torture that a fat-hating society encourages. Because of this history, I feel a strong kinship with the struggles of people of size, and I have a selfish interest in thinking critically about the fat prejudice that once poisoned my brain and damaged my body.

Critical thinking about weight issues is more necessary than ever given the growing girth of the population during the past few decades. Two thirds of American adults today are classified as "overweight" or "obese," and more than 50 percent of European adults now qualify for one of these designations.[19] Within the EU, the United Kingdom appears to be the heaviest nation, followed closely by Ireland and Spain.[20] The increasing size of many Westerners is often described as a health *crisis*. But what if we saw this "crisis" as an opportunity to interrogate the meanings assigned to fat bodies and to consider the consequences of those meanings for diversely proportioned people?

Meanings assigned to fat and thin bodies

Thinking critically begins with the recognition that the meanings of differently sized bodies are not self-evident. Being bony or plump are physical traits that *acquire* significance in particular historical and cultural contexts. In the West, soft, expansive, adipose tissue is typically considered "gross" or "disgusting" and fat people are thought to be lazy, unattractive, unhealthy, uncivilized. These stereotypes assume that being fat is a choice—that a corpulent body is evidence of overeating and thus a disordered, undisciplined self. Conversely, a lean figure represents self-mastery and control. Such virtues are tied to notions of good health, beauty, and broad cultural values like efficiency, speed, mobility—all of which reflect and support the prevailing economic system of consumer capitalism.

As Mary Douglas observed in her classic work on symbols, iconic depictions of human bodies function as microcosms of the social body, expressing and reinforcing dominant cultural values and systems through the norms they generate.[21] Her analysis suggests that we can learn a lot about our culture's priorities, anxieties, and social arrangements by studying the idealized images it produces. While fantasies of thinly sculpted bodies represent the ideal self of Western culture—i.e. Descartes' autonomous individual who is "in charge" of her or his own destiny—fat bodies stereotypically symbolize the loss of control that epitomizes a self who has failed (Figure 6.1). Whereas the well-defined contours of the lean ideal provide a symbolic antidote to the uncertainties and changes that permeate contemporary society, the less rigidly defined edges of the fat figure remind us, consciously or not, of the unpredictable, impermanent aspects of life.

The relationship between body ideals and social contexts varies. In some cultures, fat women are still associated with health, prosperity, and beauty. Fat activist Virgie Tovar describes how "at home" she felt as a big, brown, curvaceous woman when she visited the Cook Islands, where women with large breasts, thighs, and buttocks are considered beautiful:

Before visiting the Pacific, I had never been to a place where big wasn't bad, where big was normal. I had never been to a place where big, fat,

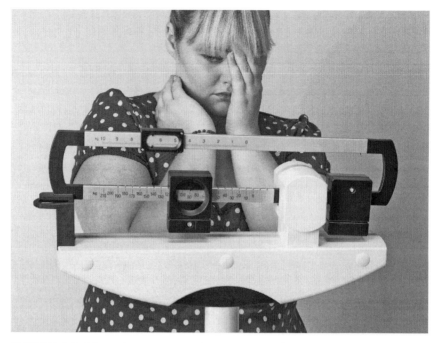

FIGURE 6.1 *Obese Teenager on Scales* © *Peter Dazeley.*
Source: Getty Images.

beautiful women walked arm in arm, smiling and sharing secrets. It turned everything I had accepted as 'just the way things are' on their head. It reminded me that fat life doesn't have to be what it is out there.[22]

Tovar's experience illustrates how disdain for fatness and desire for thinness are culturally specific. In the West, contemporary meanings of differently sized bodies are the product of a long, complex history in which religion has played a prominent role.

Historical perspectives on eating and fat shame

Historical accounts of evolving attitudes toward fat and thin bodies often start in the nineteenth century. Yet scholars of religion have shown that concerns with appetite and appearance are *much* older. Even a cursory sketch of the evolution of these concerns reveals how certain religious beliefs and practices paved the way for present-day ideas about differently sized bodies, particularly their moral meanings.

Food, appetite, and divine abundance

In *Eating to Excess*, Susan Hill explores the ancient antecedents to modern and contemporary attitudes toward appetite and body size. Her analysis of biblical and philosophical sources suggests that ancient people considered excessive consumption of food and drink (i.e. gluttony) to be immoral, and they linked such behavior with death and disease. Interestingly, however, they did not automatically associate gluttonous eating with being fat and lazy. In biblical times, physical girth was positively correlated with wealth and abundance, and, for women, fertility and desirability. Moreover, ancient people distinguished between corpulent bodies and overeating because they noticed that persons of all sizes are capable of food indulgence, and that fat people do not necessarily eat more than their slender counterparts. In the ancient period, it was gluttonous *behavior*—not a corpulent *appearance*—that was deemed morally reprehensible.[23]

In fact, in many biblical texts, fat is a symbol of God's bounty. For example, in Genesis 41, Joseph correctly interprets the attractive, fat cows and plump ears of grain that Pharaoh sees in his dream as representing the years of plenty that will proceed a time of famine—a time of scarcity symbolized in the same dream by ugly, skinny cows and thin, blighted ears of grain. In this story, the phrase "the fat of the land" (45:18) represents divine abundance—the same God-given plentitude that causes food to fall from heaven to feed the famished Israelites as they wander through the parched desert (Exodus 16). The vision of the "promised land" as a place of "milk and honey" (Deut. 11:8–17) further suggests that a satisfied appetite is not sinful.[24]

Positive depictions of food and eating permeate the gospels. For example, all four gospels recount a story in which Jesus' power becomes known when he feeds a crowd of 5,000 with a small supply of bread and fish (Matt 14:13–21; Mark 6:30–44; Luke 9:10–17; John 6:1–15). Multiple references to Jesus' table fellowship suggest that sharing and enjoying food with people assumed to be of questionable character (e.g. sinners, tax collectors, prostitutes) were symbolic actions that simultaneously embodied and anticipated the reign of God (e.g. Mark 2:13–17; Matt 9:10; Luke 7:36). Such table fellowship culminates in the story of Jesus' last supper, at which he is understood to have instituted the Eucharistic meal that would bring healing and foster community among Christians for generations to come. Eating and drinking were so central to Jesus' ministry that his critics reportedly accused him of being a glutton and a drunkard (Matthew 11:19; Luke 7:34). These gospel accounts remind us that satisfying one's appetite has not always or inevitably been seen as a mark of moral failure—at least not according to Jesus' example.

The moral dangers of idolatrous eating

Alongside biblical passages that link fat or feeding with divine abundance, there's a narrative of caution against abusing God's bounty. Several texts urge disciplined eating and portray food indulgence as a sign of spiritual and social disorder. Leviticus 3:16–17 declares, "All fat is the Lord's," thus "you must not eat any fat or any blood" because eating the fat of animals sacrificed to God would be an act of human arrogance. In Psalm 119:70 the arrogant are portrayed as possessing hearts that are "fat and gross." Several Hebrew Bible texts instruct humans to prioritize serving God and others over filling their bellies. Deuteronomy 31:20 describes people who "have eaten their fill and grown fat" as overly dedicated to eating and insufficiently committed to God.[25] Here, fat is associated with idolatrous behavior: devotion to the false gods of appetite and food.

Though silent on the issue of fat per se, several New Testament texts echo ancient Hebrew warnings against unbridled, self-centered consumption. In Luke's gospel, Jesus rebukes those who refuse to share God's bounty: "Woe unto you that are full now, for you shall hunger" (6:25). The apostle Paul cautions Christians to avoid people who "are servants not of Christ our Lord, but of their own appetites" (Romans 16:8), and warns that those whose "appetite is their god" are "heading for destruction" (Phil. 3:19).[26] According to Paul, "belly worship"—i.e. prioritizing food over God and concern for feeding oneself over sharing with others—jeopardizes not only the order of the early Christian community, but also one's prospects in the heavenly afterlife.[27] While such texts do not link indulgent eating and fatness, they depict gluttony as manifesting disordered desire—i.e. sin.

Throughout the ancient world, the immorality of eating to excess was gendered. Ancient authors associated gluttony with women's allegedly irrational, excessive, animal-like nature.[28] No biblical story better illustrates the dangers of disobedient female appetite than the second creation myth (Genesis 3), wherein the downfall of humanity is symbolically depicted through the act of a woman eating. Though the authors of this familiar story were not intending to send women a message about the perils of becoming fat, ancient associations between sin, shame, and female appetite have shaped attitudes toward women's bodies for millennia, and their influence continues today.[29]

Taming the flesh and exalting the spirit in historical Christianity

Biblical depictions of the moral dangers of unrestrained appetite informed Christian fasting in the post-biblical world. By the early third century, the influential church leader Tertullian (d. 220) suggested that emaciated bodies would have an easier time passing through the narrow gates to heaven, and that only lightweight physiques could be resurrected.[30] By the fourth and fifth centuries, ascetic Christians fasted as a means for restoring their bodies to the innocence of Eden, while preparing themselves for the incorruptible perfection of the flesh they anticipated in the heavenly hereafter.[31]

Early Christian fasting practices were influenced by Greco-Roman medical theories of the time, which linked appetite for food with sexual desire. Thus St. Jerome (d. 420) insisted it was impossible to remain chaste without fasting, arguing that a full stomach stimulates the genitals and inflames lust.[32] Female fasting was deemed particularly praiseworthy because it diminished the distinctive features of women's bodies (i.e. round breasts, hips, and belly), making them *un*attractive in the eyes of men and more appealing to Christ. Female ascetics who conquered their hunger were praised for being disciplined, virtuous, and beautiful. Conversely, gluttonous women were described as vulgar, unsightly, and unhealthy.[33]

By the late Middle Ages, fasting had become a popular method for cultivating holiness among women. From about 1200–1500, many pious women refused food as a means for identifying with the suffering of Christ. In cases of prolonged abstinence, fasting was deemed supernatural. Later historical authors called it *anorexia mirabilis*: the miraculous loss of appetite. For women like Catherine of Siena (d. 1380)—who reportedly subsisted on the Eucharist alone and stuck twigs down her throat to induce vomiting because she couldn't stand the sensation of anything in her stomach—food was the most readily available social/symbolic resource for cultivating a relationship with God and others. Catherine didn't have the option of renouncing institutional power, social prestige, or property in pursuit of holiness.[34] But the notoriety she achieved by fasting enabled her to intervene in the political and religious crises of her time, until she died of starvation.[35]

During the Protestant Reformation, Christian leaders who preached a gospel of "salvation by faith alone" condemned excessive fasting, which they associated with Catholic devotion. Protestant reformers believed that trying to win divine favor by refusing to eat exemplified a theology of "works" (i.e. trying to *earn* salvation through pious actions) that was both futile and displeasing to God. Yet reformers stopped short of abandoning fasting altogether. While Martin Luther (d. 1546) rejected exaggerated forms of self-denial, he advocated moderate food abstinence to quell desire and prepare one to serve others. John Calvin's (d. 1564) endorsement of restrained eating echoed in the Puritans' reliance on fasting as a public and private devotional method for curbing desires, preparing for prayer, and even warding off such evils as witchcraft. Food abstinence also functioned as a penitential antidote to the shame of gluttony. In *Born Again Bodies*, historian Marie Griffith quotes an eighteenth-century Puritan catechism that describes fasting as a discipline of "holy Revenge upon the Flesh or Body for its former Excesses."[36]

By the eighteenth century, Christianity's moralizing approach to appetite merged with modern/Cartesian notions of selfhood that emphasized the supremacy of reason over lust for food. In his best-selling *Poor Richard's Almanack*, American statesman Benjamin Franklin (d. 1790) blended the Puritans' distrust of pleasure with the scientific revolution's emphasis on rational calculation: "'The Difficulty lies, in finding out an exact Measure, but eat for Necessity, not Pleasure, for Lust knows not where Necessity ends.'"[37] By the mid-1800s, the spiritual and physical advantages of appetite control were explicitly linked in the theories and practices of prominent health evangelists like Sylvester Graham (d. 1851), who advised people to scrutinize and restrict their eating habits as a means for improving their bodies, cleansing their spirits, and fostering social order. By the late nineteenth century, Griffith observes, it was difficult to distinguish between "religious" and "secular" discourses on the virtues of controlled eating since their "content was virtually interchangeable."[38]

As the spiritual practice of fasting was reinvented for purposes beyond traditional religion during the eighteenth and nineteenth centuries, fat became associated with a wider variety of moral evils (beyond gluttony), including laziness, greed, stupidity, ugliness, criminality, and animality.[39] The popularity of pseudo-sciences like physiognomy and phrenology reinforced these associations by inferring virtue or vice from a person's outward appearance, including bodily contours. Long after these methods of "reading" the flesh for internal character were discredited in the late 1800s, the principle of "body-soul correspondence" lingered in modernity's faith in "mind-over-matter," the quest for somatic perfection this faith supported,[40] and the shaming of nonconforming bodies it implied.

A turning point: The modern emergence of fat shame

This historical sketch of Christian attitudes toward food and eating suggests that moral concerns about appetite and size have been recycled for millennia. That said, scholars generally agree that a major shift took place during the latter half of the nineteenth century and early decades of the twentieth century. In *Fat Shame*, historian Amy Erdman Farrell shows how social changes in this era consolidated a clear preference for slenderness and intensified hostility toward corpulence. The overlapping processes of industrialization, urbanization, and the rise of a consumer-based economy (with advertising as its central artery) made lifestyles more sedentary, food more abundant, and body norms more visible for all but the poorest people. In this context, the Protestant mandate to work hard, control desire, and delay gratification clashed with market imperatives to buy more, seek pleasure, and gratify the senses.[41] A distinctly modern version of fat stigma coalesced at the junction of these competing values. Regulating appetite and body size became a symbolic and practical means for navigating modernity's conflicting imperatives: refrain and indulge.

Modern moral concerns about managing material abundance both echoed and secularized the biblical caution against abusing God-given plentitude. By projecting these concerns onto the body's contours, modern people repurposed Christianity's warnings about the moral perils of uncontrolled eating and abandoned the tradition's view of fat as a sign of divine abundance. In 1863, William Banting published his enormously influential "Letter on Corpulence," in which he deplored the "evils of obesity" and advocated a low-carb diet.[42] By the early twentieth century, entrepreneurs mass-marketed products that capitalized on the fat-phobia that was spreading to people of all sizes. Ads for weight-loss products of this era illustrate this trend: "If you are fat or fear you are becoming so, if your figure is in any way abnormal, you need the Magic Figure Mold Garment." The money people were willing to spend on such products, and the dangerous measures some were willing to take to eliminate the "handicap" of "useless" flesh—from tapeworms to arsenic—illustrate the extent to which fat was becoming a visible/tangible symptom of shame.[43]

Yet even as the scales were tipping in favor of thinness, positive associations between plump bodies and prosperity, health, and beauty didn't die overnight. Well into the twentieth century, many doctors were suspicious of slimming regimens and assured patients that gaining weight was a natural part of growing older. Some defended adipose tissue as not only healthy but attractive for women.[44] At the same time, however, popular discourses increasingly depicted rotund bodies as disorderly. Large, fleshy figures were also associated with poor, working-class, or ethnic immigrants— especially Jews and Catholics from eastern and southern European countries or Ireland.[45] As Sander Gilman shows, scientific and cultural authorities in this era differentiated between non-Jews and Jews by the "fact" that the latter were fat.[46] By contrast, the sleek and slender form was a status symbol of bourgeois, Anglo-Saxon, Protestant privilege: a sign of upward mobility. Not surprisingly, then, dread of fat was predominantly a white, middle- and upper-class, Protestant preoccupation.[47]

Fat shame in this era continued to be gendered. Many late nineteenth- and early twentieth-century Protestant leaders promoted a "muscular Christianity," in which the masculine "virtues" of authority, assertiveness, and self-mastery were cultivated and displayed on formidable, well-defined male physiques.[48] By contrast, corpulent men were thought to be greedy (i.e. "fat cats") and effeminate: like women, they were seen to lack the rational faculties and self-control needed to refrain from excessive consumption. During this era, fat became a convenient motif for ridiculing white, middle-class women who dared transgress their proper sphere of domesticity. Anti-suffragist propaganda lampooned feminists with unflattering images of large, mannish-looking women who threatened the social order. In response, white feminist propaganda featured young, slender, Caucasian, "attractive" women as the prototype of their cause. In fact, *both* campaigns deployed images of corpulent female bodies as irrational and inferior to advance their agenda. Fat women's alleged lack of self-mastery and insufficient reason posed a serious social problem since the dominant gender ideology of the time charged females with maintaining "civilized" society—a racialized/colonial notion associated with thinness.[49]

Erdman Farrell's research illuminates how dominant views on race, ethnicity, evolution, and civilization dovetailed with anxieties about the excesses of modernity to create the fat-shaming culture we know today. Based on taxonomies that positioned lean, able-bodied, elite males of northern European descent at the pinnacle of human evolution, scientific "experts" of the era pinpointed fat as a common bodily characteristic of "primitive" people—a trait that proved their inferiority. The intersection of race, gender, culture, and body size hierarchies is apparent in these scientists' beliefs that men from "savage tribes" prefer big-bodied women, whereas "civilized" men desire women who can contain their appetites and are therefore slender. Related to this belief was the notion that body sizes and gender roles were unmistakably distinct among women and men from "enlightened" societies, but less pronounced among females and males from "less evolved" cultures. Thus the dominant culture's binary view of gender also contributed to the construction of fat bodies as uncivilized and ruled by instinct.[50] Since mainstream anthropologists and Christian leaders understood primitive, dark-skinned people to be "infidels" or "heathens," these people's alleged predisposition and taste for plump bodies would also have been seen as a sign of their spiritual inferiority and unsaved status.

Contemporary devotion to thinness

The same web of superiority complexes (racial, class, gender, religious, cultural) that consolidated fat stigma in the late nineteenth and early twentieth centuries fueled the expansion of the slender fantasy of bodily perfection throughout the twentieth century. During this time, virtually every mainstream social institution and cultural discourse joined forces to support the growing predilection for slimness and corresponding disdain for fatness. By the latter decades of the second millennium, thinness had become so incredibly meaningful, especially for women, that many pursued it with religious-like fervor.

Religious dimensions of the pursuit of slenderness

In my previous work on body image and eating problems, I coined the phrase "religion of thinness" to describe white Western culture's devotion to the slender ideal. This phrase is not meant to suggest that the quest for slenderness is, *in fact*, a religion. Rather, it aims to highlight the quasi-religious *function* this quest serves by providing a profound source of meaning, particularly among women. The phrase also calls attention to aspects of devotion to thinness that functionally resemble certain features of traditional religion (especially Christianity): the iconography of taut, sleek bodies that pervades consumer culture and preoccupies our imaginations (e.g. pictures of models and movie stars); the daily rituals that reinforce the symbolic importance of thinness (e.g. counting calories, weighing the body, exercising to shed pounds); the moral codes designating which foods (and how much) you should/shouldn't eat; the sense of community that bonding over weight-loss failures and achievements engenders; and the salvation myth that promises "you'll be happier when you're thinner." The phrase *religion of thinness* deliberately aims to cause confusion about the difference between "religious" and "secular" enticements and motivations for weight loss, suggesting there is no neat-and-tidy line delineating the two. The phrase also points to the traditional Christian narratives that echo in the present-day belief that thinner is better—i.e. narratives depicting the dangers of unruly appetite, the need for women in particular to control their carnal urges, and the future/eschatological vision of perfected flesh.

The religious dimensions of the quest for thinness are most obvious in the Christian diet movement. Comprised of mainly evangelical weight-loss programs, books, workshops, and products, this multibillion dollar endeavor is dedicated to helping people reduce their flesh to the one-and-only size God allegedly intended to be: thin. Beginning in the 1950s, titles like *Pray*

Your Weight Away (Charlie Shedd, 1957), *More of Jesus; Less of Me* (Joan Cavanaugh, 1976), *Help Lord, the Devil Wants Me Fat* (C.S. Lovett, 1982), and *What Would Jesus Eat?* (Don Colbert, 2005) preached that overeating is the devil's temptation and that fat signifies an idolatrous relationship with food.[51] Many Christian diet gurus emphasize the importance for Christian women in particular to remain slim, since being attractive is good publicity for God.[52] According to Gwen Shamblin, founder of the popular Weigh-Down Workshop, a delicate form is a sign of true Christian womanhood: thinness proves that a woman has overcome the urge to overeat and totally submitted herself to God. By demonstrating how traditional Christian narratives on gender, appetite, and physicality are alive and well in evangelical programs like Weigh Down and First Place, scholars like Lynn Gerber and Marie Griffith expose the overlap between spiritual and worldly concerns in the contemporary veneration of thinness.[53]

The same Christian narratives that blatantly support evangelical dieting underwrite some secular weight-loss plans. Emily Contois analyzes the Protestant concepts and language embedded in *Dr. Atkins' New Diet Revolution* and *The South Beach Diet*. These diet books employ moral categories to demonize certain foods (e.g. sugar is "poison," bread is "treacherous") and instill fear, guilt, and hope in the hearts of low-carb believers. Both texts use confession and testimonials as strategies for converting infidel bodies and "Spreading the Word" of thinness. Their weight-loss regimens demand "sacrifice," "commitment," and the "strength of conviction." Their authors promise that by faithfully following their guidelines, anyone can escape the disgrace of fat and enjoy the rewards of thinness. While invoking the authority of science, these diets are deeply rooted in what Contois refers to as "a church of capitalism."[54]

The religious-like function of the seemingly secular quest for thinness is also evident in the Internet subculture known as "pro-Ana." Ana (short for anorexia) is an imaginary goddess-like figure whose disciples believe that anorexia and bulimia are lifestyle choices, rather than illnesses, and that those who go to extremes in the name of thinness need not be bothered by the mediocre standards of unbelievers. This subculture's iconography consists of "thinspirational" pictures of emaciated young women posed in ways that flaunt their protruding bones. The Pro-Ana Lifestyle website has an "Ana Religion & Lifestyle" tab on its menu, which offers quasi-spiritual tools to support anorexics' crusade for thinness, including "Ana's Psalm" (parodied on Psalm 23); "Thin Commandments" (e.g. "Thou shall not eat without feeling guilty"); "Ana's Creed" ("I believe in control…"); and Ana's Laws ("Thin is beauty; therefore I must be thin…If I wish to be loved…nothing else matters").[55]

However disturbing, the philosophy and rituals of pro-Ana are merely an extreme version of the beliefs and activities of many ordinary girls and women, most of whom want to be thinner.[56] The difference between dieting and disordered eating behavior is a matter of degree, not kind. As philosopher Susan Bordo points out, full-blown eating disorders have never been the norm. The real epidemic is among those with seemingly "normal" eating habits, who regularly police their appetites, hoping to get or stay noticeably slim.[57]

Repurposing patriarchal religion

That the majority of those devoted to thinness are female is troubling given how much this secular faith has in common with patriarchal religion. In both cases, women's bodies are the focal point of their identity and value, and their salvation pivots on their ability to subdue or transcend their carnal cravings. Like patriarchal religion, the quest for slenderness encourages female suffering, sacrifice, and self-denial (i.e. hunger) as a strategy for exercising power, establishing virtue, and garnishing social approval. This quest pits "good" women against those who, having "let themselves go," lack redemption.

For several decades, feminists have critically analyzed how narrowly defined female body norms function as a form of patriarchal domination. In the words of activists from the Fat Underground: "Fear of fat is a means of social control used against all women."[58] Once women internalize the cultural imperative for thinness, they police their own bodies as if they were dangerous criminals. Although some say they feel "more confident" when they are thinner, feminists' analyses reveal how weight loss practices "empower" women by making them docile and complicit with a society that judges them based on appearance.[59] In response to Protein World's question—"Why make your insecurities our problem?"—feminists answer that physically destructive, emotionally painful, seemingly personal conflicts with size and eating are the product of internalized dysfunctional norms that ads like the beach-body-ready billboard sponsor.

Feminist critiques of the ridiculously narrow fantasy of feminine perfection have helped many women understand that their troubled relationships with food and their bodies reflect a societal—not a personal—failure. However, these critiques have not always recognized how the sexism the normative ideal perpetuates intersects with racism, wealth disparity, ableism, and theories of religious and cultural superiority. Narrowly defined female body norms not only reinscribe women's inferior position in relation to men by defining their worth through physical appearance; they also reinforce the privilege of those who are white, wealthy, able-bodied, and thin above a diversity of "others." If, as Andrea Elizabeth Shaw says in *The Embodiment of Disobedience*, slenderness is a hallmark of white Western notions of feminine beauty,[60] then white women who seek to improve their bodies by making them thinner may be colluding with a colonial legacy they consciously reject.

Neocolonial aspects of compulsory thinness

This legacy lingers in depictions of tightly contoured female bodies that support the mission of global capitalism. The same mass-produced, digitally perfected images that line the checkout stand at your local grocery store circulate around the world, spreading the white-Western gospel of thinness to nations where many people are food insecure. Functionally, these images resemble the nineteenth-century colonial "White Lady" ideal, which served as a missionizing tool for "saving brown women" from their "heathen" cultures by civilizing/converting them to the respectable norms of white Christian womanhood.[61] Like the iconic White Lady, today's slender fantasy of femininity disseminates Euro-American, "civilizing" values in the name of "helping" females around the globe attain the health, beauty, and happiness that well-toned, first-world women of privilege presumably enjoy.[62]

As a privileged white woman, I feel a responsibility to critically examine my potential complicity with the damaging effects of the globalization of the white-Western slender ideal. How might my everyday thoughts and behaviors unwittingly perpetuate this damage? Am I supporting a worldview I consciously reject when I drink a Diet Coke? How should I respond when I hear other white women praising each other for losing weight? What about those who "choose" to diet because "it makes me feel better?" How do I honor their agency and choices in light of the suffering fat-phobia engenders? To what extent is a woman's decision to diet *freely* chosen in cultures where slenderness is required for "femininity?" Does my critique of the spread of white Western body norms to women of color around the globe unintentionally reinstate the "saving brown women" colonial agenda I aim to reject? These questions don't have easy or definitive answers. Nonetheless, they can facilitate the soul-searching privileged white women need to do if we want to minimize our complicity with the prevailing symbolic system that pressures diversely configured female flesh to conform to the narrow "White Lady" ideal.

Pressures to convert are heavy among minority women in first world contexts. Womanist scholar Cheryl Townsend Gilkes recalls the mixed messages she had to navigate growing up as a "full-featured" black female. While her slender mother encouraged her to trim down by giving her appetite suppressants, enrolling her in dance classes, and monitoring her consumption of sweets, Townsend Gilkes' great-aunt and grandmothers appreciated her ample size and served her delicious meals. At school, Townsend Gilkes' black peers associated her heavy-set frame with her leadership abilities. Members of her church similarly interpreted her full-figure as evidence that she was a capable young woman. Having to negotiate these mixed messages in the context of the dominant/white cultural preference for thinness made Townsend Gilkes recognize the revolutionary wisdom of Alice Walker's definition of a "womanist" as a black feminist who "loves love and food and roundness."[63]

Despite broader appreciation for women of size within African-American, Hispanic, and lesbian communities, black, Latina, and gay women are not immune to the dominant culture's mandate for thinness. This is evident in Becky Thompson's study of racial, ethnic, religious, and sexual minorities whose eating problems developed from their efforts to minimize the stigma of their "otherness" by losing weight. For black and Latina women, weight loss was a strategy for downplaying their darkness. Among Jewish and Catholic females, dieting was a way to fit in with their "WASP" (White-Anglo-Saxon-Protestant) peers. Some of the women Thompson interviewed connected their troubled eating to a belief that "being successful heterosexually depended upon being thin." And some traced their preoccupation with food and thinness to their immigrant parents' hope for economic prosperity. For them, "fat" was not only a sign of poverty, but of being un-American.[64]

Linking patriotism and thinness makes sense when we remember how cultural, racial, religious, or economic otherness functioned in the historical development of fat stigma. Minimizing "difference" via weight loss makes one fit for "the privileges of citizenship."[65] Given the lean form's association with upward mobility, it's not surprising that body size plays a pivotal role in the real-life parables of people who have risen from nobody to somebody in the public eye. US President Barack Obama is said to have been a "chubby" teenager prior to playing basketball, and he and First Lady Michelle Obama have been outspoken advocates of weight control. Size figures prominently in the rags-to-riches tale of another prominent African-American: Oprah Winfrey has yearned and endeavored her entire career to be slimmer. While Winfrey's humanizing struggle to lose weight has endeared her to millions of sympathetic fans, in her own mind, fat still threatens to undermine all her accomplishments. In her 2009 "Weight Loss Confession," Winfrey remarks: "It [referring to money, fame, and success] doesn't mean anything if you can't fit into your clothes. It means the fat won. It means you didn't win...I am mad at myself. I am embarrassed."[66] Perhaps the saddest thing about this comment is just how difficult it is to imagine Oprah shaming others the way she shames herself.

Losing your way to salvation

The tenacity of some people's devotion to thinness reveals just how painful fat shame can be. The colonial/missionizing dynamics of this devotion, its commercial underpinnings, and its homogenizing trajectory can be seen in

FIGURE 6.2 *Girl is Happy by Achievement © NinaMalyna.*
Source: iStock.

the familiar "before-and-after" advertisements for products and programs that encourage us to lose our way to salvation. These ads juxtapose "before" pictures of an unsaved, uncivilized soul/body (usually a fat, disheveled, unhappy-looking person) with "after" images of the same person redeemed by weight loss, looking confident, joyful, and notably thinner (Figure 6.2). Sometimes these photos are accompanied by testimonials along the lines of "I once was lost…But now am found…." Such redemption narratives and images epitomize the culture of physical improvement, in which the fat are damned, the slender are saved, and everybody is encouraged to repent and reduce.

Perhaps the most popular commercial drama of "born-again bodies" today is *The Biggest Loser.* This television "reality" show features fat contestants competing to win cash prizes and, of course, the rewards of thinness. Each week, viewers watch contenders' herculean efforts to outdo each other in the quest to win by losing. Choreographed to evoke horror, fascination, and sympathy, the show's various rituals—e.g. weekly weigh-ins, public confessions about food transgressions, fraught encounters with temptations, prolonged workouts, and miniscule meals—offer average-sized spectators a reassuring sense of their own saved (i.e. "normal") status. In this regard, *The Biggest Loser* resembles the freak shows described in the previous chapter, whose exhibits often included "Fat Man" or "Fat Woman" alongside other human "monstrosities" (e.g. disabled or uncivilized people).[67] Though *Biggest Loser* contenders differ from their historical freakish counterparts, who were not concerned with reducing, the program itself serves a similar function: entertaining audiences with the dehumanizing spectacle of nonconforming flesh and generating considerable wealth for those running the show.[68]

But if the spectacle of suffering sells,[69] not all *Biggest Loser* contestants' pain is in full view. For example, the show's first winner, Ryan Benson, eventually admitted that his behind-the-scenes weight-loss methods included starving and dehydrating himself to the point where he was peeing blood. Like many other former contestants, Benson regained most of the weight he'd jeopardized his health to lose.[70] The frustrations of weight cycling (i.e. losing and regaining pounds) echo in the experiences of countless people. "I tried everything" is a recurring theme in the stories of those whose bodies refuse to stay slim. Studies indicate that the vast majority of people who lose weight dieting regain much or all of what they lost within four or five years, leading some scientists to suggest that the phrase "permanent weight loss" is oxymoronic.[71]

Human bodies are not fooled by commercial culture's eschatological promises that with the right product and sufficient discipline, losing weight is quick and easy. However lofty our spiritual, philosophical, or commercial ideals, our flesh knows the truth about evolution. Early *Homo sapiens* needed to store body fat because they couldn't just open the fridge or head to the supermarket when hunger pangs hit. Nutritionist professor Linda Bacon reminds us of the challenges our hunter/gatherer ancestors faced:

> Given the scarcity of food and the tremendous amount of calories expended catching it (think running after mammoths with spears), it's no surprise that our bodies evolved to be super-efficient at energy conservation, genetically wired to hang on to every calorie while they urge us to seek out the highest calorie food we can find.[72]

In other words, our bodies are designed to stockpile—rather than shed—adipose tissue. This tenacious, evolutionary truth has not prevented some from viewing fat as an enemy.

The war on obesity

In the late 1990s, US government authorities officially declared "war on obesity." By the early 2000s, the popular news media had joined the crusade, rallying public support for the battle with thousands of articles, reports, and stories warning Americans of the dangers of the "obesity epidemic."[73] Amid the post-9/11 climate of heightened public anxiety, the anti-fat crusade's leaders galvanized citizens to get back in control by getting fit. Shortly after the terrorist attacks, the US Secretary of Health and Human Services encouraged every American to lose 10 pounds "as a patriotic gesture." In 2002, the US Surgeon General described "obesity" as "a threat that is every bit as real to America as the weapons of mass destruction." According to the war's propaganda, children were both victims and perpetrators of the problem. In 2004, the Surgeon General announced that the rise in "childhood obesity" is "every bit as threatening to us as is the terrorist threat we face today. It is the threat from within."[74]

In the name of health

From its inception, the anti-fat mission has been predicated on the belief that "excess" fat is a killer—that being "obese" or even "overweight" (according to BMI scores) will destroy your health. On the surface, this belief makes weight a medical issue. Yet critics of the crusade have noted its moralizing overtones. The war identifies a common enemy and thus creates a shared sense of purpose. Like any battle, fighting fat gives ordinary citizens a way to feel in control, to belong, to be good. Curiously, most scholars who recognize the war's moral subtexts do not examine the religious and philosophical narratives that shape those subtexts. But where do a culture's prevailing moral attitudes and values come from if not its dominant religious and philosophical traditions?

Both Christian and Cartesian legacies are deeply embedded in the war's basic premise—that people of size need to reduce. The notion that people *should* slim down reflects traditional Christian narratives in which self-denial is virtuous, gluttony is sinful, the condition of one's body reveals the state of one's soul, and the gate to salvation is singular and narrow. And the belief that individuals *can* control their weight assumes Descartes' view of the body as separate from and subject to the sovereignty of a rational will. Both narratives underwrite the appeals to "health" that fuel the "war on obesity," tacitly lending legitimacy to the battle.

Christian and Cartesian attitudes toward physicality interface with other cultural discourses and institutions that support the mission to eliminate "excess" in the name of health. In the United States, a $60 billion a year diet industry promotes the perception that losing weight is a laudable and achievable goal—emphasis on *perception*, since, on the whole, the industry fails to help consumers keep weight off.[75] Ironically, this failure is crucial to the success of the slimming business. Though diet companies appear to back the anti-fat crusade with promises of salvation through thinness, in reality, the "obesity epidemic" is good for business. Winning the war would compromise the industry's bottom line. Nevertheless, weight-loss marketers galvanize consumers with bellicose jargon. Phrases like "Conquer Your Cravings," "Blast Belly Fat," "Banish the Bulge," and "Torch the Fat" permeate magazine, TV, and Internet commercials.

A multilevel condemnation of fat helps justify government interventions to contain the "crisis" and exterminate the "terror." With its "Call to Action" in 2001, the Department of Health and Human Services recruited soldiers from virtually every sector of society to fight the good fight. Parents, teachers, health care professionals, coaches, business and community leaders were enlisted to do their moral/civic duty not only to ensure their own fitness, but to help others, especially youngsters, take charge of their flesh.[76] Children and teens became prime targets in the war in large part because federal and medical authorities were so unsuccessful in conquering the adversary in adults. Judging from the auto-ethnographies of Greenhalgh's students, however, the anti-fat crusade has done little to foster young people's healthy relationship with food and physicality. Rather, this campaign has created a generation of youth who feel alienated from their bodies, who can't stop thinking about weight and calories, and who measure their worth on the bathroom scale.[77]

Unintended consequences

The story of one of Greenhalgh's students illustrates some of the unintended consequences of the anti-fat crusade. Tiffany is a Chinese American young woman who doesn't fit the stereotypical profile of Asian women as slim, delicate, and petite. In her essay about her struggles with weight, she recalls how a group of fifth grade girls explained why they were bullying her: "we don't like ugly Asian girls...and you are ugly and fat." Shocked and devastated by such vicious comments, Tiffany started a year-long anorexic regime of eating only a bowl of rice per day. Her starvation-induced weight loss earned her the praise of peers and teachers ("You look so much better"), which raised her confidence but deepened her dread of fat. When, a few years later, she heard rumors that a "friend" had called her "a fat and ugly bitch," Tiffany became even more anxious about staying slim. At an annual check-up, a doctor reinforced her worries by warning that even a few extra pounds posed a danger. At home, Tiffany's little brother repeatedly told her she was "fat and ugly," and her father concurred. Understandably, this litany of attacks—interspersed with praise for weight loss—left Tiffany feeling terrified of other people's judgments and deeply mistrustful of her body and her sense of reality.[78]

Collateral damage is a part of combat. Anti-fat assaults may be cruel, but they're not surprising in a nation at war with "obesity." Still, when such attacks come when one's guard is down, as is often the case in childhood, the trauma they inflict can last for decades. While most fat youth receive shaming body commentary from their peers, many also hear harsh criticism from parents who feel pressure to produce children who are acceptably thin. "My family heavily criticizes me for my weight," a college student named Jessica explains.

> My father constantly will remind me not to eat too much because I am too fat. My mother will always remind me about how beautiful I was five years ago when I was 125 pounds…[She] is also constantly saying that she is on a diet. She too is trying to lose weight.

Instead of bolstering Jessica's health, these criticisms, cautions, and enticements fueled her obsession: "The thoughts that constantly play over and over in my head deal with weight. I keep telling myself, 'if I am able to lose weight, I will look better,' 'if I am able to lose weight, people will like me better.'"[79] Like many young people, Jessica understands quite well that in the anti-fat crusade, more is at stake than a value-neutral concern with being healthy. To be thin is to be good. To be good is to be in control. And to be in control is to be godly.

Hidden and not-so-hidden supports

However secular the war on fat seems, a behind-the-scene image of a judgmental, controlling God silently sanctions its aims and strategies. Although Christian dieters reference this God most explicitly, government and medical leaders of the anti-fat crusade also assume everybody is divinely destined to be thin. Couching this destiny in the language of "health" conceals—but doesn't eliminate—its theological underpinnings. Proponents of the war would have us believe that our personal salvation (i.e. health) and national glory depend on everybody converting to the same slender standard. Lurking quietly in the background of this mission is a God who seems more concerned with trimming our waistlines than with the thousands who die daily from malnutrition; a God who punishes the sin of nonconformity with internalized shame and public derision.

When authority figures reprimand young people because of their size, they implicitly mirror the actions of this judgmental, despotic God who "loves his children" by castigating them. A number of my students have told me the first thing they hear when they go home for a weekend or semester break are their parents' critical comments about their weight. They are not alone. In Greenhalgh's study, 60 percent of female students and 40 percent of males reported being scolded by a parent for being too big.[80] Some doctors play a similarly god-like role, using their authority to perpetuate judgment. Sometimes physicians' misguided focus on fat as the root of all bodily afflictions leads them to overlook serious health problems. When fat activist Abby Weintraub saw a doctor for excessive menstrual bleeding, she was told to lose weight. "'It's a matter of how badly you want to feel better,'" a gynecologist admonished, "'It's up to you.'" Disheartened by such condescending advice, Weintraub suspended her quest for medical help. A few years later, doctors discovered a malignant tumor bigger than a grapefruit in her uterus.[81]

Weintraub's reflection on this episode illustrates the difficulties fat people face as they struggle for health and sanity amid a cacophony of blame and praise directed at their bodies. After surgery to remove the tumor, Weintraub decided to lose weight by changing her eating and exercise patterns. People lathered her with praise for being "so strong" to "beat the odds" and win not just the battle with cancer but the war on fat. But Weintraub was suspicious of this applause: "as if my access to health care reflects a kind of inner strength… as if this was the end of a lifelong struggle [for self-acceptance], as opposed to just another point in the history of my body." Interestingly, she also detected a kind of existential angst beneath people's enthusiasm for her weight loss:

[W]hat I felt from other people's praise was a strong sense of their discomfort around bodies and an effort to find solid ground where there is none. We are ungrounded in the simple fact that bodies change, grow, shrink, and gain/lose ability over the course of a lifetime.

By creating "winners" and "losers," Weintraub observes, the war on fat fosters the belief that good health is something we earn, even as it downplays the unpredictability of embodied life. "It's much more difficult to accept that our bodies are, by turns, miraculously high functioning and simply vulnerable." Eventually, Weintraub regained much of the weight she lost. But rather than cling to either praise or blame, she works "to accept the impermanence of [her body's] size, health status, and ability every day."[82]

Praise and blame are intimately linked strategies for instilling anti-fat sentiments. Disdain for fat can be transmitted in compliments (e.g. "You've lost weight—you look great!) just as surely as in put-downs ("Didn't anyone ever tell you fat girls shouldn't wear shorts?"). Some "fat-talk" aims to be educational (e.g. "Do you know how many calories muffins have?"), and some has a more biting tone (e.g. "Do you really think you need that extra helping?").[83] Undoubtedly, being praised for losing feels much better than being criticized for gaining. Yet both applause and disapproval serve the war's colonial agenda of conquering fat by converting diversely sized individuals to a supposedly universal ideal.

Parents, physicians, and other authority figures may think they are doing young people a favor by chiding heft and extolling thinness. But the "for your own good" mentality behind such commentary resembles the justifications religious missionaries used to force "uncivilized heathens" to convert to the "one true God." Needless to say, those campaigns did not end well. Countless indigenous people are still struggling with the residually harmful effects of the trauma inflicted by such morally sanctioned coercion—sugar-coated as concern. No doubt, leaders of the "war on obesity" and its faithful servants intend to "help"—not traumatize—people whose bodies are larger than average. But it's difficult to separate an organized assault on fat flesh from a unified attack on people of size.

Moreover, since "obesity" and "overweight" in the United States are disproportionately prevalent in women of color, ethnic minorities, and people who are poor, the war's collateral damage inordinately harms persons who are already socially disadvantaged.[84] Framing weight as a matter of personal responsibility, public health rhetoric condemns fat people for driving up medical costs, without critiquing the profit-driven economic system that supports the wealth disparity that significantly impacts health outcomes.[85] While the anti-fat crusade encourages African-Americans and Hispanics to assimilate to the northern-European ideal of thinness, the media proliferates stereotypes of poor black and Latina mothers as endangering their children's health through overfeeding.[86] Although the generally leaner figures of Asian Americans reinforce their status as "model minorities" in a culture that worships thinness, large-bodied members of this community often feel doubly ostracized—by white people and by their families—because of their size.[87]

The war's faulty premise and financial interests

As many scholars point out, the anti-fat mission itself was initially justified with statistics on mortality rates among fat people that have since been widely discredited.[88] More generally, a growing corpus of peer-reviewed research calls into question the war's basic premise, namely, that being fat is automatically unhealthy. In *Body Respect*, nutrition researchers Linda Bacon and Lucy Aphramor discuss this evidence, including studies indicating that "overweight" people do not die sooner than their average-size peers, that shedding pounds does not prolong life (and can actually increase the risk of dying early), that fat individuals do not necessarily consume more food than their slender peers, and that *fitness* is more important than *weight* in determining health and longevity. While heavier weights are *associated* with higher risk for certain health problems (e.g. coronary heart disease, type 2 diabetes, hypertension, some forms of cancer), being fat does not *cause* disease (and in fact protects against certain illnesses).[89]

The evidence Bacon and Aphramor present exposes the fallacy that a person's weight is strictly under her or his individual control. This fallacy ignores the powerful role genetic and environmental variables play in influencing body size. One of the many truths of biodiversity is that people's metabolisms run at different speeds.[90] In addition, a web of social, economic, and political factors affect our weight, e.g. (in)ability to purchase healthy food, time and places to exercise, family habits and cultural customs, geographic location, nutritional literacy, and so on. Even federal agricultural policies impact our size. Ironically, the same US government that wages war on fat subsidizes the mass production of soy, corn, and wheat—crops that are heavily processed into nutritionally sparse, calorie-dense products (e.g. fast foods, packaged macaroni and cheese, microwave dinners, Cheetos, Twinkies). Thanks to federal subsidies and cheap (though environmentally harmful) agricultural practices, these calorie-rich, processed foods are affordable for most people, which helps explain why Americans spend 90 percent of their food budget on them. Most Americans also say they prefer (taste-wise) processed over whole foods,[91] which makes sense considering that processed foods are typically manufactured with fats, sugars, salt, and artificial flavors that trigger our taste buds. Many of these products are intentionally designed to act like opiates, stimulating a physiological craving to consume more of them—an addictive pattern that pads both our waistlines and corporate profits.[92] The more we understand the various ways nature and nurture interact to shape the size of our bodies, the more the one-size-fits-all agenda of the anti-fat crusade makes little sense—unless we recognize some of the other interests it serves.

It boggles the mind to learn just how intimate politics, medicine, and the pursuit of profit have been in instigating and sustaining the war. Several scholars have critically examined these ties in detail.[93] Their analyses reveal how the war's leaders have had vested interests in making people worry about weight. The same "obesity experts" who run weight-loss clinics, receive millions of dollars in research grants, review submissions for medical journals, and serve on government panels that define public health priorities have had close ties (as paid consultants and board members) with diet companies like Weight Watchers and corporate giants like Eli Lilly, Knoll Pharmaceuticals, and Wyeth-Ayerst, which manufacture and market weight-loss drugs.[94]

More harmful than healthful

Both the profitability of the war and its tendency to do more harm than good are evident in the growing popularity of weight-loss surgery as a "treatment" for fat people. The average price of procedures ranges from $17,000 to $50,000,[95] but those numbers don't include the nonmonetary costs—including risk of death—of having parts of your internal organs removed.[96] The dangers surrounding bariatric surgery illustrate the "by any means necessary" mentality the "war on obesity" promotes, and the desperation many large-bodied people feel as living targets of this crusade.[97] This mentality was common among Greenhalgh's students, many of whom used laxatives, diet pills, excessive exercise, starving, purging, smoking, and even cocaine in their efforts to lose weight, often with little concern about the hazards of such behavior.[98]

Even less drastic slenderizing measures can be more detrimental than beneficial. Despite short-term "victories," dieting is often counterproductive in the long run. By slowing the body's metabolism, intensifying its efficiency at calorie absorption, and increasing hunger and cravings for high-calorie foods, underfeeding can catalyze a "yo-yo" pattern of losing-regaining-losing-regaining that's hard on a body.[99] Weight-loss rituals also tend to foster an adversarial, master/slave relationship between mind and body. Assuming the sovereignty of the rational will, diets typically instruct you to eat certain foods, in limited amounts, at specified times, in a calculated manner—regardless of what your body wants or needs. This externally directed, controlling approach to eating erodes people's capacity to notice feelings of hunger or satiety, thereby exacerbating the mind/body dissociation many who struggle with weight already experience.

Though fought with a vengeance, America's crusade against fat appears to be a losing battle—but not with regard to weight. Despite enormous investments of private and public resources to defeat the enemy, "obesity" rates have barely budged since the war's inception.[100] Instead of changing strategies, however, the plan seems to be: full steam ahead. The US government continues to spend hundreds of millions on research each year to find a way to fix fat people, while ignoring the hidden costs the war inflicts.[101] If medical, political, and moral leaders really wanted to promote physical well-being, they would have to encourage us to change something larger than our bodies—namely, our assumptions about health and weight variation. Ultimately, these leaders would have to recognize that there is more than one path to salvation: that health is possible at a variety of sizes.

Introducing HAES (Health at Every Size)

This is the insight of Health at Every Size (HAES), a grassroots movement comprised of activists, academics, therapists, health care professionals, and others who oppose the "war on obesity" and advocate an alternative approach to wellness. HAES is based on the principles of respect for somatic diversity, appreciation for embodied knowledge, critique of social injustices that perpetuate poor health, and compassionate self-care based on mindful eating and exercise.[102] Needless to say, this approach challenges stereotypical views of fat as unhealthy, unattractive, and symptomatic of moral or character dysfunction. Moving beyond an individualistic view of good health as a reward for virtuous behavior, HAES proffers an ethical perspective and practical path for well-being that is not contingent on size. Not surprisingly, HAES is a crucial resource within the fat acceptance movement.

The clinicians who developed HAES were motivated by the suffering they witnessed both among those targeted by the war on fat and among those struggling with anorexia and bulimia. In their eyes, it didn't make sense to prescribe the same practices for heavier people that were diagnosed as eating disorders in thinner people.[103] In addition to drawing on peer-reviewed research that exposes the myth that health=thinness, they conducted their own studies, the results of which confirm that a nonviolent approach to wellness—one that doesn't target appetite, calories, and fat as enemies— fosters greater physical and mental health than fighting "obesity."[104] Some who follow the HAES model do lose weight. But reducing is not the goal. The aim is encourage lifelong health-promoting practices—regardless of size. Taking the emphasis *off* weight liberates people's mental, moral, and physical energies so they can be channeled into more creative, life-giving endeavors.

HAES signals a significant paradigm shift: from controlling the body to nurturing it wisely. Instead of forcing our flesh to comply with cultural expectations and torturing ourselves for not achieving that goal, HAES encourages us to honor, appreciate, and enjoy our bodies' particularities, to listen attentively to the wisdom of our flesh, and to devote ourselves to creating a world in which everybody is respected and cared for. Ultimately, HAES can be seen as a kind of peace movement, one that aims to help us reconcile with the biodiversity, impermanence, interdependence, and vulnerability of embodied life by urging nonviolent, noncooperation with the crusade to make everyone the same boring size.

The practical wisdom of a nonviolent approach to health

Though HAES is a nonsectarian movement for peace, many of its principles and strategies segue with the pragmatic wisdom found in traditional religions.

For example, HAES's emphasis on accepting your body *as it is* resonates with the Buddhist teaching on *nonattachment*. In Buddhism, clinging (i.e. attaching) to a fixed idea of how something (or someone) is *supposed* to be creates suffering. From this perspective, much of the mental and physical anguish people experience in relation to weight stems from the cultural/internalized expectation that everybody can/should be slender.[105] Relinquishing such narrow expectations frees us not only from the exhausting burden of trying to achieve the impossible, but also from the self-contempt that frequently follows our bodies' refusal to cooperate with that task.

In calling for a cease-fire in the war on fat, HAES proponents are not advising people to abandon the quest for physical well-being. They advocate healthy eating and exercising, but caution that these behaviors will not magically make fat people skinny. While they take blood pressure, blood sugar levels, and cholesterol readings seriously, they see the number on the scale as a dubious barometer of fitness.[106] Rather than fixate on weight, HAES encourages "compassionate self-care" through "attuned" eating and movement: forms of mindfulness practice that involve listening to and trusting your body's internal signals to guide decisions about food and activity. Learning to distinguish between physical and emotional hunger, eating what your body tells you it wants/needs (instead of what you think you *should* eat), experimenting with stopping when you're full, and finding ways to exercise that are enjoyable (rather than punishing) are examples of attuned eating and movement.[107] This method of paying attention—without judgment—to internal thoughts, feelings, and physical sensations in order to nurture the body's actual needs resembles the Buddhist precept of "mindful consumption," a moral guideline for choosing foods and activities that nourish one's body/mind while supporting the welfare of others.[108]

As a guide for ethical/healthy living, mindful consumption respects the interrelated nature of embodied life: how mental, emotional, and physical states influence each other, and how our personal well-being is inseparable from the health of others, our social milieu, and the earth. For example, it's no coincidence that foods that are closer to their original state (e.g. whole, organic, or locally grown) tend to be better for our bodies and for the environment. But is it fair that only the wealthy can afford such foods? The truth of interdependence challenges individualistic definitions of "health" and illuminates the intersecting forms of oppression that diminish people's well-being (e.g. poverty, racism, sexism, ableism, homophobia, sizeism, environmental destruction). While no one person can remedy this tangle of social ills, HAES practitioners urge each of us to use whatever power/privilege we have to create a more compassionate society.[109] We can nurture the health of the social body through our daily choices—mindful choices about how we feed and move our bodies, how we think/feel about our flesh, and how we relate to the biodiversity of others. Through such choices, we can make the struggle for peace and dignity for people of size integral to all social justice movements.

Members of a compassionate society do not turn their backs on the suffering of others because they have learned how to take care of suffering in themselves. In Buddhism, formal mindfulness practice (i.e. meditation) is a method for developing the capacity to stay present to internal distress. Sitting quietly, feeling your breathing, and observing the contents of your mind without judgment is an effective way to cultivate nonattachment—to relinquish the desire for control that the war on fat exploits and perpetuates—and experience self-acceptance. But you needn't practice formal meditation or be a Buddhist to build a more mindful, friendly relationship with food and your body. In the context of HAES, staying present might mean being curious about guilty feelings that arise when you stop counting calories, probing such feelings without morally labeling or trying to suppress them. Practicing mindfulness could also mean noticing when you're engaging in comparative thinking—measuring yourself or others based on the normative ideal—and realizing how such thinking triggers painful self-judgments and judgments of others.[110]

Whatever form it takes, the practice of staying present differs from the control-and-conform, competitive training we receive from the culture of physical improvement. In fact, practicing mindfulness can be thought of as a "vacation" from the never-ending task of self-enhancement. From a Buddhist perspective, there is no "self" to improve—at least not the autonomous, individual ego most Westerners are taught to identify with and perfect via weight loss.[111] The Buddhist teaching on non-self (*anatta*) may seem lofty and tangential, but it's actually quite relevant to the pursuit of health at every size. For it's our implicit view of the *self* as an autonomous, individual ruling over a compliant body that make us believe that being fat is a choice and that everybody can/should be thin.

Feminist theology and the fat Jesus

For decades, feminist theologians have critiqued this modern Western notion of self as created in the image of the elite, white, able-bodied men whose interests it serves.[112] Their alternative view of the self—as diversely incarnated and constructed in the context of interpersonal relationships and social/symbolic systems, as interdependent, evolving, and soft-around-the-edges—supports the principles of HAES and the work of the broader fat acceptance movement. Appreciation for embodied diversity is explicit in the womanist affirmation of redemptive self-love (including love for "food and roundness"), and it's implicit in postcolonial feminist critiques of the mission to save "uncivilized" women by converting them to white-Western femininity norms. More generally, feminist theology's epistemological shift—from relying on external/established (typically male) religious rules and authorities as sources of truth, to trusting the inner/collective wisdom of diverse women's experiences—affirms HAES's emphasis on embodied knowledge and its communally oriented definition of health.

This shift is evident in *The Fat Jesus*, in which Lisa Isherwood gives the soft, voluptuous bodies of fat women a privileged place in reflections on God. More specifically, Isherwood's feminist incarnational theology envisions corpulent, capacious female flesh as manifesting the erotic, sensuous, life-affirming power of divine love.[113] Rejecting Christian narratives that equate feminine virtue with self-deprivation and that envision God as an invincible, unchanging, judgmental masculine authority, she retrieves the biblical view of food and eating as expressions of divine abundance and human hospitality. Her analysis invites women to stop playing "the size game"—the spoken or unspoken competition to see who's the thinnest—and start enjoying the sensual pleasures of embodied life. Indeed, she encourages us to experience such pleasures as manifestations of divine pleasure. By granting women permission to stop regulating their appetites in pursuit of some highly questionable moral ideal, and by critiquing social/symbolic systems that privilege some bodies at the expense of others, Isherwood's incarnational theology makes Christianity a resource—rather than an obstacle—for those seeking to affirm fat female flesh.

Isherwood's incarnational appreciation for well-cushioned female bodies culminates in her invitation for us to behold "the Fat Jesus." The edges of this "Christ of womanly abundance" are soft and flexible, not hard and rigidly defined like traditional hypermasculine images of God. The Fat Jesus does not call us to police our appetites or conquer our bodies for the sake of other-worldly perfection. In fact, the corpulent Christ invites Christians "to heal the split between body and mind" by committing themselves to passionately appreciating, equitably sharing, and responsibly stewarding the earth's abundant resources. Ultimately, the Fat Jesus calls on all heretical bodies "to obscenely declare 'screw you' to the myriad manifestations of patriarchal conformity that enslave us and narrow the glory of our abundant life and our liberative praxis."[114]

"Revolting bodies"

Several insights and themes in Isherwood's fat liberation theology—including this "screw you" attitude—are palpable in the broader fat acceptance movement. Her summons to celebrate, rather than fear, sensuous female physicality echoes and affirms the liberation women of size experience as they tap the revolutionary potential of their "revolting bodies."[115] Like many fat-positive females, Virgie Tovar refuses to capitulate to the politics of fear and shame. "The f-word is used to scare women," she observes, "but it doesn't scare me." Instead of apologizing for her girth, Tovar embraces its subversive/sensual potential. For her, claiming the pleasure and beauty of large, soft, female flesh is an act of civil disobedience—one that defies cultural/internalized scripts that shrivel women's bodies and distort their imaginations. Tovar urges women of substance to come out of hiding and replace their strivings to be "good" with decisions to be "fierce."

This call to ferocity challenges conventional gender socialization, particularly the residual "White Lady" requirement for females to suppress their anger and passion. Culturally and religiously socialized to please others, many women stifle the very energy we need to be whole, including feelings of anger that can prompt us to struggle *on behalf of* our bodies and each other—rather than *against* our bodies and each other.[116] To illustrate the revolutionary power of fierce fat women, Tovar recounts an incident on a commuter train where she overheard a thin woman telling her boyfriend that she (Tovar) was too fat to be wearing the outfit she had on. Rather than swallow such shaming commentary, Tovar approached her critic and calmly explained that she was quite capable of deciding how to dress, that she thought her outfit looked great, and that no one needs to feel threatened by a fat woman wearing a short skirt. "I did not insult her or berate her," Tovar recalls,

> I simply felt it polite to inform her that the era of fat-girl apologies and tastelessly retrograde fatphobic remarks is coming to a close and the day of the fierce, too-much-to-handle fat girl is close at hand. And then, I sat down…right next to her. We sat there in silence for forty-five minutes from downtown San Francisco all the way to the…end of the line. I felt like Rosa Parks of fat that day.[117]

Tovar's nonviolent noncooperation with her own oppression exemplifies the "outrageous, audacious, courageous, and willful behavior" that womanist theologians have long affirmed[118]—behavior that manifests the unconditional, redemptive self-love that brings healing to others. Such fierce, unlady-like behavior demonstrates the "the power of anger in the work of love." This is Christian feminist ethicist Beverly Harrison's classic description of the divine energy that is present in oppressed people's embodied knowledge of their own dignity and in the struggles for justice this knowledge inspires. For Harrison, anger is not a deadly sin. Nor is it the opposite of love. Anger is a moral "feeling-signal that all is not well in our relation to other[s]" and "that change is called for." Denying anger can stunt one's growth, clinging to it can make one bitter. But when anger energy is rooted in an understanding that all of life is intricately interrelated and a corollary commitment to respect the dignity of others, such energy has the moral potential to generate loving action—behavior that promotes care and respect for self and others.[119]

For fierce fat women, practicing self-care and respect means relinquishing the eschatology of a better/thinner future. The redemption/revolution Tovar proclaims is already at hand. It is this-worldly, it is liberating, and it includes pleasure:

> Life happens now, not fifteen or thirty or one hundred pounds from now. You can wear that bikini now. You can go on a date now. You can play in the ocean now…You can dance in your underwear now. You can savor and gasp-with-delight while eating that double crème brie…You have permission not to waste another hour on self-denial.[120]

Ultimately, what big-bodied women really need to lose isn't weight, but shame. Tovar calls on curvy sisters everywhere to abandon their painfully futile efforts to pass through the narrow gate of feminine perfection, to enjoy every pound and inch of their carnal abundance, to become "models of corporeal anarchy," and, most importantly, to dedicate themselves to "the path to self-love."[121]

The saving path of self-love

This path is not easy for people of size. Often, Marilyn Wann says, fat people have to practice the Golden Rule in reverse: "Do unto yourself as you would do unto others."[122] And yet, loving yourself is controversial when you are fat. Many thin or average-sized individuals find it hard to believe that people of size are capable—much less deserving—of self-love. Why is this? Fat activist Jes Baker explores this conundrum in a blog about Tess Munster, a happy, successful, 5′5″, size-22 model who has attracted a lot of public attention, some of it positive, but much of it vitriolic. As Baker notes, the idea that happiness=thinness is so deeply engrained in most people's psyches that a happy fat person like Munster messes with their worldview. Being fat and happy seems not only *impossible*, but *unfair*—especially to those who dedicate time, energy, and money to the goal of getting or staying slim. When you've sacrificed so much in order to be happy/skinny, it's easy to feel angry with those who appear to have "cheated the system and found the pot of gold without doing *any* of the goddamn work."[123] By showing that it's possible to love yourself without losing weight, Munster, Baker, Tovar, and other fat-positive people expose the myth of salvation through thinness to be an illusion.

In *Fat!So?* Wann deconstructs this illusion by listing responses from an online survey she conducted in which she asked, "What do you *like* about being fat?" These are just a few of the thousands of illuminating answers she received:

- My friends like me for who I am
- I'm unique, not a cookie-cutter person…
- People like to hug a soft person…
- I'm not tiny and helpless
- I feel substantial
- It taught me to think for myself and not rely on the crowd
- It made me more accepting of other people
- It's a built-in jerk detector[124]

As these comments suggest, loving fatness in a world that worships thinness generates an alternative consciousness. Rooted in the wisdom of unrepentant, unconventional flesh, this atypical thinking interrupts our religiously/culturally conditioned habit of "demonizing difference"[125] and appreciates humans' biodiversity.

Masada articulates this prophetic perspective by challenging us to recognize the spiritual consequences of the war on fat: "many people born today will die hating themselves for their fatness, and some of them will have thin bodies that they or others perceive as fat."[126] Whether directed at oneself or others, fat-hatred is soul-killing because it diminishes one's ability to trust the goodness of life, oneself/body, and others. For too long, Masada says, people of faith have tacitly supported such hatred:

> We have let anti-fatness become part of religion, a religion in itself, the state religion, with fat phobic doctors, scientists, politicians and other secular leaders as clergy…We have let people's morality be judged by their weight, and by whether their beliefs and behaviors were likely to cause weight gain or loss. We have connected fatness and food with sin…placed thinness next to Godliness…[and] estranged people from their own bodies.

Masada calls on religious people to recognize and confess their complicity with fat oppression, to embrace the "good news" of somatic diversity, to challenge narratives that seek to minimize people of size, and to see the intersections between various kinds of superiority complexes.[127]

Masada's prophetic perspective invites us to wrestle with the question: Why is unorthodox flesh so scary? Perhaps nonconforming bodies make us uncomfortable because they reveal our unexamined assumptions—and ultimately, our ignorance—about how things are supposed to be, e.g. how bodies are supposed to look, act, and feel. Perhaps by embodying the unknown, divergent, unpredictable nature of life, irregular bodies (whether our own or others') show us that the security we crave is as tentative as the satisfaction of our appetites. Maybe the "corporeal anarchy" of fat bodies can be unsettling because it reminds us that the somatic laws we habitually obey are constructed, not God-given. Perhaps "revolting" bodies trigger feelings of vulnerability by stirring our tender yearnings to belong, to not be the last kid chosen for kick ball. Maybe transgressive flesh scares us because, in its refusal to be controlled and converted, such flesh makes it hard to deny that life is fundamentally a mystery, in the face of which we get to choose between love and fear.

Communal/revolutionary dimensions of self-love

For fat women, choosing love is an ongoing practice. Theoretical acceptance is not sufficient. Intellectual critique is not enough. You can brilliantly deconstruct media images of feminine perfection and still cringe at the sight of yourself in the mirror. Tovar suggests that although self-love is an inborn capacity, it's also a skill that develops with practice. The goal is not perfection: "you will make many…sweet mistakes long the way." Nor is self-love a once-and-for-all achievement. For women of size, self-love is a "minute-to-minute" process, because "[i]t never stops being hard to love yourself in a world that tells you you'll never be good enough."[128] Fat-positive performance artist Emma Corbett-Ashby elaborates the dynamic, nonlinear quality of this path: "Body shame runs deep. Even the most upbeat and self-loving fatties feel they're on shaky ground every now and then." Yet despite internal and external obstacles, "Tough, nuanced women aren't afraid to go deep." Sometimes, going deep means locating that inner strength that empowers you to see the beauty of stretch marks, and to behold them with "reverence." Sometimes, going deep means honestly admitting that self-love can be a struggle. Making peace with the struggle is, Corbett-Ashby suggests, just another part of the journey.[129]

Self-love is not a path one travels alone. Many self-described women of substance recount how the fat acceptance movement facilitated their conversion from self-hatred to self-love. Fat activist Emily Anderson narrates the communal dimensions of her rebirth in an essay about her experiences at the gym. Without referencing religion explicitly, a "born again" subtext permeates the transformation she describes. "In my pre-fat acceptance (PFA) life, I felt caught in the paradox of being fat at the gym: the fear that I didn't belong in its hallowed, sweaty halls, but if I didn't go, I would never become un-fat and finally worthy." After years of failed diets and imprisoning shame, Anderson discovered the fat acceptance movement, where she learned to value herself "not *despite* my body, but *for* my body and for my personhood and my laughter and for all of me." Emboldened by the fat-friendly examples of others, she returned to the gym "as a fatty who loved her fat and wasn't trying to undo her body, or to become un-fat." No longer suffocating in a "haze of apology," she now enjoys "the transgressive thrill of exercising without the goal or effort to lose weight." She doesn't hesitate to wipe sweat off her face with the bottom of her shirt (exposing her belly), or to wear tight shorts that reveal her thighs touching. These acts of personal empowerment have a communal dimension. By being "that fat woman who won't stop singing along to Beyoncé while she's running," by being "happy in a place where she's supposed to be self-flagellating," Anderson hopes to be a role model for other fat females, to offer them the same support that saved her from self-destruction. Together, she says, they can accomplish something far more valuable than burning calories.[130]

What women like Anderson are accomplishing is a revolution—one that changes the way we see, value, and experience somatic diversity. This revolutionary redemption connects the power of self-love to the quest for social justice by affirming the equal dignity and worth of all persons; by prophetically interrogating the moral underpinnings of the "war on obesity"; by examining our complicity with fat prejudice and related/intersecting forms of oppression; by making care and respect for unorthodox bodies non-surprising and noncontroversial; by promoting sanity, health, happiness, and peace not only for people of size, but for everybody who has suffered under the weight of cultural expectations about how a body is supposed to be. In this sense, the very fat, disorderly flesh our society has damned has the potential to save us all.

7

The shame of chronic pain and illness

A few summers ago, my friends Mary and Dale invited my husband and me over for a visit. It was a beautiful day in early June, the kind northern Minnesotans don't take for granted. The frigid winters we survive make the warm sunshine, purple, yellow, and lavender irises, chartreuse trees, and singing birds nothing short of a miracle. Mary is the former office administrator for my department. Dale used to direct the college's Financial Aid Office and the Native American Outreach Program. They had both retired, and Dale was living with stage IV liver cancer.

It had already been a rough day for Dale by the time we arrived around noon. His body felt achy and weak from the chemo treatment two days earlier. One of Dale's gifts was that he didn't try to hide his illness or the uncomfortable consequences of treating the cancer. His lack of pretense was disarming. After chatting a while, I sensed Dale's discomfort and fatigue increasing and decided it was time to leave. On our way out, Dale asked me how I was feeling. He knew about my hip and noticed I was limping. "Not so good," I responded. "Lately the pain has been relentless." It was a relief to be able to tell the truth without worrying that Dale would feel sorry for me. Instead of offering platitudes and pity, he just nodded and kept listening. "As much as I dread it," I continued, "I think I'm going to have surgery." Dale could tell I was on the verge of tears, but he didn't rush to rescue me from my sadness. He just looked at me reassuringly through his own pain and said, "We don't always get to choose."

What choice do we have?

The idea that we don't always have a choice—that we can't control how the dramas of our bodies unfold—runs contrary to the messages we receive from mainstream society. Sure, I could decide whether or not to have a hip replacement. But I didn't get to choose whether or not to have osteoarthritis, any more than Dale got to choose whether or not to have cancer. And Dale didn't even have the option of having surgery to resolve his condition. Though not the whole story, the fact that we can't totally determine our physical destiny is an abiding aspect of embodied life—a partial truth many of us, myself included, have spent a lot of energy resisting.

It's hard to accept what we cannot willfully change about our physiology when the messages we receive from our culture constantly tell us we have dominion over our flesh. The language and images that shape our relationship to our bodies assure us we can power through somatic setbacks like chronic illness and pain. We can battle cancer, defeat heart disease, fight asthma, conquer arthritis, and triumph over the discomfort surrounding these and myriad other maladies—or prevent them from happening in the first place. In many ways, popular medical, self-help, and commercial discourses collapse notions of choice and control, (mis)leading us to believe we can dictate the outcome of our decisions about our bodies.

We have seen how the salvation myth of a better body is constructed through a military mentality that advocates antagonistic strategies for physical improvement. In this chapter, I examine how the same colonial paradigm that supports the myth of overcoming disability and the war on obesity is deployed to rally sick bodies back to health. By exploring the terrain of chronic pain and illness against the backdrop of the culture of physical improvement, I encourage us to rethink our beliefs about health and healing, particularly with regard to flesh that refuses to get well.

Because chronic disease and discomfort are lodged in bodies, it's tempting to view them as purely biological experiences, the natural response to which is a desire to make them go away. The undesirability of cancer, diabetes, migraines, arthritis, and heart disease (to give a few examples) is so obvious that it may seem that energy expended reflecting on meanings assigned to these conditions would be better spent trying to cure them. Biochemistry becomes imbalanced, neurons and neurotransmitters misfire, cell development goes awry, immune systems malfunction. No one wants these afflictions (Figure 7.1). What else do we need to know?

However unwanted persistent pain and illness may be, these conditions are worth investigating because how we think about them and the meanings we assign to them are integral to how we (or others) experience them. Like physical impairment and weight, experiences of intractable pain and sickness are shaped by popular discourses about them, which bear the imprint of the culture in which they circulate.[1] In developed Western societies, the beliefs that "healthy people have more fun!" and that "Better health means a better

FIGURE 7.1 *Headache Woman © Media for Medical.*
Source: Getty Images.

life"[2] influence both *perceptions* and *experiences* of persistent pain and illness.

At the heart of my exploration in this chapter are the experiences of people who are losing the battle against chronic pain and illness, including those who consciously choose not to fight. These experiences challenge us to soul search our way through a variety of questions: How do dominant cultural, religious, and philosophical narratives shape our understanding of health and sickness? What constitutes healing? Who decides? Given that chronic disease and discomfort are just that—*chronic*—why do many charitable organizations, self-help programs, commercial products, and doctors promise that you can conquer these afflictions? What understandings of "body" and "self" support that promise? Are there ways to envision somatic afflictions, other than as alien intruders to be vanquished or as punishment for poor choices? Before exploring these questions, we need to understand some basic terms.

Chronic illness and pain: Diagnoses and distinctions

In *The Illness Narratives*, Arthur Kleinman distinguishes between *disease* and *illness*.[3] Whereas disease connotes a medical view of what is not well in an ailing body, illness refers to the patient's subjective (though culturally influenced) experience of unwellness. Thus disease is understood as something that happens to the body, while illness is what happens to the person. This distinction illuminates the tension between *discourses about* chronic pain and disease and individuals' *experiences of* these afflictions, and this tension is central to my analysis in this chapter. However, since most of my sources do not explicitly employ Kleinman's disease/illness rubric, neither do I. Instead, I use terms like chronic disease, sickness, and illness interchangeably.

Illnesses and pain that are "chronic" are not subject to quick fixes. Something chronic (from the Greek, *chronos*) lasts a long time, is recurrent, and may never go away. In medical terms, *chronic* pain and disease are distinguished from *acute* conditions, which can usually be resolved in less than three-to-six months.[4] Some long-lasting maladies are progressive (i.e. getting worse over time); but this is not always the case. Some are terminal (i.e. ending in death); but many are not. Some chronic diseases, such as cancer, also come in non-chronic forms. Despite their vast diversity—e.g. heart disease, diabetes, cancer, and asthma (which are the most common), as well as arthritis, lupus, multiple sclerosis, Crohn's disease, colitis, fibromyalgia, epilepsy, and countless others—*chronic* sicknesses share the common fate of being "treatable but not curable."[5] As such, they both stimulate and frustrate the pursuit of physical improvement—blending the longing to be healthy with the reality of obstinate illness.

The pain that often accompanies chronic disease varies in magnitude and kind. The hurt can be dull, aching, tight, burning, or stabbing, depending on the condition one has, one's activity and stress levels on any given day, and even the weather. Whatever the sensation, the experience of pain is both highly subjective and influenced by social attitudes and standards. You may have seen the "Pain Measurement Scale" in your doctor's office—with the happy/smiling face at one end (0/"No Pain") and the unhappy/crying face at the other (10/"Worst Pain"). For many people with chronic pain, this scaling is so familiar that it becomes habitual to notice not just the numerical severity of the pain sensation at any given moment, but the happiness level correlated with the number. Prior to having hip surgery, for example, I regularly had involuntary thoughts like, "glad it's only three...not so bad," "four-and-a-half...could be worse," "six-and-a-half, maybe seven...I'm so sick of this!" Unwittingly,

I numerically tracked my shifting pain and corresponding moods throughout the day. Obviously, the continuum of happy/unhappy faces did not cause my shifting moods; but they reinforced the varying degrees of animosity I felt toward the hurt.

Chronic disease and discomfort are often—but not always—related. For example, my dad has a slow-progressing form of cancer called chronic lymphocytic leukemia (CLL). Although many forms of cancer are pain producing, so far his hasn't been. In my case, however, continuous pain and illness were intimately related. X-rays revealed that the distress I felt for years in my left hip was an obvious symptom of osteoarthritis, a disease well known for making joints hurt. Though having a hip replacement eliminated that perennial discomfort, new pain I've noticed in my right hip and other joints reminds me that surgery did not cure my arthritis. Sometimes, prolonged discomfort can be traced to a specific injury, rather than an underlying illness. And sometimes pain is the consequence of treating disease, as is often the case for chemotherapy patients. Interestingly, many physicians now understand chronic pain as a neurological disease in itself, rather than a symptom of some underlying condition.[6] This view validates the experience of unrelenting hurt, particularly when its source remains unknown.

The lack of a clear-cut diagnosis for an enduring malady can exacerbate the suffering surrounding that affliction. A woman Laurie Edwards interviewed for her book, *In the Kingdom of the Sick*, describes the difficulties she experiences not knowing the cause of the pervasive pain and intense fatigue with which she lives:

> Healthy people don't understand how a person can be sick for months and years and have doctors still not know what's wrong with her. Some people get a funny look in their eye, like they think it must be all in my head because otherwise wouldn't I have a diagnosis by now?[7]

In a society that values the certainty scientific labels seem to provide, not knowing how to answer what Edwards refers to as the "inevitable question"—"*So, what's wrong with you, anyway?*"[8]—can compound the frustration, depression, and anxiety that often shadow chronic pain and illness. The absence of a diagnosis can also generate self-doubt and self-blame, e.g. "Am I just imagining this pain, fatigue, dizziness?" or "What's wrong with me?" Not having a name for what's wrong also makes it hard to explain your situation to others, including agencies or offices that handle benefits and work accommodations.

While a clear-cut diagnosis lends credibility to chronic hurt and illness, it can be a double-edged sword given the stigma attached to sickness. Like bodies that are fat, old, or disabled, those classified as "diseased" by medical authorities are vulnerable to prejudice, shame, and dread—from without and from within. Illness has long been associated with weakness and is commonly perceived as an inferior form of embodiment. A woman who suffers from migraine speaks to this association and perception:

> The assumption that I am in some way weaker and less capable due to my illness…drives me nuts (even though it's sometimes true). People without chronic illness cannot know what it's like to live with it every day; even when pain or other symptoms aren't present, they linger like ghosts, ready to come out of the woodwork when we least expect it…Healthy people don't live with these specters.[9]

The feeling that "you can't understand" the difficulties of ongoing illness unless you've experienced them adds to the sense of isolation many people with chronic afflictions feel.

This feeling of isolation led Susan Sontag to observe that unhealthy bodies inhabit "the kingdom of the sick"—a world apart from and inferior to "the kingdom of the well," i.e. where healthy bodies live.[10] Although, at least in the United States, people with chronic diseases do not constitute a numerical minority,[11] the practical and physical challenges their sicknesses present, coupled with disparaging meanings assigned to pain and illness, subject them to various forms of systemic discrimination and internalized oppression. Factor in the reality that chronic ailments disproportionately affect people of color, women, and those who are poor, and the multiple layers of suffering surrounding these afflictions become clear. Not coincidentally, the lesser kingdom chronically sick people inhabit also resembles—and intersects with—the second-class universe people with disabilities occupy.

Chronic disease/discomfort and disability

The overlap between disability and chronic disease is significant, yet hard to pin down. Incurable pain and illness can be debilitating, but there's no absolute line demarcating when such a condition qualifies one as "disabled." Susan Wendell attempts to clarify the ambiguities by distinguishing between the "healthy disabled" (people with disabilities who are not chronically sick or in pain) and the "unhealthy disabled" (those whose disabilities are rooted in chronic illness).[12] But this distinction is fluid. For example, Edwards, who has lung and autoimmune diseases, lives in the "gray area" between chronic disease and disability. For her, this area includes the normalcy of being ambulatory and having a family and career, and the interruptions of breathing difficulties and frequent doctor visits.[13]

The invisibility of many forms of debilitating pain and illness means that people with these conditions can often "pass" as able-bodied, which may seem like a blessing in a culture that places a high premium on physical appearance. But passing can also be a burden. A person who *feels* ill much, most, or all of the time but does not *look* sick has to navigate the same ableist world that disadvantages people with visible disabilities. In *Hoping for More*, theologian Deanna Thompson lists "*You don't look sick*" among the *un*helpful comments people said to her upon learning she had stage IV breast cancer. "It seems that because I did not have the requisite indicators of breast cancer—a bald head, a missing breast—my situation wasn't as bad as they had thought."[14] Having to explain or remind people of one's unseen limitations and needs for special accommodations can feel alienating and humiliating.[15] In the end, the invisibility of persistent pain and many kinds of chronic illness challenges assumptions about what able-bodied normalcy looks like and reminds us that "disability" and "disease" are porous categories.

Despite the overlap between chronic pain, sickness, and disability, some people with incurable conditions are reluctant to identify as "disabled." They may not see their health problems as significant as those of the "truly disabled," or they may want to avoid the shame associated with disability.[16] For others, however, the continuities between incurable illness and disability are too obvious to deny. Bruce Kramer, who lost the ability to walk, move, and breathe on his own as ALS (amyotrophic lateral sclerosis, a kind of motor neuron disease) took over his body, realized how unaware he had been of his able-bodied privilege and the disparaging view of disability he had internalized prior to his illness. Kramer refers to this way of viewing—but not really seeing—people with disabilities as "The Look":

> We see the guy on crutches, on a cane, the woman in a wheelchair. But The Look goes right through them. We are afraid to acknowledge their disabled regalia, how they struggle, walk without balance, or don't have a free hand when one is needed. In my old normal, I gave The Look as often as I didn't, secure and confident in my able-bodiedness…I'd look right through disability, and I wouldn't have to face its possibility in the person that I'd looked through.[17]

The experiences of people like Kramer have prompted some activists and scholars to call for a broader concept of "disability," one that fosters greater inclusion, understanding, and advocacy on behalf of people with *invisible disabilities* like debilitating pain and illness. For example, Alison Kafer sees disability "less as a diagnostic category and more as a collective affinity"—a political orientation rooted in a commitment to support the struggles of those whose physical nonconformity makes them vulnerable in an able-bodied society.[18]

This commitment involves an affirmation of somatic diversity that goes beyond appreciating people's different colors, sizes, abilities, and sexual orientations to include acceptance of, and accommodations for, those living with infirmities that won't go away. To recognize deeply entrenched somatic pain and illness as manifestations of human biodiversity is not to say that we shouldn't strive to find ways to alleviate the suffering these conditions create. Rather, it is to acknowledge the reality that some people have disease and discomfort that, like it or not, *cannot be cured*. This reality compels us to ask: What is the most helpful way to view chronic conditions and those who have them? Before exploring this question directly, let's consider another continuity between disability and chronic pain and illness: their shared historical association with punishment and sin.

Associations between sickness/sin, pain/punishment

Like disability, disease is often linked to sin, impurity, and chastisement in the biblical tradition. A prominent Christian narrative depicts physical ailments as the punitive consequences of moral transgression.[19] (In fact, "pain" is from the Latin *poena*, meaning "punishment"[20]). Biblical associations between sin/sickness and pain/punishment reflect the mindset of the ancient world that did not sharply distinguish between natural and supernatural causes and events—the same mindset that coupled disability and impurity. Like physical impairment, somatic illness is often portrayed as the result and sign of immoral behavior—either personal sin (in the case of acquired sickness) or collective sin (in the case of congenital illness).[21] In the Hebrew Scriptures, good health is tied to keeping the Lord's commandments (e.g. Ex. 15:26), and disobedience is punished with disease (e.g. Numbers, 12:1–15; Deut. 7:12–15). Several New Testament passages that affiliate sin and disability also link immorality with illness (e.g. John 9.2-3; John 5.1–16; Luke 5.20–26).[22]

Correspondingly, a number of biblical texts highlight the value of being cured and conjoin proper faith and healing. Several "Penitential Psalms" (e.g. Psalms 32, 38, 51, 102) suggest that sorrow for and confession of one's sins brings healing. Moreover, the healing=curing conflation we saw in stories where Jesus enables the lame to walk and the blind to see also operates in gospel texts where people with other kinds of infirmities (e.g. leprosy, epilepsy, hemorrhaging) are cured. As with disability narratives, healing/curing leads to inclusion since disease compromises one's access to God and to the community.[23] Additionally, the phrase "Your faith has made you well" is frequently attributed to Jesus after he performs miraculous healings (e.g. Mark 5.34; Luke 17.19; Luke 7.50; Luke 8.48; Matthew 9.22). While the meaning of this saying needs considerable unpacking, throughout Christian history the idea that faith, righteousness, healing, and curing were continuous supported the belief that the condition of your soul determines the health of your body.

Despite the prominence of biblical narrative associating pain and sickness with punishment and sin, another biblical storyline suggests that the origins of disease are unknown or inexplicable. There are examples of this in the New Testament (e.g. Mark 1:30–31; Mark 5:21–24, 35–43),[24] but the most famous biblical tale that affirms the mysterious source and meaning of sickness is the story of Job. This story poses a major problem to the theory that if you do everything right, God will spare (or heal) you from physical affliction. Inversely stated, it challenges the common assumption that people get what they deserve—i.e. that the world is fair. Job is an "upright and blameless" man (1:8) who nevertheless must endure an assortment of calamities as part of a bargain God makes with Satan to test Job's faithfulness. In addition to losing both his wealth and family, he is plagued with a chronically painful disease. After an initial stage of acceptance, Job angrily interrogates God, demanding some explanation for his suffering. In the end, however, this narrative has no easy answers, no ready-made fixes, no "God has a purpose" explanations. Only mystery.

Physical affliction as spiritual opportunity

Throughout Christian history, narratives depicting illness and pain either as the punishment for sin or as symptomatic of life's inscrutable mysteries coexisted and (to some extent) comingled with another storyline that viewed physical maladies as pivotal spiritual opportunities.[25] From this vantage point, pain and illness were to be probed and wrestled with as they offered opportunities to imitate and identify with the transformative suffering of Christ—an agony in which death was metabolized into new life for the benefit of others. Grappling with the meaning of that suffering was a profound act of faith: while such struggle reflected an active relationship with the mysterious power of life, pain and illness deepened one's sense of dependence on God and increased one's empathy for the bodily afflictions of others.

In historical Christianity, this narrative was vividly played out in the practices of ascetics, who welcomed and cultivated somatic distress as a means for fostering virtue. In the centuries following Christianity's legalization in 313, some ascetics struggled with "demons" disguised as disease in their pursuit of righteousness. Through the process of wrestling with physical ailments, some acquired the power to heal others' illnesses.[26] Significantly, the aim of such wrestling was not to conquer these afflictions. Although controlling the flesh is a recurrent theme in ascetic Christianity, the target of such mastery was not disease or discomfort, but desire—including the desire to escape disease and discomfort. Instead of shunning or trying to avoid pain and illness, ascetics contended with bodily afflictions as life-changing opportunities.

In the later medieval era, some Christian women became especially known for creating sacred meaning from experiences of pain and sickness. The spiritual awakenings and authority of several of the most well-known holy women of this era began in excruciating experiences of illness. Hildegard of Bingen (d. 1179), famous for the lucid visions she received from God about the nature of creation and redemption, was sickly from birth and suffered from severe headaches throughout her life. Catherine of Siena (d. 1380) became ill (or made herself sick) after eating. This "infirmity" (her word) caused her tremendous pain, which she experienced as connecting her with the passion of Christ and with the sufferings of people on the margins of her society. In the midst of a life-threatening sickness, Julian of Norwich (d. 1416) received sixteen "Revelations" of God's love, in which she witnessed/experienced Christ as a kind, nurturing mother.

Women's traditional association with the weaknesses of the flesh no doubt factored into the prominence of pain and illness in their spiritual experiences in this context. Compared to their male peers, medieval women's devotion was more likely to involve physical self-denial, sickness, and self-inflicted injury.[27] Compared to ordinary women, female ascetics and mystics who experienced life-changing illnesses had a greater degree of influence in their own lives and the lives of others. Some had followers and gave spiritual counsel; some founded convents and hospitals; and some ministered to the needs of the sick. Transgressing the boundaries dividing healthy and unhealthy bodies, they took care of people who were quarantined. Some of them literally embraced diseased bodies, licking their open sores and pus. Angela Foligno went so far as to drink the water with which she had washed a leper! Ultimately, the meaning women's physical suffering acquired in relation to the agony of Christ empowered them to help heal "the broken body of humanity."[28] As a pivotal opportunity for holiness, medieval women's sickness had the added advantage of muting the very power it promoted: its association with physical frailty diminished the threat a spiritually confident woman posed in a male-dominated society.

Echoes and assumptions of a theology of curing

Despite the undeniable power of the narrative of pain and illness as spiritually meaningful opportunities, the storyline associating sickness/pain with sin/

punishment was prominent throughout Christian history, in part because it supported the eschatological vision of redemption as contingent on the eradication of physical afflictions. In the celestial afterlife, diseased and hurting bodies would be restored to good health, which is what "salvation" (from the Latin, *salve*) literally means. Resurrected flesh would enjoy the rewards of heaven in a pain-free, disease-free state of perfection—a forward-looking, flawless state that simultaneously mirrored the innocence of Eden. Needless to say, the notion of "eschatologically cleansed" bodies as free of iniquity and infirmity implies that earthly flesh still stuck in the muck of pain or illness is manifestly mired in sin.[29]

Theologies depicting pain and sickness as punishments for moral transgressions, healing as contingent on faith, and heaven as a place where infirmities have been vanquished may be relics of an ancient past, but they are not hard to come by today. They can be found in obvious venues, such as evangelical faith healing forums where the sick are invited to be cured via faith in the power of Christ. Thousands of websites feature evangelists preaching on the nexus between pain, illness, and perdition. One cyberspace pastor explains: "God uses sickness in our lives as a way to…rebuke us."[30] Another warns: "*sin* is the cause for the existence of *sickness* in the world. There was no sickness in the Garden of Eden, and none of us expect to find either sin or infirmity in heaven."[31] Many "holistic" or New Age approaches also predicate corporeal health on spiritual well-being.[32] Even some mainstream Western doctors harbor assumptions about the role of proper religious belief in healing, like the physician who told a woman suffering from chronic pain that she wasn't getting better "because you don't have enough faith in God."[33]

It's worth pondering what the narrative of disease as divine retribution for moral weakness assumes about God, humans, and the interaction between them. This storyline is based on a classic Christian view of divinity as a separate, controlling entity who acts externally on human beings/bodies, judging their actions and distributing rewards and punishments as "He" sees fit. As ecofeminist Ivone Gebara points out, this model of God has implications for how body and spirit are to be understood, namely, as dualistically divided, hierarchically arranged (i.e. "mind over matter"), and oriented toward a singular, normative, moral perfection achieved by subduing the flesh. Whether this perfection is nostalgically envisioned (i.e. looking backward to a state of paradise) or futuristically imagined (as a state of heavenly bliss), humans are understood as destined for a better place/better body—free of pain, sickness, and suffering. As Gebara points out, "[t]he story of our denial of earth in favor of heaven is very old."[34]

This ancient story is also very current, and its influence is not limited to recognizably religious discourses. The mythic character of Christian eschatology makes it difficult to see this drama playing out in the contemporary salvation story of physical improvement, but the plotline is surprisingly familiar: fallen flesh in need of redemption, sick or hurting bodies in need of healing/curing. Elements of this storyline are tacitly embedded in popular health discourses that depict disease and discomfort

- as "enemies" to be fought and defeated;

- as the antithesis of health and happiness;

- as the result of poor behavior and lifestyle choices; and

- as symptomatic of emotional problems or character weaknesses

In different ways, these contemporary health narratives recycle antiquated religious associations between sin/sickness and pain/punishment by incorporating the modern Cartesian belief that you can control your body with the proper application of will.

Going to war with chronic pain and illness

One of the most common approaches to health and healing in commercial, self-help, charitable, and medical perspectives encourages a war-like mentality to combat the infamy of persistent pain and illness. This colonial paradigm is evident in self-help texts like *Chronic Pain for Dummies*, whose stated goal is "to help you understand and conquer your pain." The book emphasizes the link between "knowledge" about somatic affliction and the "power" to defeat it: "You need to know some basics about the pain enemy before you can vanquish her."[35] That pain here is gendered female is not coincidental. Not only do women represent a disproportionate number of the 116 million of Americans living with chronic pain,[36] but in our culture pain is associated with weakness, and I don't need to tell you who has been designated the "weaker" sex. Nor do I need to point out how the conquest method for dealing with this weakness draws on stereotypes of masculine dominance.

This approach envisions unrelenting pain as an adversary that needs to be "put...in its place," as a Wal-Mart ad for pain-relieving medications states. In *Chronic Pain for Dummies*, long-lasting discomfort is also personified as morally deviant characters (e.g. "villain," "wild demon"). Readers are encouraged to have multiple "strategies in [their] anti-pain war chest" to battle this foe.[37] This bellicose language echoes in other self-help books on the topic. For example, *Defeat Chronic Pain Now!* has chapters entitled "Beating Your Back Pain," "Fighting Fibromyalgia," and "Conquering Arthritis." Books aren't the only way an adversarial approach is encouraged. Consider the common term "painkiller," which covers a variety of pharmaceuticals designed to terminate somatic discomfort.

Popular discourses about chronic illness deploy the same combative jargon. Just googling the phrase "fight cancer" gets 223,000,000 hits.[38] The perception of cancer as evil morally justifies this belligerent approach. The Cancer Resource Center rallies us to "Unite and Fight Cancer" by participating in a variety of fund-raising events.[39] There's an entire line of "Warriors in Pink"™ clothing, proceeds of the sales of which go to Susan G. Komen for the Cure™ "to help fight breast cancer" because "the battle rages on."[40] Even the language of "survivor," though potentially helpful, reflects the combat mentality surrounding cancer.[41] The homepage for the American Cancer Society assures that "Your monthly donation will make a difference in the fight against cancer."[42] Thanks to such charitable efforts to support research, "we are starting to win the war against breast cancer," a *Health* magazine article declares.[43] As these examples suggest, warfare terminology aims not only to galvanize the courage of those living with cancer, but also to rally their supporters to open their wallets.

The economics of this war are astounding, as S. Lochlann Jain demonstrates in *Malignant*. In the United States, for example, annual medical costs of cancer care are currently about $125 billion and expected to increase to $173 billion by 2020. Those amounts double when the price of related factors (e.g. lost productivity) is considered. Despite (or because of) these costs, cancer boosts the financial health of powerful industries and professions. In the later decades of the twentieth century, cancer became a multibillion dollar business in the United States, creating enormous wealth for a few while leaving millions in debt. This dynamic helped make America's health care system the most profitable industry in the US economy. Lochlann Jain questions whether it makes sense to trust our health to for-profit corporations, "whose binding legal concern is stockholder profit." The fact that some of the same companies that manufacture drugs to treat cancer also dump known carcinogens into the environment justifies her suspicion. In the end, she suggests that the business of cancer is so significant that winning the war could seriously damage the US economy.[44] Like other military expeditions, the anti-cancer crusade has strong ties to monetary interests.

Cancer may be the disease most associated with the combat lexicon, but there's no shortage of adversarial lingo in popular discourses on other chronic conditions. To give just a few examples: a *Women's Health* article characterizes chronic inflammation as "The Enemy Inside You" and recommends several "Top Inflammation Fighters" to subdue this invisible assailant.[45] A MedHelp blog is entitled "Battling Asthma," and the American Lung Association encourages you to "Take Control" of this intractable disease.[46] The Arthritis Foundation describes itself as "fighting for you, fighting for your family and fighting for a cure." The logo for this organization encourages you to "Take Control," and its mission is clear: "We exist to conquer arthritis."[47] Even some "natural" approaches to healing depict illness as an enemy. For example, the products advertised on the New Age Medical Research website are "GUARANTEED to Destroy Disease Quickly."[48]

A variation of the conquest storyline promises a return to the happiness of a normal life—i.e. life as it was before pain and sickness took over. This enticement is explicit in a Tylenol ad campaign that promises to get you "back to normal." You can find a link to these ads at http://www.bloomsbury.com/uk/shameful-bodies-9781472594945/ under "Chapter Seven." Though not couched in acrimonious language, a controlling subtext still operates in the "back-to-normal" storyline insofar as the promise of returning to life before the fall into chronic pain suggests that you *should* be able to subdue the insubordinate energy of a hurting body.

The problem with a fight-or-flight approach

Without question, millions of people are well served by pharmaceuticals, charities, self-help literature, and medical research dedicated to better understanding and treating chronic disease and discomfort. I have benefited personally from drugs, studies, and technologies that have made hip replacement surgery routinely successful. By calling attention to the combative language that permeates popular health discourses, I do not mean to diminish the value of such knowledge and therapies; rather, I aim to expose the imperial paradigm through which they are commonly framed in order to examine what this approach presumes, obscures, and implies with regard to bodies that refuse to be cured.

As Bruce Kramer suggests, the strategies the military paradigm advocates reflect what brain scientists and psychologists refer to as the "fight-and-flight" response. The product of evolution's efforts to ensure survival, this response is rooted in the reptilian part of our brains that instinctively reacts to threats or perceived dangers by releasing hormones that prompt us to attack or escape.[49] While popular health discourses mainly promote the "fight" response, one could argue that "flight" (i.e. avoidance) is also implicit in the conquest approach to chronic illness, insofar as waging war against an incurable condition involves some measure of denial. In any case, perceiving persistent pain and sickness as enemies we must vanquish or escape is understandable given the genuine threats they pose to our well-being. But does a military approach really help people whose somatic maladies cannot be conquered? "I do not want to feel like a failure about something beyond my control," a woman with terminal cancer reflects. "I refuse to believe my death will be because I didn't battle hard enough."[50]

By rallying us to fight our way to physical well-being, the conquest paradigm diverts our attention away from the invisible violence of industrial pollution that sickens our bodies and the planet. Lochlann Jain uses the example of the asbestos industry to illustrate this kind of anonymous assault: "It is as if a gun was shot into a crowd, and fifty years later someone from that crowd keeled over and died."[51] The fighting lexicon conceals the irony that the same corporations that join the pink ribbon crusade are allowed (by laws created by politicians they lobbied) to pour known carcinogens into the Earth. Reflecting on these political realities in light of her own struggle with cancer, Lochlann Jain wonders:

> What would it mean to acknowledge—*really acknowledge*—the sheer number of people who literally rot from the inside out each year, with no way to stop it, while so many known causes of cancer continue to be pumped into the environment?[52]

Unfortunately, the colonial approach to chronic disease and discomfort preempts such critical inquiry by keeping us fixated on fighting these (perceived) foes.

Pain-free/disease-free visions of the "healthy" body

To understand why the conquest paradigm is so popular, we need to see it in the context of consumer culture's wider obsession with controlling and fixing bodies. Going to war against incurable disease and discomfort makes sense in a society where health is synonymous with happiness and beauty and visualized as the absence of pain and illness. This vision permeates the iconography of the culture of physical improvement.

Commercial images of smiling, presumably healthy physiques illustrate this aspect of the better body story. Look at the cover of any popular magazine with "health" or "fitness" in its title and you're likely to see such an image next to articles containing instructions for how to achieve such wholesome perfection. Like able-bodied youth and thinness, the presumed absence of pain and illness is a defining feature of our culture's somatic ideal. Actually, this ideal's pain-free/disease-free status is quite ironic given that the rituals employed to produce the stereotypical image of fitness can be considerably painful, even sickening, involving restrictive diets, endless hours at the gym, botox, breast implants, and the like. Yet like the beauty and happiness with which it is associated, health is visually and ritually constructed as a "natural" occurrence.

Because it's largely invisible, the better body's pain-free/disease-free status relies on familiar visual cues associated with fitness and beauty (e.g. youth, social privilege, slenderness, and able-bodiness). With the help of these cues, images of ritually produced well-looking bodies tacitly reinforce the rhetorical promises of the conquest storyline: you can conquer infirmity and enjoy the health and happiness you deserve. At the same time, the ideal body's healthy status is visually constructed in relation to what it defines as undesirable: the weakness, disgust, shame, and ugliness associated with flesh that is diseased.[53] To the extent that they can pass as normal, bodies with incurable illness or pain may not be cast into the "physiognomic bottomlands" of the empire of public appearance.[54] But like flesh that is fat, old, or visibly impaired, sick bodies represent the antithesis of the normative vision of health, happiness, and beauty that permeates the culture of physical improvement.

The aesthetics of women's health—its ties to beliefs about feminine beauty—are apparent in the social imperative for female cancer survivors to camouflage their sickness. Consider the "Look Good…Feel Better" program, which aims to "help" female chemo patients resolve beauty problems—and thereby boost confidence—via makeup and wigs (Figure 7.2). Though wearing lipstick to "brighten your looks and lift your spirits" may function as "an act of resistance to the social exclusions" and "othering" that women with cancer often experience, such a strategy cannot disguise the anguished uncertainty surrounding the disease. Moreover, as Lochlann Jain points out, the goal of looking good in spite of cancer obscures the irony that the cosmetic industry that sponsors the Look Good…Feel Better program spends "millions on political lobbying to prevent regulation, or even labeling, of the known and possible carcinogens commonly found in its products."[55] Thus under the guise of benevolence, the beauty industry extends its business of constructing beautiful/ugly, healthy/diseased female bodies and keeping women preoccupied with improving their appearance—even amid life-threatening sickness.[56]

Scientific approaches to health and disease

The health aesthetics that permeate the visual landscape of popular culture find support in conventional medical definitions of wellness as the absence of pain and illness. This understanding evolved during the modern period, as medical science replaced theology as the authoritative rubric for interpreting human physiology. During the nineteenth century, for example, scientists

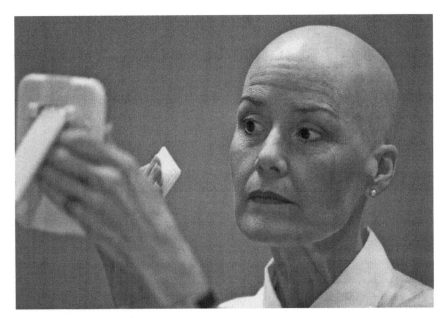

FIGURE 7.2. *"LS.gift.mirror.0902. Newport Beach...a volunteer with the Look Good, Feel Better campaign" © Rick Loomis.*
Source: Getty Images.

discovered the biological roots of disease, thereby undermining theories of pain and illness as divine retribution. At the same time, however, doctors began to pay more attention to behavioral/lifestyle choices and psychological traits in the etiology of chronic conditions. These new emphases implied that sick people were to some extent culpable for their ailments.[57] A view of cancer as the result of a degenerate lifestyle was common just a few generations ago. More recently, HIV/AIDS has been seen as the consequence of morally reprehensible behavior.[58] While mainstream medical views today don't blame God for sending chronic pain and illness to teach us a lesson, some imply, however unwittingly, that chronic health problems are the punitive consequences of unwholesome choices or psychic weaknesses. This is evident in self-help rhetoric that promotes the pursuit of wellness as a personal responsibility rooted in self-control.

Disease-proofing your body: Health as personal duty and achievement

To some extent, framing health as a personal responsibility makes sense because behavioral and lifestyle choices inevitably impact one's physical well-being. Countless studies document this point. David Katz discusses some of these studies in *Disease-Proof*, a self-help book that variously reflects, challenges, and reproduces familiar themes in the culture of physical improvement. In it, Katz aims to help you "take control of the master levers of your medical destiny" by "using lifestyle as medicine." By exercising "personal responsibility" with regard to eating, weight, tobacco use, and activity level, we can "exert incredible power over both the number of years in our lives and the quality of those years"; we can "sidestep illness and health risks," "combat chronic disease," and "seize control over...our medical destiny."[59]

I'm not a medical doctor, but I can't help but wonder: can we really "disease-proof" our bodies? Even if we eat all the right foods, exercise daily, get plenty of rest, do yoga, meditate, and never touch tobacco, is it possible to determine the *outcome* of our choices? Guarantee immunity from pain and sickness? Why promise something that can't be delivered? Interestingly, Katz's language becomes notably less militant and more nuanced in the chapters following his "Introduction." The promise that you can "seize control over" your physical destiny gives way to softer claims that "you *may* be able to alter your genes" (emphasis added), "reduce risk" for certain diseases, and "refashion" your medical fate by making healthy choices.[60] These more qualified assertions are, it seems to me, much more truthful than the assurance that you can "disease-proof" your body. But perhaps more honest, nuanced claims don't sell well in our sound-bite society. Maybe the combative tone of Katz's "Introduction" is designed to capture reader's attention. Perhaps his book's title tells us what we want to hear.

In many ways, Katz's initially heavy reliance on the conquest narrative and his (arguably) overstated title reflect the extent to which medical professionals are influenced by commercial culture. His use of controlling rhetoric also illustrates just how much the Cartesian legacy lives on in mainstream Western medicine. Although Katz's thesis—that our lifestyle decisions dictate our physical well-being—challenges the mind/body dualism, his description of how health works resurrects a ghost-in-the-machine view of human beings: "your body is the plane and you are the captain."[61] This image suggests that 1) you (the pilot) are separate from your body (the plane), and 2) as captain, you determine the aircraft's course and destination. But what happens when the plane has a mind of its own? Deanna Thompson describes an experience common to many who struggle with chronic disease and discomfort: "Every time I started thinking I was gaining on cancer, it seemed to reassert itself to make sure I knew who was calling the shots."[62]

In addition to downplaying "the will of the body,"[63] defining patient responsibility through Cartesian notions of individual self-control obscures the social, environmental, geographic, hereditary, and demographic variables that enhance or diminish our physical well-being. Wellness and illness are influenced not simply by personal decisions, but by a web of injustices and unearned privileges that structure behavioral and lifestyle "choices." Affluent people have health-promoting opportunities that those who are socially disadvantaged can scarcely imagine, from fitness club memberships to the ability to purchase organic produce. For many people, the stresses of poverty, racism, sexism, and homophobia exacerbate the difficulties of inadequate health care and insurance, or lack of nutritious food. The disproportionate prevalence of chronic ailments among poor and minority populations illustrates this point.[64] So does a study that found nearly 80 percent of nurses preferring not to touch gay and lesbian patients.[65] People from poor and minority communities often don't have the option of calling in sick on days when illness is all-consuming. For centuries, economically impoverished and colonized people have had to show up for work, their families, and life—despite devastating disease and discomfort.[66]

To be fair, Katz is more attentive than many medical/self-help authors to the role environmental factors play in shaping lifestyle and behavior choices.[67] Nonetheless, his insistence that your choices "determine" your somatic destiny[68]—that you are the pilot driving your body—plays right into the master narrative defining health as the absence of pain and illness, as achieved through individual combat and control, as a reward for good behavior, and as synonymous with happiness and virtue. While the metaphysical assumptions framing this storyline are not stated in philosophical or religious terms, they are nonetheless moralizing insofar as they imply that people with unresolvable pain and illness are somehow to blame for their afflictions.

When the "plane" colludes and collides with gender norms

Health discourses that encourage you to "seize control" of your medical destiny may be well-intended, but when they conflict with the lived experience of pain or illness that won't go away, they can add layers of suffering to chronic conditions, including feelings of depression, shame, and isolation. A woman with migraine disease explains:

> I felt I was supposed to be happy, energetic, successful, and active all the time, and often, I was. The only dark spot on those times? My headache. Things may have been easier on me had I not kept the pain a secret. The majority of my closest friends had no idea I was suffering.[69]

Women in particular may spend years in the closet of chronic pain and sickness, isolated from the emotional and medical support they need for fear of not being taken seriously or being seen as complaining too much. A woman with Crohn's disease explains: "Usually, I minimized my pain because I didn't want to be perceived as whiny and weak."[70] During the 1970s, the women's health movement in the United States worked to dispel patriarchal medicine's views of female physicality as inherently fragile and inferior, while empowering women to know their own bodies and be proactive in keeping them well. But the relative success of this movement has created a dilemma for some women insofar as female bodies are more vulnerable to certain pain conditions (e.g. chronic fatigue syndrome, irritable bowel syndrome, migraines and chronic daily headaches, to name a few), and recognizing this vulnerability may seem like capitulating to patriarchal perspectives.[71]

Moreover, research reveals that women's narratives of persistent pain are taken less seriously than men's. Whereas men are more likely to be prescribed pain-relief medication for their symptoms, women are more likely to be referred to psychotherapists or given antidepressants. Discomfort, fatigue, and other symptoms in female bodies are repeatedly trivialized as "emotional," "psychogenic," and "not real."[72] This pattern is especially common among patients with fibromyalgia, a chronic musculoskeletal pain condition that causes extreme fatigue and occurs mostly in females. In *All in My Head*, Paula Kamen reports on her conversations with many women suffering with this condition, all of whom had stories of doctors belittling or dismissing their symptoms as manipulative attempts to get attention. These "Tired Girls," as Kamen empathetically calls them, were "usually isolated with and shamed by their problems." The more Tired Girls that "came out" to Kamen about their never-ending pain and fatigue, the more she realized that there's an entire subculture of women "living secret lives" for fear of being seen as "hysterical."[73]

As feminist playwright and activist Eve Ensler reminds us, *hysteria* (derived from the Greek word for "uterus") is a term typically deployed "to make women feel insane for knowing what they know."[74] In the late nineteenth and early twentieth centuries, male doctors applied the label to women whose recurring physical maladies defied physiological explanations. These physicians identified the culprits for such inexplicable afflictions to be women's emotional instability, repressed sexuality, nervous tendencies, and resistance to standard gender norms. They interpreted hysterical symptoms as unconscious strategies for getting attention and expressing emotions— feelings, feminists have pointed out, that couldn't be voiced directly according to the dictates of Victorian womanhood. As it turns out, a number of women manifesting enigmatic symptoms were survivors of sexual abuse, though physicians like Freud waffled on acknowledging such experiences.[75] Although "hysteria" is no longer an official diagnostic category, its legacy lingers in many women's experiences of chronic pain and sickness. Kamen regularly encountered sexist stereotypes in her quest to relieve her daily headaches, leading her to remark that these "old-time Victorian prejudices about women and illness…compound the guilt and shame that chronic pain sufferers may already feel about our 'deviances,' pushing us deeper into the closet."[76]

For men, the shame of illness is exacerbated by cultural norms of masculinity requiring them to be stoic in the face of infirmity.[77] Symbolically associated with rationality and spirit, men are expected to exercise "mind over matter," rather than succumb to the weakness associated with disease and involuntary pain—the same weakness affiliated with the fragility of female flesh. In fact, appearing to be weak was the number one "shame trigger" among the hundreds of men Brené Brown interviewed for her research on shame.[78] Given the associations between pain, illness, and weakness, along with conventional male socialization to be "in charge," if not invincible, it's not surprising that many men find it difficult to admit to and deal constructively with persistent afflictions.

For both men and women, efforts to hide, deny, or minimize ongoing disease and discomfort reflect the widespread belief that as captain, you should be able to get your aircraft back on course. A woman diagnosed with multiple chronic pain-producing conditions expresses frustration at this expectation:

> The fact that you're just not going to get better seems unbelievable to most people…It's easier for them to believe that there is something you can control…There must be something you can do that you aren't doing! Eating raw foods, forcing yourself to exercise, thinking your way out of it, trying the latest drugs that promise a cure in their commercial: something should work, and if you're not better, then you're not working hard enough.[79]

Part of what makes chronic illness and pain so difficult is the widespread and easily internalized judgments that popular health narratives promote, namely, that pain and sickness are *bad* and that you *shouldn't* have to experience them because you *should* be able to defeat them, to take a pill, read a book, eat some kale, change your lifestyle, do *something* to make them go away. But to experience disease or discomfort that are chronic is to live in a body that obeys neither the commands of the self nor the dictates of culture.

Moralizing assumptions about chronic pain and illness

The sense of failure many people feel in relation to this disobedience is predicated not only on the belief that we can control our physical destiny, but also on our religious/cultural conditioning to equate control with virtue. Reflecting on his experience with cancer, Arthur Frank considers the moral implications of this conditioning: "Every day society sends us messages that the body can and ought to be controlled…Control is good manners as well as a moral duty; to lose control is to fail socially and morally. But then along comes illness, and the body goes out of control."[80] The perceived shame of chronic pain or illness reflects a lingering view of health and sickness as *moral issues.*

Even elevated stress, which is known to suppress a body's immune system and increase physical distress, can be an occasion for judgment. "Stress is more morally charged than other [pain] triggers, such as certain foods or weather changes," Kamen observes.[81] Presumably, people with sufficient inner discipline can rise above anxiety. Even a patient recovering from cancer may be instructed by her doctor to "reduce your stress load," as if such a feat is simply an act of will.[82] Any analysis of stress as a factor in chronic pain and illness must take into account the dehumanizing speed and often unreasonable work expectations that structure our society, paying particular attention to how this turbo pace and pressure intensify the stressors already compromising the well-being of people who are poor or ethnic, sexual, religious, or cultural minorities.

In a culture that celebrates and rewards productivity, self-sufficiency, conquering adversity, and mastering the flesh, incurable pain and sickness are tantamount to failure, punishment, and defeat. "I was ashamed of having cancer," Sandy Boucher writes in *Hidden Spring*. "Secretly, I had nurtured the idea that only losers get this disease."[83] Lochlann Jain had similar feelings in response to her diagnosis. Walking down the hospital's chemotherapy hallway, she tried to pass as a doctor so as not to be associated with "the slumped-over sick people crowded in the waiting room."[84] Ensler also describes her resistance to having cancer and the negative meanings attached to infirmity:

> I didn't like sick people. First of all, they were sick. Sick was not well, not able, not working, not making things better. Sick was surrendering, caving in. Sick was wasting time, not adding up. Sick was alone and stuck as the rest of the well world moved by.[85]

None of these women is endorsing the disparaging view of disease she had internalized. On the contrary, each of them is de-internalizing the shame associated with sickness by openly naming it as a culturally conditioned belief, rather than a personal truth.

For many people, moralizing judgments about illness are compounded by economic challenges. Health care expenses account for 60 percent of personal bankruptcies in the United States.[86] The blatant greed of some drug companies only adds insult to ailing bodies. In 2015, for example, Turing Pharmaceutical increased the price of a 62-year-old drug (Daraprim, used to treat toxoplasmosis) by more than 4000 percent, raising the cost of a pill from

$13.50 to $750.[87] Even people with relative privilege often feel stressed or humiliated by disease-induced financial hardships. Although she appreciated the safety net of her middle-class family background, Kamen describes the "dread of dependence" she felt when her daily headaches, along with the medications she took to alleviate the pain, made it impossible for her to work and forced her to rely financially on her parents. Eventually, Kamen swallowed her pride and applied for Social Security Disability Insurance, only to discover she was ineligible for the $550 monthly payments because she had earned more than $800 dollars the previous *year* (the cut-off line for qualifying for assistance). Reflecting on her failure to live up to society's definition of "success," Kamen observes: "Much of my suffering stemmed not from the [headache] pain itself but from the constant roller coaster of frustration, shame, and havoc that it created in so many areas."[88]

The same pull-yourself-up-by-your-bootstraps ideology that links economic status with moral virtue—i.e. "rich people worked hard to earn what they have"—fosters the belief that, when it comes to health and illness, you get what you deserve. If, as so many popular discourses promise, you *can* take charge of your health, then living with prolonged pain and sickness must be a choice, or the upshot of a faulty disposition. Such logic is implicit in one cancer survivor's self-help assurance that "with a positive attitude and hope, you can conquer anything."[89] This bootstraps mentality prevents some people who are well from empathizing with those who are not. A man with Crohn's disease describes a mentality he often encounters: "There is a sizable minority in this country which believes either explicitly or subconsciously that people deserve what they get. If you're sick, it must be because you did something awful, or are an awful person."[90] As this remark suggests, narratives depicting illness as retribution for sin linger on in contemporary perceptions of sickness—either as symptomatic of immoral behavior ("you *did* something awful") or as evidence of character dysfunction ("you *are* an awful person").

Whether couched in religious or scientific terms, the belief that you get what you deserve implies that people who are well merit their place in the higher kingdom. During his struggle with cancer, Frank noticed that many healthy people harbor an attitude similar to that of Job's accusers, who blamed Job for his afflictions as a way of "protect[ing] themselves from thinking that what had happened to him could happen to them." Similarly, Frank says, many people who are well

> believe that they control their health and that they have earned it. Those who have cancer must have done something wrong, which the healthy can then avoid. The sick person must have participated in sickness…Otherwise illness is an intolerable reminder of how risky life is.[91]

Interpreting good health as a reward for righteous behavior, an index of discipline and virtue, fosters a sense of physical/psychological/moral superiority among those who are well, a sense that shields them—at least temporarily—from the fragility of embodied life.

Psychologizing theories of illness and complicating blame

Often the shame people experience in relation to persistent pain and illness stems from a view of their affliction as manifesting not just moral failure but some deep psychological problem. For example, when Kamen sought medical help for her unrelenting headache, a doctor told her that she had a "migraine personality," which she later learned meant that she was too "ambitious, inward, intolerant of error, rather rigidly organized, and perfectionistic." Needless to say, the self-blame and -doubt Kamen felt in the wake of that diagnosis did little to relieve her suffering.[92]

In *Illness as Metaphor*, Susan Sontag critiqued theories that rooted somatic illness in psychic problems. Her analysis reveals the extent to which modern psychological explanations of disease resurrect religious narratives that attribute illness to internal weaknesses. For example, a nineteenth-century doctor understood breast cancer not as punishment for sin but as symptomatic of an overabundance of anxiety and grief. During the twentieth century, some doctors believed cancer to be rooted in a manic or repressed character type (depending on the decade). As Sontag pointed out, psychologizing explanations stigmatize sickness by consolidating moral and medical meanings. Analyzing this conflation, she noted that the less doctors understand the etiology of a disease, the more likely they are to see it as "caused by mental states and... cured by willpower."[93]

If some doctors are more comfortable incriminating patients than admitting to the limits of their capacity to cure, some patients are more than willing to accept the blame. Ensler calls attention to this self-accusing pattern in an amusing yet serious chapter entitled "How'd I Get It [Cancer]?" Most of the possibilities she considers indict herself:

>...Was it failing at marriage twice? Was it never having babies? Was it having an abortion and a miscarriage?...Was it worry every day for fifty-seven years that I wasn't good enough?...Was it the exhaustion of trying to change? Was it my father dying slowly and never calling to say goodbye?... Was it sleeping with men who were married?...Was it Tab? I drank a lot

of Tab after I got sober…Was it drinking water out of plastic bottles?…TV dinners?…Was it that I didn't cry enough? Or cried too much?…[94]

These (and other) questions Ensler poses expose the futility of this (mostly) self-blaming quest for origins—as if knowing the precise cause of her cancer were possible, as if identifying what or who to blame would make everything okay.

Admittedly not knowing anything for certain, Ensler nonetheless shares her theory on why she got sick. On the surface, her thinking seems to resemble the psychosomatic, psychologizing view of illness that Sontag rejects. Ensler describes her cancerous tumor as a "flesh monument" her body had "sculpted" over the years, drawing its raw materials from the trauma of having been raped repeatedly by her father when she was a girl, and from the gut-wrenching tales of women she had been listening to for decades—women who had survived unimaginable brutality.[95] Ensler suggests that the memories of such horrific violence found expression through cancer in her body. As if to support this hypothesis, her doctors note the unbelievable coincidence—or is it a "mystery"?—that her cancerous tumor, nestled between her vagina and the bowel, had "fistulated" her rectum, which means that it "had done exactly what rape had done to so many thousands of women in the Congo," whose experiences and stories were the focus of Ensler's activism at that time.[96]

The difference between Ensler's understanding of her cancer as connected to a history of female trauma and the psychologizing theories Sontag critiques is that Ensler doesn't blame herself for getting sick. Rather, she sees her illness as a somatic expression of the suffering she has survived—a suffering that connects her with millions of women who struggle in the body of a world in crisis, a body/world plagued by the sins of violence, greed, and addiction to a way of life that is destroying the very Earth on which we depend.[97] In a chapter describing a life-threatening infection she gets in the course of treatment, Ensler juxtaposes a CAT scan that reveals poop and pus leaking from a rupture inside her postsurgical body with images of the BP oil spill poisoning the gulf coast (the BP disaster made news the same day her infection was discovered). Instead of blaming herself for getting cancer, Ensler interrogates approaches to health that pathologize *individuals* while ignoring systemic cruelty and disease: "What would be the appropriate nonhysterical response," she asks, to the insanity and devastation humans inflict on each other and on planet? Like her medieval foresisters, Ensler makes meaning from her sickness—not in relation to the suffering of Christ (she's an atheist)—but in connection with the suffering of the earth and the anguish of women in the Congo, most of whom, she acknowledges, "are not lucky enough to be given bags" to deal with the incontinence caused by fistulas.[98]

The complexities of health and healing that emerge in the stories of Ensler and women in the Congo are obscured by the commercially sponsored, medically endorsed, self-help fantasy that we can achieve such a level of self-mastery and somatic perfection that we become invulnerable to the unpredictability of the flesh, including the possibility of getting sick or feeling pain. Margaret Mohrmann refers to this fantasy as the "idolatry of health"— our cultural devotion to somatic fitness as an end in itself, rather than as part of a larger life purpose of serving others. As a practicing physician and professor of pediatrics who is also a religious ethicist, Mohrmann advocates being "good stewards of the bodies we have been given." But she cautions against believing we can make ourselves immune to pain and illness by avoiding every carcinogen and purging every toxin. So often, she says, the pursuit of health is predicated on the denial of death: "It is the unspoken, but strong and pervasive, belief that if we just learn enough, do enough, prevent enough, exercise enough, eat the right stuff, purify our air and water and food, none of us will have to die." Ultimately, Mohrmann observes, the idolatry of health signals "a failure of trust"—trust in the intelligence of our flesh, in the power of life that sustains it, and in the knowledge that "death is the natural end to our earthly stories."[99]

Rethinking salvation, health, redemption, and healing

In *We Know How This Ends*, Bruce Kramer shares his experience of living while dying with ALS. Shortly after his diagnosis, trying to fathom the enormity of what lay before him, he asks: "What do you do when the news is bad and will only get worse?"[100] Not all incurable illnesses progress to the kind of agonizing end ALS guarantees. Still, Kramer's query is meaningful for anyone who struggles with unrelenting illness. In fact, his question has relevance for people in good health as well. For although catastrophic sickness and hurt manifest in some bodies and not others, everyone experiences *dis ease*. Human suffering is a *chronic* condition. This turns out to be "the greatest revelation" of Kramer's incurable pain and illness: everybody has some version of ALS.[101]

Embracing chronic pain and disease

Whether we experience *dis ease* in our flesh, in our lives, or "in the body of the world" (Ensler), we inevitably have to decide how to respond to suffering.

Given our evolutionary and cultural programming, it's understandable that our fight-or-flight mechanism kicks in. "Embracing the disease is the farthest thing from our minds," Kramer acknowledges, especially when there's "no reasonable possibility that a cure can be found." The problem is, he continues, "Neither fight nor flight possesses the nuance for the complexity and inevitably the loss that cannot and will not be fixed. Instead, they suggest a vulnerability that most of us find hard to face."[102]

Vulnerability of the flesh is at the core of experiences of chronic pain and sickness. These afflictions are typically seen as the antithesis of health. But what if reconciling with physical frailty is a crucial component of well-being? What if instead of seeing enduring pain and disease as enemies to be conquered, we saw them as uninvited yet pivotal opportunities for growth and healing, even as we sought to alleviate the suffering surrounding them? What if a body's refusal to live up to the dream of the Cartesian self ruling over an eschatologically purified body makes it a valuable asset for critiquing the idolatrous fantasy of perfect health and the dysfunctional systems that chimera serves? And what if the sin/punishment associated with sickness were understood not in terms of individual transgressions but as the harm inflicted on vulnerable bodies by social/symbolic hierarchies?

Such questions suggest that even the most abhorrent experiences of pain and illness may contain seeds for self-discovery and prophetic critique. Whether we experience them first hand, or encounter them in the lives of others, these afflictions have transformative potential to the extent that they are intentionally explored—rather than demonized. *If consciously engaged*, the experience of living in the kingdom of the sick can generate an atypical vantage point that challenges assumptions and norms we habitually take for granted, renews our sense of what really matters, and helps us wrestle and reconcile with the parts of our bodies/our lives we can't control.

The fragility of salvation, health, redemption, and healing

This perspective finds support in the work of Ivone Gebara, for whom health and healing are spiritual priorities. Gebara's work as a postcolonial, Catholic nun/ecotheologian who lives alongside the poorest women in Brazil may seem far removed from the first-world struggles of people who are chronically sick. But her critique of religious, philosophical, and cultural narratives that sanction aggression toward vulnerable bodies, coupled with her affirmation of biodiversity, interdependence, fragility, and impermanence, suggest an alternative approach to salvation that can help us rethink the experiences of incurable pain and illness. Following Gebara's suggestion that we explore the existential and experiential meanings of traditional religious categories,[103] I use the terms "salvation" and "health," "redemption" and "healing" interchangeably in the remainder of this chapter, not as nouns but as embodied processes. In so doing, I aim to breathe new life and relevancy into traditional religious terms while illuminating aspects of the pursuit of well-being that secular discourses typically overlook.

The understanding of salvation Gebara develops in *Out of the Depths* reflects the Christian narrative in which suffering has transformative potential. Though the suffering Gebara describes stems from the systemic evils of injustice, her vision of redemption is instructive for people struggling with chronic pain and illness. It is salvation not beyond the body, not outside this life, not once and for all, not universal, and not as a "happy outcome." Instead, it is redemption *in* the flesh, healing "in the here and now." It is salvation "intermingled with the confusion of life," "mixed with suffering," experienced in the "complete acceptance of our corporal [sic] historic reality," including our mortality. It is the "fragile redemption" that "we find in the everyday life of every person…like a glass of water that quenches thirst for the moment, but thirst comes again, sometimes stronger than before." It is "[t]emporary redemption…that gives back eagerness for living [and]…is not bound by moral judgments." It is "micro- and macro-salvation," calling us to embrace the imperfect wholeness that's already present, even as we work to build a more just society.[104]

Gebara's embodied, this-worldly, non-perfectionistic view of salvation provides a crucial caveat to seeing ill health as a spiritual opportunity because it avoids theological clichés and platitudes that too easily give injustice or debilitating sickness a positive spin. To suggest that the suffering surrounding pain and illness may become meaningful does not assume it is divinely given, inherently praiseworthy, or "good for the soul." As Gebara points out, redemptive suffering narratives have been used to sanctify the subjugation of women and disenfranchised men.[105] Reconciling with the frailty of the flesh is especially tricky for people whose bodies are already vulnerable to the structural violence of racism, sexism, colonialism, and poverty. Thus any understanding of disease as potentially spiritually transformative must be developed in ways that do not recycle oppressive, placating narratives of redemptive suffering. "[Pain] does not ennoble you," Audre Lorde observes, reiterating womanists' caution about the dangers of romanticizing adversity by spiritualizing its purpose.[106] Deanne Thompson shares this critique when she challenges the notion that "cancer is a gift": "Knowing the odds are strong that cancer will kill me in the near future, I am unable to see—or embrace— the gift character of cancer." Though not denying that "sometimes suffering is educational," and that "life with cancer has been rich with gifts," Thompson resists viewing her illness itself as a blessing in disguise.[107]

In fact, the idea that "God has a purpose for giving you cancer" is near the top of Thompson's list of well-intended but not-helpful things people say about the disease. While she admits to being "a better person today than [she] was before the cancer" because of her increased gratitude for life, she says she would "take it all back" if she could. "When I was sick, I hated being so out of control, so vulnerable, so weak. In remission, I'm terrified of becoming that vulnerable again." Thompson not only refuses to romanticize her struggle with chronic illness; she "doubt[s] cancer has a purpose in [her] life," even as she strives "to make meaning in cancer's wake."[108]

Thompson's subtle distinction—between cancer as a blessing and cancer as a brutal experience with educational potential—is helpful for thinking about health and healing as pivotal spiritual opportunities. This distinction illuminates the difference between believing God gives you chronic illness as a punishment, test, or gift (a belief that makes God cruel) and striving to make meaning from a grueling disease whose origins are uncertain. It marks the difference between thinking you got sick because you didn't eat your broccoli or because of your neurotic tendencies (beliefs that promote self-blame) and accepting that you may never know the causes of your disease and it may never go away, but that there's something to learn from the experience. Thompson's distinction makes it possible to recycle the narrative that enabled medieval women to probe the meaning of their afflictions, without interpreting pain and illness as part of a divine conspiracy. In short, this distinction suggests a Job-like theodicy* reminiscent of the colloquial expression, "shit happens," even as it leaves open the possibility of salvation amid the dung.

Refusing shame

In *The Cancer Journals*, black lesbian feminist poet and activist Audre Lorde shares her non-sentimentalized struggle to harvest some lessons from the devastation of her disease. Her story combines self-examination with prophetic critique, exchanging the self-blame, antagonism, isolation, and denial that so often surround experiences of intractable disease for the honesty, integration, accountability, and solidarity that make healing possible—even in the face of death. In the years she lived while dying from cancer, Lorde sought to scrutinize the significance of her illness and to incorporate—rather than conquer—the crisis it created in her life. Taunted with desires to return to normalcy, to choose oblivion, to give into despair and fear, Lorde stayed

---

* "Theodicy" involves theories about God's role in orchestrating (or not) suffering and evil in the world.

present to the emotional and physical pain of cancer, and "in the process of losing a breast," became "a more whole person."[109]

Lorde's experience challenges a view of illness and healing as mutually exclusive. Gebara articulates this challenge in Christian terms: "the cross and the resurrection coexist in the same body."[110] Both women insist that "listening to the wisdom of our bodies, even with all its contradictions," provides knowledge necessary for healing.[111] Both refuse a carrot-and-stick eschatology of health and opt instead for a strategy for female well-being based on women's daily lives as "the training ground" for transforming silence and difficulty into language and action. This strategy links personal survival with growth with social critique. By writing candidly about her excruciating struggles with cancer, Lorde turns our culture's shaming gaze back on itself.[112]

Perhaps the best illustration of Lorde's refusal to be silenced by the shame of sickness was her unwillingness to wear a prosthetic breast. It was the late 1970s and pressure to return to normative femininity post-mastectomy was huge. As Lorde was leaving the hospital, the head nurse wanted to know why she wasn't wearing "a form" (i.e. "a lambswool puff" inserted in the bra to create the impression of having a breast). "You will feel so much better with it on," a Reach for Recovery volunteer assured her, adding that not wearing the form is "bad for the morale of the office." In Lorde's translation, what the volunteer was really saying (on behalf of society) was that with an artificial breast, "Nobody will know the difference." As if there were something shameful about having cancer, something indecent about being a one-breasted woman. Lorde responds to this message, saying "it is that very difference which I wish to affirm, because I have lived it, and survived it, and wish to share that strength with other women."[113]

Lorde shares that strength by challenging the "nobody will know the difference" message and the shame it implies and instills. She starts by indicting society's view of women as decorative objects that the cosmetic fix of an artificial breast perpetuates. "Women have been programmed to view our bodies only in terms of how they look and feel to others, rather than how they feel to ourselves." Lorde says she is "affronted by the message that I am only acceptable if I look 'right' or 'normal'… [w]here 'normal' means the 'right' color, shape, size, or number of breasts."[114] In addition, pressure to prostheticize encourages post-mastectomy women to avoid "com[ing] to terms with their own pain and loss, and thereby, with their own strength." For Lorde, grieving and facing mortality are opportunities to move through the fear that alienates women from their own power and prevents them from coming together to protest systemic injustices—injustices that decrease the chances of surviving breast cancer "if you are poor, Black, or in any other way part of the underside of this society." Given its increasing incidence, Lorde says, women can't afford to treat breast cancer "as a private or personal problem," any more than they can afford the illusory comfort of a lambswool puff.[115]

Lorde's critique of a culture that encourages post-mastectomy women to improve their bodies by wearing artificial breasts is not meant to judge women who choose "the path of prosthesis." She recognizes the "pressures of conformity and the loneliness of difference" that, for many women, make this path a decision by "default." Rather than blame individual women for "wish[ing]...to be the same as before," she directs her critique at social/symbolic hierarchies that perpetuate fear of somatic diversity and make women susceptible to false promises of empowerment through a better body.[116] At the same time, she suggests that for healing to happen, the losses surrounding the experience of breast cancer "must be integrated into a new sense of self."[117] Women must wrestle with—rather than deny—the difference cancer makes in their lives.

Trading the fight for the struggle

The healing strength Lorde experiences comes not from fighting and defeating cancer—the disease eventually kills her—but from wrestling with its meaning for her life and the lives of other women. I'm choosing my metaphors carefully here. In my mind, *wrestling* or *struggling* with chronic illness and pain are not the same as fighting or trying to conquer them. This distinction is subtle but important. Whereas the conquest approach relies on one of our culture's most common methods for problem solving (i.e. force and violence) in an effort to control disobedient flesh, a wrestling paradigm recognizes the mutual agency of those aspects of ourselves we typically refer to as body, mind, and spirit. To speak of someone's *struggle* with sickness is to configure agency in a way that highlights her need and capacity for self-determination without implying that she can dictate or force the outcome of every decision. Wrestling allows us to speak of her suffering without implying victimhood. As a metaphor, wrestling illuminates the never-ending scrimmage between what we can influence and what eludes our control, between what we can and cannot fix. It names the tentative, evolving, imperfect, and fragile nature of the salvation Gebara describes.[118] Finally, by acknowledging an opponent without turning that opponent into an enemy, wrestling leaves room for reconciliation.

The idea of wrestling with—rather than fighting—illness makes sense when we realize that agency is a partial truth, and that combat is not a sustainable method for pursuing health because it aims to destroy the very organism it seeks to preserve. As counterintuitive as it sounds, reconciliation with illness by wrestling with it may well be a more effective strategy for healing. This strategy resonates with Buddhism's teaching that the best way to alleviate suffering is to stay present to it. Buddhist feminist Sandy Boucher experienced this truth when, amid agonizing back pain following surgery for colon cancer, she decided to give her undivided attention to the burning sensation, rather than fight it, which was only making it worse. The more she directed her consciousness to the searing pain, tuning into how it actually felt, the less solid it became.[119] Staying present to her pain didn't make it go away, but it alleviated the suffering surrounding her desperation for it to end. "Wrestling" is not a term typically associated with Buddhist practice, but it speaks to the agency on which the capacity to stay present depends.

The most famous wrestling match in the biblical tradition is between Jacob and an angel. Jacob meets the angel on his way home to visit his estranged brother, who he cheated in his youth (Genesis 32.22–32). There are various ways to interpret the story. With what or whom is Jacob wrestling? Does the angel represent God? Humanity? Some part of Jacob himself? What seems clear is that the struggle involves Jacob's effort to come to terms with his own losses and failures. He wrestles all night and in the end survives but is wounded in the hip. Though injured, he refuses to let go of his unidentified opponent until he receives a blessing ("I will not let you go unless you bless me"), at which point the angel renames Jacob "Israel," literally, "one who wrestles with God."

During his final year with ALS, amid physical pain that left him semiconscious, Kramer felt himself wrestling with angels. Like Jacob, he wasn't sure of their identity, and eventually realized he was "wrestling with the unknown," which is perhaps a way of talking about the divine. Like Jacob, Kramer insists on receiving a blessing before letting go, knowing that his pain, lost capacity, and sadness have changed him forever. The encounter doesn't cure him, but the wrestling helps Kramer reconcile with his losses, enabling him to be acutely present to what's left of his life. "I have gazed upon the face of God," Kramer says, "wrestled with her—not to win, not to lose, but to live as fully as I possibly can."[120]

This struggle to live fully with incurable pain and illness suggests that as a strategy for healing, reconciling with somatic vulnerability is not the same as giving up. On a physical level, opting out of combat mode does not mean doing nothing to alleviate physical distress. To varying degrees, most chronic conditions can benefit from treatments—from pharmaceuticals, to chemotherapy, to surgery, to alternative therapies like massage, yoga, acupuncture, and meditation. On a spiritual level, reconciling with persistent illness or pain is not the same as resignation. Even as she embraces her dire situation, Lorde sees herself as a "warrior" rather than a "passive victim"; and Ensler says she's "not going down without a fight."[121] Occasionally, both women employ combat language to describe their struggles with cancer. But when they do, the antagonist is not disease itself, but the fear and despair surrounding it, *and*, the industries that poison our environment and our bodies with the toxic waste of their greed.[122] Ultimately, accepting and wrestling with such inner demons and external forces turn out to be empowering: "What is there possibly to be afraid of?" Lorde asks. "Once I accept the existence of dying, as a life process, who can ever have power over me again?"[123]

Challenging our culturally induced illusions

Examining the struggles of people with incurable disease and discomfort has been incredibly humbling. My own encounter with chronic pain, though utterly maddening in the years leading up to surgery, was a mosquito bite compared to what many people go through. The ache in my hip has been so dramatically reduced thanks to surgery that even though I still experience mild discomfort in some of my joints and my arthritis is certain to worsen with age, I no longer inhabit the kingdom of the sick. I'd be lying if I said I miss that netherworld. Still, I'm drawn to the lessons one can learn there about the vulnerable, diverse, interdependent, and impermanent character of embodied life. For it seems to me such lessons have the iconoclastic potential to "cure" us of—or at least to help us identify, resist, and recover from—some of the cultural illusions that diminish our well-being.

The illusion of perfection and the "grace that Is"

Incurable pain and disease have the potential to "loosen the soil of our certainties," to borrow a phrase from Gebara. To the extent that we allow them to unearth "the illusion that…we can defeat the powers of change, flexibility, and creativity that are inherent in all vital processes,"[124] these afflictions can even become a means for healing. Like so many women, Thompson wrestled with the powers of impermanence as she yearned to return to her "almost perfect life" prior to her cancer diagnosis. She experienced this yearning in a vision that visited her repeatedly: she walks up to an appointment desk in an oncology waiting room and politely tells the receptionist, "*I'm ready to give back my diagnosis. I've tried this cancer life on for size, and unfortunately, it doesn't fit my lifestyle.*" Reflecting on this vision, Thompson says, "I was sick of being sick…I wanted *out*…of this world of cancer. I wanted to go back to…a time when life was good."[125] Despite nostalgia for normalcy, Thompson sees this mirage for what it is and moves deeper into the unknown of her disease, clinging to the Easter hope of her faith that "brokenness is not the end of the story."[126] As the title

Hoping for More suggests, elements of classic Christian eschatology shape Thompson's account of her struggle with cancer. In the end, however, the redemption she experiences is not a return to Eden, but a this-worldly "salvation in the midst of wretchedness," a healing based on "acceptance of the grace that *is* rather than the grace that *could be.*"[127]

The paradox of "salvation in the midst of wretchedness," of serious illness as a venue for healing, frames Kramer's account of his struggle with ALS. He describes his spiraling descent from "the arrogance of [his]…able-bodied existence," in which he imagines himself to be master of his own destiny, into an ever-dwindling "new normal," characterized by daily losses in physical functioning and a corresponding realization that control is an illusion. From this new vantage point, "fixing is a lie," fragility is the truth, and "embrac[ing] vulnerability" is the only viable path for healing as his physical condition rapidly deteriorates. This very deterioration catalyzes his spiritual "rebirth":

I KNOW what is important now. I know that every experience has multiple layers, each to be felt and analyzed and kept…There is no time to hold grudges, be afraid, and not forgive. There is no time for games…I just don't have time for bullshit anymore.

ALS compels Kramer to abandon the niceties and pretenses of the dream of normalcy and be fully present to his life as it is: "The autopilot of living from event to event is completely gone. Pay attention!"[128]

The illusion of "individual omnipotence"

The healing that comes from paying attention to "the grace that *is*" defies not only the illusion of health as the prize for self-mastery and good behavior, but also the myth that health is a personal achievement. If illness unmasks "the illusion of our individual omnipotence" (Gebara),[129] healing reveals our interdependence with others. Immediately after her diagnosis, for example, Thompson is flooded with the care of family, friends, church members, coworkers, and even acquaintances, who bring meals to her family, do their laundry, and offer constant prayers. She recognizes how much privilege saturates her situation and struggles not to feel guilty for the efforts of this "real-life communion of saints," who "incarnate the hands and feet of divine love."[130] For Lorde, these saints are women of various colors, ages, and sexual orientations, united in battle not against cancer but "against the tyrannies of silence" Lorde dedicated her life to exposing: the fear, shame, and injustices that threaten to stunt women's growth through the difficulties of their lives. "Wrapped in a web of woman love and strong wishes of faith and hope,"

Lorde evolved through her disease for more than a decade. During those years, she shared with others the salvation that comes from knowing you are not alone in wrestling with fear, and the liberation that comes from "learning to put fear into perspective."[131]

Ensler's struggle with cancer also catalyzed a communally mediated experience of redemption. In an epiphany that rivals the *Revelations of Divine Love* Julian of Norwich received while she was sick, Ensler discovers a healing truth: the love she had spent her whole life pursuing and failing to achieve— i.e. enduring romance between two people—isn't necessarily the highest expression of love. While she had been busy dreaming of, waiting for, and chasing after what she believed to be "the ultimate love, the love that would sweep me off my feet," she had neglected to notice the bonds of love already in her midst. The saving care and commitment expressed by friends, fellow activists, and family members who cooked her breakfast, rubbed her feet, brought her pajamas, sent her poems, and so on revealed that the "big huge love" she had tried so hard to find and create already pervaded her life.[132]

Deciding/discovering what really matters

Ensler's illness-induced epiphany calls into question common cultural assumptions about what it takes to be happy. In our consumer-driven, achievement-oriented culture, happiness is predicated on acquiring something else or getting someplace more important. Chronic sickness exposes the delusionary quality of these beliefs. Thompson recounts an especially difficult winter afternoon during her struggle with cancer when her 12-year-old daughter, book in hand, crawled into bed with her and read out loud for over 2 hours. As you can imagine, this "subtle display of love nourished [her] for months to come."[133] This display of love also contains a prophetic critique of the "standard of productivity" by which most healthy people measure their success—and self-worth.[134]

A similar critique is implicit in Virginia Woolf's reflections on the "tremendous spiritual change" that illness can instigate. Woolf was a late-nineteenth-century literary genius who suffered from debilitating headaches, fevers, and faints, coupled with bouts of agitation and depression. In "On Being Ill," she bears witness to "the daily drama of the body," with its "unending procession of changes," and she marvels at the "undiscovered countries" that sickness discloses: "we [the sick] go down to the pit of death and feel the waters of annihilation close above our heads." Illness plunges you beneath the superficial world, Woolf observes, enabling you to see and name things as they really are. In health, "the genial pretense must be kept up," but "in illness this make-believe ceases…truths [are] blurted out, which the cautious respectability of health conceals."[135] Unfit for respectable society, the sick "cease to be soldiers in the army of the upright." While healthy people "march to battle," the sick "float with the sticks on the stream; helter-skelter with the dead leaves on the lawn, irresponsible and disinterested and able, perhaps for the first time for years, to look round, to look up—to look, for example, at the sky." This capacity to look deeply and appreciate what most people take for granted is a strength that illness grants. As deserters in the "army of the upright," the sick can do things many healthy people can't, like take time to see the sky, read in bed, or appreciate the company of others.[136]

Seriously ill people challenge the way the rest of us live simply by "teach[ing] us the value of being alive." Recalling the worst days of his illness, Arthur Frank says,

> I often wish I could live a bit more as I did then, without having to have cancer. Illness, and perhaps only illness, gives us permission to slow down...When I was ill I valued just being with others. Too often now I think of people as intruding on my work.[137]

Ensler suggests that cancer saved her by forcing her "to let go of everything that didn't matter." Paradoxically, the excruciating disease gave her a "second wind," a new breath for life—minus the fear. The wisdom she accumulates through this transformation illuminates the crucial difference between letting go and giving up. Here's a sampling of that wisdom, which reads like a contemporary beatitudes for people with social privilege:

> Do not be afraid, no, death will not be our end. Indifference will be, dissociation will be, collateral damage, polar caps melting, endless hunger, mass rapes, grotesque wealth. The change will come from those who know they do not exist separately but as part of the river...The only salvation is kindness. The only way out is care...Step off the wheel of winning and losing...Lose everything. That is where it begins.[138]

The soul-searching process of deciding and discovering what really matters differs from what Lorde calls the "superficial spirituality" of "looking on the bright side of things."[139] A spiritual approach to health and healing that refuses to recognize mass rapes, wealth disparity, and melting ice caps promotes complicity with society that is sick.

For both Ensler and Lorde, salvation is not simply a matter of personal happiness, any more than health is an individual achievement. It's easier to tell people to be happy than to clean up the environment, Lorde observes, as if personal happiness can save us from the systemic injustices that sicken the flesh of those on society's bottom. As if individual well-being can prevent profit-driven corporations from polluting the earth with toxins that the National Cancer Institute says are responsible for two-thirds of cancer cases. "The only really happy people I have ever met," Lorde says, "are those of us who work against these deaths with all the energy of our living, recognizing the deep and fundamental unhappiness with which we are surrounded, at the same time as we fight to keep from being submerged by it."[140]

Lorde's criticism of superficial spirituality speaks to any number of cancer clichés—e.g. "What doesn't kill you makes you stronger," "God is trying to teach you something"[141] —and reminds us to keep whatever personal truths disease teaches tethered to prophetic critique. Ensler connects these micro/macro aspects of salvation when she speculates that perhaps our lives are "precious only up to a point." She is deliberating whether to go through with chemotherapy in the aftermath of a harrowing recovery from surgery. She ponders all the resources that went into saving her life so far, as she remembers the female survivors of violence in the Congo, whose well-being seems to matter little in the eyes of the world. While utterly grateful to be alive, surviving cancer gives her an unusual viewpoint: "What if we held [our lives] loosely and understood that there were no guarantees?"[142]

To understand our lives as "precious only up to a point" is to see them not just in relation to the lives of women in the Congo (and other suffering, vulnerable bodies), but also in the context of the evolutionary movement of life itself: the creative–destructive process Gebara describes as fundamentally mysterious.[143] This perspective illuminates the mystery of life manifesting itself in flesh that is diversely and precariously configured: sick, healthy, young, old, fat, thin, impaired, nondisabled, straight, gay, brown, black, beige—and everything in between. From this vantage point, we can affirm the tentative preciousness of our vulnerable and evolving flesh, wrestle with the choices we do and do not have, struggle to reduce suffering in ourselves and in the body of the world, and reconcile with the imperfection of salvation. As we shall see in the next chapter, a crucial aspect of the health and healing this perspective offers is embracing the realities of aging and, ultimately, death.

8

The shame of getting old

On January 1, 2016, my mom texted my siblings and me to inform us that the new year was off to a rough start. She had taken my 80-year-old father to the hospital emergency room that morning because he wasn't feeling well and was having trouble remembering things. I called immediately to find out more. Mom tried to be brave as she explained that Dad had suffered a transient ischemic attack (TIA)—a stroke-like episode in which blood flow to part of the brain temporarily stops. The attack lasted a few hours, during which my father was fully conscious, but confused. At one point, he didn't know who the president was. Mom assured me that the TIA was over. Dad's memory was back, he felt fine, and was sitting in his favorite rocker watching football on TV, as if nothing had happened.

Wanting to trust my mother's optimism, my thoughts settled on the word *transient*, which means "temporary" or "short-lived." I felt relieved that this term was in the title of Dad's diagnosis: *transient* ischemic attack. But later that night, I did some online research. According to the National Stroke Association, TIAs do not cause permanent brain damage, but "they are a serious warning sign that a stroke may happen in the future."[1] Suddenly, the idea of transience lost its appeal.

Getting old can be hard and scary

When we examine our fierce desire for our loved ones to live forever, we can begin to understand our culture's deep-seated fear of aging. Old age and death are connected not just in theory, but reality: eventually, the former leads to the latter. Getting old reminds us that we, and the people we love, are mortal. The thought of mortality raises questions about the purpose of life: Why are we here? What really matters in the end? Old age can be an incredibly rich chapter of life, but it can also be physically debilitating, not to mention mentally, emotionally, and spiritually difficult—both for those who are elderly and for those who care for them. Ultimately, old age requires us to let go of people, places, abilities, and activities we treasure. Though living a long life can be a tremendous privilege, there are reasons why, as a society and as individuals, we often avert our gaze from the evidence of aging. Buddhist writer Susan Moon puts the matter succinctly: "getting old is hard. Getting old is scary."[2]

The culture of physical improvement exploits the fears and difficulties surrounding the process of aging by promoting fantasies of immortality and eternal youth. This chapter interrogates those fantasies, along with the ageist stereotypes they generate and the anti-aging pursuits they inspire. I analyze how self-help and commercial enticements to escape, conquer, or conceal bodily signs of aging reflect and reinforce medical discourses that pathologize the entropy (i.e. breakdown, weakening) that happens as bodies grow old. This analysis highlights the religious and philosophical narratives that tacitly support disparaging views of aging, including the idealization of "imperishable" bodies in Christian eschatology, and the Cartesian view of the self as an autonomous individual. Finally, I propose a different perspective on aging, in which the frailties, metamorphoses, and limited futures of elderly flesh become opportunities for introspection and prophetic critique.

Ambiguities of aging bodies

The poet May Sarton compares old age to "a foreign country," a place that's "not interesting until one gets there."[3] If you are a college student, or someone in your twenties or thirties, chances are you've not given much thought to this territory. Likewise, you may not have noticed just how central youth is to our culture's better body story. Somatic norms often remain hidden—until you transgress them. Just as many healthy, able-bodied, or thin people don't notice how dominant social/symbolic systems privilege them, so many young adults don't recognize the challenges elderly persons face as foreigners in "youth-worshipping culture."[4]

During the first few decades of my life, I didn't give a second thought to getting old. Now in the middle of middle age, I find our culture's idealization of young bodies impossible to miss. I've not yet officially joined the ranks of "senior," but it's been a long time since I've been carded, and no one confuses me for a student anymore. My graying hair and deepening facial lines are a dead give-away that I've outlived the golden era of youth. Although I've not yet had to endure the worst insults and indignities of getting old in a society obsessed with looking/feeling youthful, I only need to remember my artificial hip to feel a strong kinship with people more advanced in years—those whose flesh refuses to "stay forever young."

Stereotypical meanings assigned to old and young flesh

Did you ever notice that Bob Dylan, the legendary folk singer-songwriter, didn't write a song encouraging his beloved to "stay forever old?" *Of course not*, you might be thinking. *No one aspires to be geriatric, gray-headed, hunched-over, and wrinkled.* In developed Western societies, "old" is outdated, old-fashioned, obsolete. Old is rusty, withered, weak; decrepit, debilitated, and dependent. Old is feeble, fragile, infirm, in contrast to "young," which is strong, vigorous, and sexy. Young is fresh and fit, radiant and resilient, growing and green, budding, burgeoning, and buoyant. Young is innocent, tender, and rife with possibility.[5]

In a culture where *better* means *younger*, the age of one's flesh is not value-neutral. The same prominent societal values we saw operating in shaming views of disabled, fat, chronically sick, and painful bodies—control, speed, productivity, and self-sufficiency—imply virtues and vices for young and old physiques, generating stereotypes that ignore diversity within each group. Seniors are thought to be impaired in body and mind, sluggish, crotchety, lonely, dependent, unproductive, weak. Alternatively, young adults are assumed to be healthy, independent, energetic, efficient, happy, and attractive. (Compare, for example, Figures 8.1 and 8.2). These stereotypes perpetuate an age-segregated and stratified society. In fact, there's evidence that children internalize them by age 2 or 3.[6]

We may not consciously subscribe to ageist stereotypes, but our repeated exposure to them trains us to lower our expectations when we see or interact with older people.[7] In *Aging Our Way*, sociologist Meika Loe interviewed a 94-year-old woman named Alice, who notices that most of the time when she meets young people, "they immediately pull the curtains down…They don't think of me as a person." Although these encounters are painful, Alice recalls feeling a similar "not-me" aversion when she was younger: "I remember as a thirty-something visiting old people who would hold onto my hand, and I just wanted to get away,"[8] as if the frailty of older flesh were contagious.

Some social psychologists understand ageism as "an unconscious defense strategy" for dealing with unacknowledged fear of mortality. This perspective highlights the existential roots of ageism and its function as a "death-denying coping mechanism." Research suggests that younger adults associate elderly bodies with mortality, and that they "adopt agist [sic] attitudes and behaviors

FIGURE 8.1 *Older woman holding a cane* © *Matt Cardy.*
Source: Getty Images.

to distance themselves from older people in order to deny the reality that they, too, will eventually…die." This research also indicates that for the not-yet-elderly, the most terrifying aspect of old age is the prospect of physical deterioration.[9]

Cross-cultural, historical, and biblical perspectives on old age

The dread directed at older bodies is not universal. Despite evidence that ageism is on the rise in collectivist societies,[10] in traditional African, Asian, South American, and indigenous cultures, elders have been revered because of the knowledge and maturity they are believed to have acquired over the years. In these contexts, aging is not typically fraught with anxiety, and bodies don't depreciate in value as they advance in years. Senior women are not expected to color their hair or wear make-up to hide their wrinkles.[11] Elderly family members are not sequestered away in nursing homes because their stories and wisdom are considered valuable resources for younger generations.

Old age also had positive meanings in earlier historical periods in the West. In seventeenth-century America and Europe, privileged people wore powdered

FIGURE 8.2 *Bikini Girl jumping at the beach* © *Vasileios Economou.*
Source: Getty Images.

white wigs because they wanted to appear older and more authoritative.[12] We find similarly favorable attitudes in ancient history. In the Bible, older characters are often exemplars of faith, and the elderly are to be honored and cared for, not treated as objects of condescension and pity.[13] According to Proverbs 20:29, "the beauty of the aged is their gray hair," and Proverbs 16:31 says "Gray hair is a crown of glory"—a reward for righteousness. Several other passages from the Hebrew Bible link old age with wisdom, male authority, and divine favor. Adam is said to have lived to be 930, Noah 950, Abraham 175, Moses 120. Such longevity was not meant to be understood literally. Rather, it communicated the elevated status these mythical/spiritual

FIGURE 8.3 *Michelangelo's "Creation of Adam" © Lucas Schifres.*
Source: Getty Images.

ancestors had among the ancient Israelites.[14] Later in the biblical tradition, associations between old age and holiness gave rise to the image of God as an old man—a depiction that reflects one of Yahweh's titles: "the Ancient of Days" (Dan. 7:9).[15] In the New Testament, this image resurfaces when a triumphant Jesus appears with "white hair" in *Revelations* (1:14).[16] Famously portrayed in Michelangelo's *The Creation of Adam*, a personified image of God as a white-bearded, grandfatherly figure continues to shape the imaginations of many Sunday school students today (Figure 8.3).

As this image suggests, in the biblical tradition, the virtue and authority associated with seniority are gender specific. In both testaments, the term "elder" is most often used to describe a spiritually mature person in a *public* leadership position—a role the texts reserve primarily (though not exclusively) for men. Titus 2:3–5 instructs older women to set a holy example for younger females by demonstrating domestic skills, self-control, kindness, chastity, and submissiveness to their husbands. Similarly, the "good works" the author of I Timothy stipulates for elderly widows involve household duties, not institutional authority.[17] Yet these texts were *prescribing* behavior, rather than reflecting reality. Historical evidence suggests that some churches did in fact ordain older widows as deaconesses.[18] The gospels also cast some elderly women in prophetic roles—e.g. Elizabeth, mother of John the Baptist, identifies Mary as "the mother of my Lord," and the elderly Anna recognizes the redemptive power of Jesus (Luke 1:42–43; 2:38).

Despite these examples of older women's spiritual power in early Christianity, the virtue and authority of old age is more typically associated with men. Given females' identification with physicality, and the specific importance placed on their reproductive capacities, women's value in the biblical tradition tended to diminish as they matured beyond their childbearing years.[19] The exceptional stories of characters like Sarah and Elizabeth, both of whom miraculously conceive in old age, reinscribe rather than undermine this pattern.

Defining "old" and "aging"

If the denigration of elderly flesh is neither universal, nor timeless, nor gender-neutral, definitions of *aging* and *old* are similarly ambiguous. Technically, humans at every stage of life are aging, not just retired grandparents. From cuddly infants to defiant adolescents, from twenty-something searchers to middle-aged workers—minute by minute, all of us make the irreversible passage through time known as aging. Typically, however, *aging* describes the process of getting older during the second half of life. Still, *old* is a matter of perspective that's shaped by one's personal, cultural, and social location.

When I was a child, teenagers were "old" to me. In my twenties, forty-somethings seemed "over the hill." Now solidly in my fifties, 65—the age at which one becomes a "senior citizen" in the United States—doesn't seem *that* old. Like many Americans, I associate *old* with people 85 or older. But these ideas are culturally conditioned. According to the World Health Organization, most developed nations define "elderly" as starting at 65, but the threshold in most African countries is 50 or 55. The United Nations uses the cut-off of 60+ when referring to older people. The U.S. Census Bureau describes individuals over 85 as the "oldest old."[20] The absence of universal agreement on who is *old* reminds us that concepts like "aging" and "elderly" are social constructions.

Biological and chronological aging

The ambiguity of such terms is complicated by the fact that the entropy that happens in older bodies (technically called *senescence*) affects people differently, thanks to diverse combinations of genetic inheritances, environmental influences, exposure to disease, and emotional dispositions. This variability means there is no universal correspondence between chronological age (i.e. how long you have lived) and biological age (i.e. your body's "wear and tear"). For example, most people don't develop severe osteoarthritis by age 47, but I did. And while 90 percent of American seniors experience some chronic condition, many centenarians (people who outlive their hundredth birthday) remain remarkably healthy until their final days.[21]

It's precisely the tension between the *inevitability* and the *variability* of aging that the culture of physical improvement exploits with its constant "you-don't-have-to-look-your-age" message.

Despite this message, bodies invariably undergo changes in structure and functioning as they age—with or without our consent. "Changes" may seem like a euphemism, since these shifts typically include loss of muscle strength, bone mass, motor control, and respiratory efficiency; lowered immunity; increased difficulty in swallowing; diminished hearing and vision; decreased elastin and collagen in the skin; more frequent constipation and incontinence—and this is a short list. Older bodies are also more susceptible to diseases like osteoarthritis, osteoporosis, diabetes, and dementia, as well as cardiovascular and pulmonary illnesses.[22] The debilitating effects of the atrophy that elders' bodies eventually experience underscore the intersections between disability, chronic illness, and aging issues.

Losing independence

Much of what makes aging so frightening and frustrating is the loss of independence that happens as older flesh becomes increasingly impaired. Although elders' health statuses vary considerably—from robust, to frail, to dying[23]—the trajectory of aging generally moves in the direction of greater dependence. Diminishing physical or cognitive functioning forces some elders to relocate (e.g. to an assisted living community, nursing home, or family member's residence). Many have to relinquish their car keys, often a highly contentious issue since driving represents the autonomy we equate with adulthood.[24] And though seniors' health has generally improved since the 1980s,[25] the average 85-year-old American will spend over two years at the end of her or his life completely dependent on others for help with getting out of bed, bathing, dressing, eating, and going to the bathroom.[26]

In *A Bittersweet Season*, journalist Jane Gross cites studies that show how this trajectory toward dependence creates an ageist hierarchy that elders themselves often internalize. Many high-functioning seniors look down on those who need more assistance, projecting their own fears of dependency/mortality onto the bodies of their peers. Gross witnessed this pattern in her own elderly mother, who, when she was still healthy, didn't want to mingle with "those people"—the elders living in the section of her retirement community reserved for the most needy. But as her health deteriorated in her mid-eighties, Gross's mother found herself on the bottom tier of this aging/debility ranking system. Her dinner companions at the nursing home where she had moved wanted her banned from the table because she had lost her ability to converse and couldn't feed herself without making a mess.[27]

In a culture where being grown up means being self-sufficient, where bodily control is a cardinal virtue and needing help is a weakness, losing one's independence can feel shameful. In this context, it's hard not to interpret the somatic changes related to aging as a one-way movement of decline. Even seemingly objective medical descriptions of these developments deploy terms like "deterioration," "loss," "worsening," "diminished," and "compromised," which sound more negative than neutral. As I was writing this chapter, I found it difficult to avoid using such pessimistic-sounding language, even as I'm aware of its potential to reinforce the stigma of aging. The challenge is to honestly acknowledge the limits and losses that happen with aging without perpetuating what longevity expert Laura Cartensen refers to as "the misery myth."[28]

Demographic changes and challenges

Understanding the complexities of old age is more necessary than ever given the "graying of the population." Thanks to advances in medical knowledge and technology, average life expectancy increased some 30 years in the United States and Western Europe during the twentieth century. The fastest growing segment of the population in the United States today is people 85 and older, the majority of whom are white, middle- or upper class, and female. It's estimated that by 2050, twenty percent of Americans will be in that cohort.[29]

As their numbers grew during the twentieth century, elders came to be seen as social burdens, and their bodies became associated with dependency and decay.[30] Previously, most seniors were tended to by multigenerational family systems. But as the population aged, elderly care became increasingly institutionalized. Today, most Americans are "aging in place" (in their homes with the help of caregivers).[31] Even so, many spend their final years in nursing homes. While the quality of these facilities varies considerably, most prioritize safety, sterility, and order over residents' inner needs (e.g. for relationships, a sense of purpose, beauty).[32] In *Another Country*, psychologist Mary Pipher describes her visit with Sonja, a 93-year-old nursing home resident who wanted nothing more than to go outside and see the flowers popping through the earth on that cool spring morning. The staff had been too busy to take her out, and her son told her it was too cold anyway. "All the time we talked," Pipher recalled, "Sonja never stopped hungrily looking outside at the parking lot." She lingered at the windows in the facility's common space because her roommate insisted on keeping the shades in their room closed.[33]

Despite the high premium our society places on longevity, the oldest old face a number of difficulties, as do those who care for them. Gross recounts the overwhelming challenges she and her brother encountered when their mother's health diminished: the exorbitant expenses of assisted living facilities and nursing homes; the emotional roller coasters of guilt, grief, and exhaustion; the incessant interruptions of their professional and personal lives; the difficulties of negotiating the best medical options, arranging health care aides, deciphering insurance details, and so on. Not wanting to feel like a burden, Gross's mother resisted her slide into dependency even when the trajectory of her weakening health was clearly irreversible. By the end of her life, she was paralyzed, incontinent, unable to speak, barely able to swallow, and wanting nothing more than a way to die with dignity. From Gross's mother's perspective, "we live too long and die too slowly."[34]

As middle-aged children struggle with the practical and existential challenges of caring for elderly parents, scientists and government officials commonly describe the aging of the population as a *crisis*. One professor of medicine refers to it as "a pandemic."[35] In the United States, such rhetoric reflects concerns that our health care system is woefully ill-equipped to serve the diverse needs of the escalating number of older bodies, while the Social Security Trust Fund is currently headed for bankruptcy.[36] Indeed, getting old has become increasingly unaffordable: while the median annual income for people over 80 is roughly $15,000, the average cost of room/board in assisted living residences is over $43,000 per year, and the price of a semi-private nursing home bed is over $80,000.[37] As hospice volunteer and author of *The Good Death*, Ann Neumann, observes, "Entire life savings are being spent on nursing homes, medications, medical equipment, and home health aides. And that's the families lucky enough to have savings."[38]

As a society, we face unprecedented challenges as we confront the political, economic, and medical implications of an aging population, not to mention the psychological and spiritual hardships that often diminish older people's well-being (e.g. loneliness, depression, anxiety, loss of a sense of purpose and worth). But when concerns about this demographic trend do not take into account the broad, structural injustices that make older persons (especially female, low-income, or minority seniors) physically, socially, financially, and psychically vulnerable, they foster stereotypes of the elderly as unproductive burdens who use too many societal resources.[39] Moreover, using terms like "pandemic" to describe the aging of the population suggests that growing old is a disease that needs to be contained or cured. Actually, this view is not uncommon in the field of medicine.

Biomedical approaches to aging

Since the nineteenth century, when trained physicians began managing the health of a growing portion of the population in the West, the transformations that happen in older bodies have come to be understood as medical conditions, indicative of pathology and needing treatment.[40] For example, some doctors still see menopause (the time in a woman's life when hormonal changes lead to the cessation of menstruation) as a diseased state—a view that presumes a younger, pre-menopausal female body as the standard/healthy ideal for women.[41]

To understand how younger bodies provide the unstated norm in traditional biomedical approaches to aging, consider the section on "The Aging Breast" in a book by a medical professor. The discussion focuses on *ptosis*, "the medical term for drooping or sagging female breasts." The author describes ptosis as a natural result of aging, but notes that "in cases of more successful aging…there is less sagging and nipples remain above the fold and projecting forward." According to the author, the only remedy for less successfully aging breasts is cosmetic reconstructive surgery. For two pages, he details the causes, categories, and cure for sagging breasts, without mentioning older women's higher susceptibility to breast cancer. In fact, the single paragraph devoted to breast cancer discusses the less common incidence of this disease in men.[42] Now, I doubt that this author intentionally prioritized aesthetic over health concerns among elderly women. But his hyper-attention to ptosis, his inattention to breast cancer in older women, and his definition of "successful" aging in breasts assume a younger female body as the normative ideal and imply that the metamorphoses that typically happen in mature women's breasts are unhealthy. It's also noteworthy that there's no parallel attention to drooping penises in this book's preceding discussion of men's aging reproductive system.

The quest for medical immortality

Geriatric doctors are much less inclined to view the physiological process of aging as pathological. But certified geriatricians are increasingly hard to come by in the United States, where many medical students are opting for higher-paying specialties in which they are less likely to confront the litany of "unfixables" that elders' bodies present.[43]

In fact, the number of doctors gravitating to a relatively new specialization called "anti-aging medicine" is swelling—from about 17,000 in 2008 to 26,000 in 2014.[44] These physicians advocate technologies and remedies that "retard and optimize the human aging process." According to the American Academy of Anti-Aging Medicine (A4M) website, "Aging is NOT inevitable—Together we can END AGING in our own lifespan."[45] Anti-aging doctors' faith in the fantasy of eternal youth includes attention to diet and exercise and often involves costly hormone treatments to boost patients' energy, libido, and weight loss. Collaborating with biotech corporations and rejuvenation clinics around the globe, anti-aging medicine has become an $88 billion-a-year business. Early promoters advertised its miracles in the *Robb Report*, a magazine for millionaires. In *Selling the Fountain of Youth*, journalist Arlene Weintraub exposes the commercial interests that drive anti-aging medicine, and the ethical violations of some of its founders, who have been convicted of negligence, incompetence, improper prescribing, and tax evasion.[46]

Despite its scientific orientation, anti-aging medicine embodies a kind of "immortality narrative," which philosopher Stephen Cave describes as the quest to stay alive indefinitely by discovering the "elixir that will defeat disease and debility for good." In this quest, aging and death are solvable problems, not nonnegotiable limits. As mythical as it sounds, the pursuit of "medical immortality" (immunity to aging and disease) reflects science's long-standing goal of deciphering and mastering the powers of decay and death. According to Cave, Descartes—one of the founding fathers of the scientific method— "talked openly of seeking knowledge that would 'render ourselves the lords and possessors of nature,'" and he was preoccupied with extending life.[47] In fact, it was Descartes' desire to prove the immortality of the soul—i.e. that individuals outlived the demise of their biodegradable flesh—that led him to view the mind and body as separate entities. From the perspective of modern science, a discipline dedicated to understanding and controlling the physical universe, the human body's propensity to grow old and die is the epitome of failure.

The view of aging as a pathological process that requires pharmaceutical, surgical, or technological interventions reflects the same biomedical paradigm that pathologize disability and "obesity" and that understands chronic pain and illness as avoidable maladies. Assuming a young, nondisabled, disease-free physique as the normative ideal, and treating bodies as objects in isolation from their minds, environments, and relationships with others, this approach construes aging as a physiological process of deterioration individuals undergo in the privacy of their own skin under the authoritative care of medical experts. In this model, an elder's body is like my old, rusty Subaru—visibly worn, weathered, and weakened by time and miles—and the physician is a mechanic who tries to reverse, repair, or at least limit the damage.[48]

Problems with prolonging life indefinitely

In *Being Mortal*, physician Atul Gawande reflects on this paradigm's merits and limits:

> I am in a profession that has succeeded because of its ability to fix. If your problem is fixable, we know just what to do. But if it's not? The fact that we have had no adequate answers to this question is troubling and has caused callousness, inhumanity, and extraordinary suffering.[49]

Susan Moon witnessed this suffering when a breathing tube was forced down her 84-year-old mother's throat in an attempt to prolong her life following surgery to remove her ruptured spleen.

> It was clear she wanted to be unhooked. Her wrists were tethered to the bed rails to keep her from pulling out the breathing tube, but she kept raising an agitated hand in the direction of her mouth. A plastic clamp was wrapped around her face to hold the tube in place; it was tight across her upper lip below her nose, and the pink flesh of her lip swelled out beneath it like a bubble.

Moon and her siblings questioned the wisdom of keeping their mother miserably tethered to the oxygen machine; but a doctor persuaded them that such measures *could* help her stay alive. With no evidence to the contrary, the adult children helplessly stood around their mother's hospital bed, singing to her and hoping they would know if/when it was time to surrender.[50]

Doctors' efforts to stop at nothing to prolong life reflect the standard training most received in medical school, where, as Muriel Gillick writes in *The Denial of Aging*, students learn that "death is the enemy" and that the goal of medicine is to thwart this adversary. We can appreciate this goal when medical intervention saves or extends the lives of those we love. Too often, however, the mission to defy death prompts physicians "to summon the heavy artillery," to "keep on fighting" even when the battle is futile and overtreatment intensifies patients' suffering.[51] Sometimes, patients themselves urge doctors on in their war against death. But more often, it's family members who are unable to let go. In essence, many doctors, patients, and their families find it difficult to accept mortality. Gawande observes:

> Being mortal is about the struggle to cope with the constraints of our biology, with the limits set by genes and cells and flesh and bone. Medical science has given us remarkable power to push against these limits. [But]

I have seen the damage we in medicine do when we fail to acknowledge that such power is finite and always will be.[52]

Besides exacerbating the suffering they aim to alleviate, medical practices that deny mortality are expensive. In 2008, Medicare spent over $50 billion trying to keep intensive care patients alive during the last two months of their lives.[53]

The Tithonus dilemma

Despite their undeniable benefits, advances in medical knowledge and technology have created a Tithonus dilemma. In Greek mythology, Tithonus is the handsome young mortal with whom the goddess Eos falls in love. Aflame with passion, Eos can't stand the idea of Tithonus growing old and dying, and so she begs Zeus to make him immortal like herself—but she forgets to ask that her lover also be granted eternal youth. Thus Tithonus grows older and weaker without ever dying—a fate so miserable that, out of compassion, Eos finally turns him into a cicada.[54] As this story suggests, delaying death creates problems when the physical afflictions that create suffering in old age are not disappearing.[55]

In the trenches, physicians who treat elderly bodies regularly confront the harrowing question of when "to fiddle and fix" and when "to accept that the battle is lost." Older patients and their families often face the impossible decision of whether to risk sacrificing the quality of life now in exchange for the nebulous possibility of more time later.[56] In the absence of a neat and tidy mathematical formula for resolving these issues, Gawande advocates having difficult, sensitive, candid conversations about mortality *before* elders reach their final hours, while they are still able to articulate what matters most to them. Such discussions may not prolong patients' life spans. But they can enable those at the sunset of their lives to experience the dignity of determining their meaning—to narrate their own stories even if they can't dictate the ending or control the outcome.[57] Such conversations may also help elderly persons and their loved ones resist that ever-so-seductive response to aging the culture of physical improvement encourages: denial.

Manifestations and roots of denial

When it comes to getting old, Gross writes, "denial [is]...the widespread notion that our parents, and by extension ourselves, will beat the odds, play tennis at eighty or ninety, and then drop dead with no fuss and bother." She attributes such denial to the mainstream media, whose stories of happy aging—i.e. centenarians getting married, elderly people climbing mountains and running marathons, nursing homes encouraging consensual sex between residents—obscure the arduous realities of growing old and caring for elders.[58] Some AARP (American Association of Retired Persons) literature promotes a corollary fantasy of retirement as a kind of "extended vacation"—a time for personal gratification spent wining and dining and cruising the globe. While such uplifting images challenge negative stereotypes of seniors, they celebrate a very specific vision of old age—one characterized by financial security and the absence of physical/mental debility.[59]

Taken together, the popular media's reluctance to recount the difficulties of growing old and the scientific quest to cure senescence foster our collective delusion that we, and the people we love, will remain able-bodied, self-sufficient, and healthy right up to our dying day. But the roots of our denial may run even deeper, drawing on traditional religious narratives in which the meaning of old age is ambiguous, but the overriding trajectory aims at the triumph over death and the corollary promise of eternal life in a body that never changes.

Christian narratives on immortality and aging

We have seen how biblical narratives generally associate old age with wisdom, righteousness, spiritual maturity, and leadership (especially in men). Yet on the whole, the Christian Scriptures say relatively little about the *process* of aging per se, probably because the New Testament authors believed the world was coming to an end, and this expectation would have overshadowed concerns about growing old. Moreover, aging was not necessarily the biggest threat to life since people in the ancient world regularly died in their youth. For early Christians, the problem wasn't aging. The problem was death.[60]

Mortality as the "enemy" and salvation as "victory" over death

The most influential early church leader, the apostle Paul, was not so much preoccupied with preventing death (something Jesus chose not to do) as he was interested in understanding its meaning. In his letters to fellow Christians, Paul interprets mortality as the ultimate punishment for sin, the final payback ("wages") for the evil humans are prone to do left to their own devices (Romans 6:23). For Paul, death was the "final enemy" that needed to be destroyed (I Cor. 15:26), and this is precisely what Christ accomplished by dying and rising.

Jesus' resurrection signaled God's victory over mortality and sin and paved the way for his followers to be raised from the dead at the end of time. In this narrative, death is evil, but mortality is optional, since eternal life is possible for those who trust God's promise of redemption. For Paul, this redemption includes the body. In the final Resurrection, the broken, earthly, *corruptible* flesh of the faithful departed will be gloriously transfigured into spiritually *incorruptible* bodies—bodies that never decay or die (I Cor. 15:53).

Contemporary Christians may not be accustomed to thinking about the story of Jesus' death and resurrection as an immortality myth. Today, "myth" often has the connotation of "false." But in the ancient world, myths were stories that revealed a larger, archetypal truth, and they were not intended to be taken literally. During the first centuries of the Common Era, the mythic story of a divine figure who dies and rises was hardly unique to Christianity.[61] But the claim that the decomposing flesh of corpses could be revived, reconstituted, and perfected into imperishable bodies was surprising. Historian Margaret Miles points out that in the Greco-Roman world in which Christianity emerged, "[t]he Greek word for body (*so sōma*) was used as a synonym for slave (*ho doulos*)," an equivalency that underscores the low status of physicality (and people associated with physicality) in that context.[62] Thus, despite Paul's negative view of human bodies' perishable propensities, his teaching on bodily resurrection represented a countercultural affirmation of the flesh. Corporeality was such an integral part of his understanding of the human condition that he couldn't imagine eternal life without it. Significantly, Paul spoke of the redemption *of* the body, not *from* the body (Romans 8:23). For him, mortal flesh was not just a problem, but an opportunity.

"Imperishable bodies": Excluding old flesh from heaven

Despite this ambiguity, however, Paul's depiction of resurrected bodies as *imperishable* laid the ground for an eschatological narrative that linked anti-dying to anti-aging. In the fourth century, Augustine characterizes the perfection of heavenly bodies as restored to—and frozen in—the "prime" of their lives. Even if you were very old when you died and your flesh was weak and shriveled, your resurrected body will be young, radiant, and fit for paradise. Specifically, your celestial physique will be the "perfect age" of Christ: "about thirty." According to Augustine, "the bodies of the dead will rise neither younger nor older than Christ. They will be of the same age [as Christ], the same prime of life."[63] Early and Medieval theologians also imagined that Adam and Eve were created at this perfect age.[64]

By linking immortality to eternal youth, Augustine solves the Tithonus problem. But in so doing, he establishes the nondiseased, nondisabled, young adult physique as the spiritual/normative ideal—an ideal that excludes from paradise bodies that have begun, in Augustine's words, their "downhill" descent "towards middle age and senility."[65] Implicitly, Augustine's eschatological vision diverges from the Christian narrative that associates old age with authority and virtue by depicting elderly flesh as needing redemption.

By the late Middle Ages, Christianity's association between sin and mortality lent support to more disparaging views of bodies that were visibly closer to death. Although some pastoral theologians depicted old age as an ideal time to prepare for the final judgment by performing good works and doing penance, many church leaders characterized this stage of life as a time of loss and misery. For example, in *On the Wretchedness of the Human Condition*, the future Pope Innocent III (d. 1216) lamented the bodily and moral decline that accumulates with years: the rotting teeth, foggy vision, weakness of heart, and bodily pain, along with greed, depression, irritability, and anxiousness.[66] The torments associated with old age led both the philosopher/theologian, Thomas Aquinas (d. 1274), and the poet/statesman, Dante Alighieri (d. 1321), to surmise that Christ chose to die in the "prime" of his life because it would have been unfitting for his divinity to be manifest in feeble flesh.[67]

Church leaders' depictions of death and aging do not tell us how all (or even most) Christians actually experienced the process of growing old, but they do give us a glimpse of some prominent beliefs about aging that shaped social arrangements and perceptions of older/younger bodies. The concrete effects of these "master narratives" become clear when we consider a popular late medieval treatise called *Women's Secrets*. Intended to teach celibate monks about such delicate matters as human reproduction, this text traces women's immoral tendencies to their inferior, sin-prone bodies.[68] For example, it characterizes menstrual blood as unclean and possessing pernicious power, and suggests that older/postmenopausal women, who are "incapable of eliminating the superfluous matter," are dangerous because "[t]he retention of menses engenders many evil humours." Elderly women who are poor, "who live on nothing but coarse meat," are said to be especially "venomous." Given the intersection of misogyny, ageism, and classism that this widely circulated text promoted, it's not hard to imagine why the majority of those identified and killed as "witches" in the following centuries were poor, old, and female.[69]

Echoes of immortality and everlasting youth

This late medieval example of the denigration of older female bodies represents one of several competing narratives about aging in Christian history. Such narratives do not form a single, unified story about the virtues or vices of older bodies, but a complex picture in which the meaning of old age is ambiguous. Despite this ambiguity, however, associations between finitude and sin, impermanence and impurity, death and evil made age-prone, mortal bodies spiritually suspect in the eyes of church leaders, who solved this problem by making bodily imperishability part of God's plan for eternal salvation. Thus while Christianity's narrative of incorruptible bodies in the resurrection affirms the value of physicality, this storyline also links anti-aging and anti-dying by idealizing flesh that never changes.

The teaching of the bodily resurrection is so central to Christianity that it achieved the status of doctrine early in the church's history. Millions of Christians continue to affirm it today when they recite the end of the Nicene Creed: "…we look for the resurrection of the dead, and the life of the world to come." Yet many contemporary Christians are only vaguely aware of the centrality of this doctrine in their tradition. In the United States, where Christians comprise roughly 70 percent of the population, only 30 percent of those surveyed said they believe their dead bodies will be resurrected at the end of time.[70] The gap between official teaching and popular belief about bodily resurrection is not terribly surprising given the prominence of the scientific worldview in societies like the United States. What is very interesting is the extent to which parts of Christianity's immortality narrative echo in the secular crusade to defy the powers of death and aging.

Commercial culture's veneration of youthful bodies

Elements of this story reverberate not only in the longevity pursuits of anti-aging scientists, but also in the commercially propelled quest to fight, conquer, and—if all else fails—conceal the effects of aging. The anti-aging images, beliefs, rituals, and moral codes that permeate popular culture recycle and modify elements of Christianity's classic narratives—particularly the eschatological vision of perfect bodies that never grow old, and the view of change-prone female flesh as especially needing redemption.

Insufficient femininity

Usually, the message that older female bodies are unattractive/unredeemed is not expressed explicitly. You don't see many advertisements blatantly stating that gray hair and wrinkles are ugly. What you see are commercials for products to help women hide their gray hair and wrinkles—presumably because these visible signs of transience are less than lovely, and maybe even shameful. You also see—albeit, perhaps without noticing—that over 70 percent of females on American television are under 30 (while 1.5 percent of TV characters are elderly),[71] and that nearly all feminine icons of commercial culture (i.e. models, celebrities, movie stars) are somatically juvenile. The message that older women's physiques are undesirable need not be stated explicitly for its meaning to be abundantly clear.

Such bodies commit the same corporeal sin of insubordination as the nonconforming flesh of females who are disabled, fat, or chronically sick: they are insufficiently feminine by dominant cultural norms. Anthropologist Margo DeMello notes that in the West, many standard characteristics of feminine beauty "are actually just signs of youth: large eyes, puffy red lips, pink cheeks, thick hair, and clear skin are all indicators of youth in girls"[72] (Figure 8.4). One might add to this list: inflated breasts, lean legs, flat stomachs, and able-bodiedness—all of which are more common (though far from universal) in younger female bodies. Youth-oriented fantasies of femininity are circulated by TV, magazine, and online commercials for products that promise to camouflage or contain evidence of the body's impermanence. The cumulative

FIGURE 8.4 *Portrait of a young/smooth female face © Nadya Lukic.*
Source: Getty Images.

message from these ads' rhetoric and images is that a soft, glowing, wrinkle-free appearance is essential for feminine health and beauty. Rather than interrogate this message, many of us learn to resent our bodies for aging—as if by getting older our flesh were somehow betraying or failing us. Through repeated exposure to the salvation myth of eternal youth, many women come to see the manifestations of time on their bodies as not only "unfeminine," but repulsive.

The cost of radiance: Class dimensions of (anti)aging

The shame many women feel about their aging flesh explains why some are willing to spend a fortune in order to look younger. In *I See You Made an Effort*, comedian Annabelle Gurwitch uses humor to expose the absurdity of this exchange. She tells a story of buying concealer to hide the traces of aging on her then 49-year-old face. This concealer "not only promises to restore the under-eye area to a refreshing brightness, but dotted across my chin, it will serve to cover the stray broken capillaries and little bumps that I am loath to admit are, in fact, hair follicles." At the store, Gurwitch locates "the least intimidatingly attractive salesperson" and gives her the name, number, and manufacturer of the product, which she has written down so as not to purchase the wrong shade. As the salesclerk surveys the information, Gurwitch silently reminds herself to "stick to the list." The concealer is ridiculously expensive—$120 an ounce—and she doesn't want to let the saleswoman talk her into buying additional products she doesn't *really need*. As she's waiting, Gurwitch briefly reflects on the economic inequalities around the globe, and on her own precarious financial future. Silently acknowledging that her struggle to look younger is a "first world problem," she hands her credit card to the salesperson, who by then has convinced her to spend an additional 50 dollars on a fruit exfoliant that will make her skin glow. Leaving the store, Gurwitch realizes that "age gifts you with invisibility in all but monetary transactions."[73]

Gurwitch's story exposes the class dimensions of middle- and upper-class women's anti-aging efforts. Looking youthful when you're not is an expensive, time-consuming undertaking—requiring more resources than many low-income and minority elders can afford. In *A Different Shade of Gray*, Katherine Newman demonstrates how the experience of growing old in America differs dramatically, depending on whether you are white or a person of color, middle-class or poor, living in a suburb or the inner city. Based on the lives of older African-Americans and Latinos/Latinas in New York City, her study shows how ageism intersects with racism and poverty in ways that lead to premature aging.[74]

Anti-aging industries help sustain this matrix of inequalities, exploiting the very shame about aging they encourage women to feel by suggesting that growing old is both dreadful and optional. In addition to pricey skin creams, make-up, and hair dyes, there are expensive nutritional supplements, diet plans, and drug therapies to rescue older female bodies from impending doom. For those who can afford them, there are also age-defying surgical procedures, including face-, brow-, and eyelid lifts, laser resurfacing, fat transfers, cheek tightening, lip enlargements, Botox and collagen injections.[75] During the past few decades, the business of creating imperishable-looking bodies has become enormously profitable, with global sales for youth-perpetuating products and services increasing from $162 billion in 2009 to $261.9 billion in 2013. Botulinum treatments alone skyrocketed 680 percent between 2000 and 2012 (Figure 8.5).[76]

The reality that none of the products or rituals designed to mask the marks of time can stop or reverse the body's senescence underscores the crucial role denial and delusion play in commercial culture's reinvention of Christianity's myths of immortality and eternal youth. The fuzzy lines between denial and hope, delusion and faith are evident in the "philosophy" of "Hope in a Jar," an anti-aging skin cream whose container reads: "where there is hope there can be faith. where there is faith miracles can occur." Among the miracles

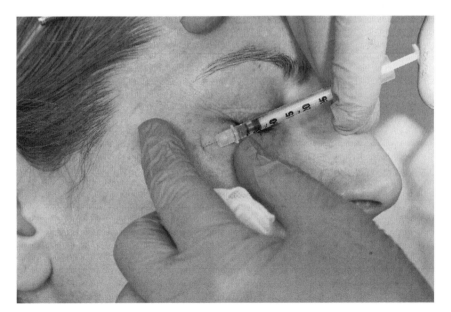

FIGURE 8.5 *Botox injection* © *Isa Foltin.*
Source: Getty Images.

this moisturizer performs: skin rejuvenation that leads to a healthier, more radiant appearance.[77] The quasi-religious language used to market this youth-restoring elixir suggests that advertisers recognize the more-than-physical stakes in women's age-fighting efforts. Given the proximity between death and aging, something as seemingly trivial as anti-aging skin cream can have existential significance.[78]

"Why is Hillary using a walker?"

Cultivating a fresh, energetic, younger-looking appearance can also be a way for senior women to stay relevant and wield power in the public sphere. The political perils of female aging are evident in the social media hype over the June 2014 cover of *People* magazine, which featured a smiling Hillary Clinton. To view this image, go to the link at http://www.bloomsbury.com/uk/shameful-bodies-9781472594945/ and look under "Chapter Eight."

At that time, Clinton was undecided about whether to run for president. Nonetheless, the photo became an opportunity for critics to express concerns about her capacity to serve in the highest office. The picture showed the former Secretary of State, Senator, and First Lady standing in her backyard with her hands resting on…something—the object was unidentifiable because of how the picture was cropped. The conservative news site, *The Drudge Report*, was among the first to Tweet the question—"Is Clinton holding a walker?"

This query elicited multiple responses. The editorial director of *People* clarified that the object in question was just a patio chair. A former White House photographer explained the artistic challenge of what to do with a subject's hands when shooting a full-length portrait. Still, a right-wing commentator persisted: "It DOES look like she's using a walker." Such comments played into some people's preexisting skepticism about Clinton's fitness for the role of president because of her age. While supporters advised Clinton to *lean in*[§]—not *on*—as she pursued the path to the White House, political opponents pointed out that, if elected, she would be 69 on Inauguration Day.[79] Never mind that former president Ronald Reagan was pushing 70 when he was sworn in.

Gender, aging, and (in)visibility

This example illustrates the residual effects of traditional religious associations between male seniority and public authority, coupled with women's historical association with physicality and corresponding exclusion from public

---

[§] This was a reference to the popular feminist text *Lean In: Women, Work, and the Will to Lead* (New York: Alfred A. Knopf, 2013), by Facebook's COO, Sheryl Sandberg.

leadership. From the time they are young, most females are still socialized to cultivate their power and worth by making their bodies resemble the feminine ideal. As they grow old, their bodies' refusal to conform to this fantasy diminishes women's value—both in their own estimation and in the eyes of others. Conversely, men's historic association with rationality, mind, and spirit has largely spared them from needing to find meaning and prove their worth by staying eternally youthful.

This is not to say men are immune to the pressure to look and feel younger than they really are. While economically and racially privileged males in the West gain authority as they move through middle age, there are limits to this trajectory. It's not the signs of transience on the body's surface that present the biggest existential threats to men's identity and worth, it's the loss of virility stereotypically associated with manhood and expressed through sexual prowess. According to DeMello, this is why erectile dysfunction can be so terrifying: the loss of sexual potency signals a loss of the social power, control, and self-determination traditionally associated with masculinity. Thus ads for erectile dysfunction drugs (e.g. Viagra, Cialis) frequently feature healthy-, confident-looking men who are mature in age (but not too old), surrounded by markers of masculinity: sports, cars, alcohol, and (of course) adoring, conventionally attractive, younger-looking women.[80]

In *This is Getting Old*, Susan Moon recounts several stories that illustrate how sexism and ageism intersect in gender double standards for maturing bodies. These stories highlight how aging invisibilizes women. At a planning meeting, a male coworker reiterated a suggestion Moon had made, but credited it to another male colleague, who also happened to be in his sixties. "Is it just my imagination," Moon wonders, "or did my words carry more weight when I was younger and prettier?" Later, at a conference for Buddhist teachers, a gray-haired man shared his observation with Moon (whose hair was also gray) that there were far more gray-haired men than women at the gathering, even though participants of both genders were roughly the same age. The man couldn't fathom why Buddhist women—particularly those who were teachers—would color their hair. Why, he asked, wouldn't a Buddhist woman want to practice accepting her body as it is? Moon explained that "[i]t's not so much that *she* doesn't accept herself as she is but that others don't. It's the invisibility factor." When you're female, "[g]ray hair shrouds you in fog, and you want to shout, 'I'm still here! I still have a physical body! I still have ideas in my head!'"[81]

Deliberations and complicity questions

Moon's story hits home, as I deliberate whether or not to color my rapidly graying hair. Intellectually, I know there's nothing intrinsically unbecoming about gray hair. Still, I can't help but notice how lovely my female colleagues' professional color jobs look. Some wise part of me realizes that my worth isn't contingent on my appearance, that I'm in my fifties, and—darn it!—I've earned the right to have gray hair! But sometimes this audacious wisdom has to contend with a more socially compliant inner voice that says: "You really should make more of an effort if you want your students, your kids, and the world to take you seriously." Then I remember: this is the world I want to change—a world that invisibilizes women as they age! And how can I encourage others to deconstruct our culture's disparaging views of older female bodies if I can't do this for myself?

As I probe these questions and conflicting voices, I find myself agreeing with Moon's conclusion that women's efforts to camouflage their gray hair and wrinkles can be seen as attempts to stay relevant in a culture that projects its fears of aging and death onto the very flesh that is capable of bringing forth new life. From this perspective, "Getting a facelift could be less an act of counterfeiting than an attempt—however futile—to be real, to tear away the veil that society projects onto our faces."[82] In fact, some scholarship suggests that older women's beauty rituals can function as resistance to the invisibility they experience in a sexist/ageist culture.[83] But even as I empathize with women who feel compelled to preserve their power by erasing the passage of time from their bodies, I worry that we collude with our own oppression when we buy into the notion that in order to be valued and visible, mature women must appear younger than we are. Moreover, I wonder: what are the unintended, hidden consequences of this potential complicity for women who are not protected by the privileges of being white, able-bodied, and affluent?

The issues get even more complex when we critically interrogate the varying levels and forms of complicity of which we are capable. Am I consenting to our culture's denigration of elderly flesh when I use face cream that claims to have "anti-aging" properties? What if I use the cream, but not with the *intention* of looking youthful? Or, what if I opt to have Botox injected into the crevices of my wrinkles because I feel more confident when I look younger? Does that make me complicit with the ageism/sexism I consciously reject? What if I simply entertain the *idea* of having Botox injections, imagining how nice it would be to fill in a few facial furrows, without actually going through with the procedure? Am I guilty by desire of unwittingly perpetuating the social/symbolic hierarchies that privilege some bodies at the expense of others?

I raise these queries not with the aim of finding unambiguous answers, but in the hopes of stirring conversations among women of various ages, colors, classes, cultures, sizes, and (dis)abilities. Only if a diversity of women deliberates these questions can they generate practical wisdom. And only if these deliberations take into account the intersecting forms of oppression (e.g. racism, classism, ableism, homophobia, sexism, religious bigotry, sizeism, ageism) that variously harm women will this wisdom be applicable to more than a privileged few. Instead of discovering definitive, universal answers, the aim of such a conversation would be *deinternalizing* the shame assigned to older female flesh, and exploring the dread of dying that lurks beneath our culture's aversion to aging.

Self-help strategies for denying aging

It's difficult for women to recognize and wrestle with the fear that links anti-aging to anti-dying when best-selling authors promise that we are not doomed to grow "old," that we can control and prevent aging with a positive outlook, behavioral changes, and joyous living. This is Christiane Northrup's claim in *Goddesses Never Age*, a book that secularizes/updates Christianity's myth of incorruptible bodies by incorporating the modern belief that individuals are masters of their fate. "The real fountain of youth is the fountain of happiness," Northrup declares. Her "principles of ageless living" and "14-day Ageless Goddess Program" are designed to help women tap this reservoir so they can look and feel powerful and fabulous at any age.[84]

Northrup is a certified physician. But as a best-selling author and woman's health guru, her language often sounds more mythical than medical: "you have the power to be an ageless goddess...to be a living, breathing embodiment of joyful, ageless living."[85] In Northrup's lexicon, "ageless" means "to never grow 'old'—to never feel as if the best days of your life are behind you." The book's chapters elaborate the qualities of ageless/goddess women— e.g. "Goddesses Know the Power of Pleasure," "Goddesses Are Sexy and Sensual," "Goddesses Move Joyously," "Goddesses are Gorgeous." With this celebratory, mythic rhetoric, Northrup reclaims menopause as a time when "your creative juices are flowing!" The secret to harnessing this energy—and avoiding the fate of women who spend their last days tethered to an oxygen tank—is choosing the right attitude and lifestyle.[86]

Getting older "without deteriorating" is possible because "the state of our health is dictated far more by our beliefs than our biology." To cultivate youth-preserving convictions, Northrup recommends self-affirmations, e.g. "*I am eternally youthful and vibrant*," "*I am a goddess of divine pleasure, beauty, and passion.*"[87] She also encourages meditation as method for sustaining youth— ironically so, since, traditionally at least, meditation is the practice of letting go of attachments (e.g. looking/feeling younger), not striving to obtain them. Northrup's mind-over-matter method for cultivating everlasting youth mixes New Age spirituality with Cartesian individualism to situate her female reader "at a crossroads" where she must decide: "are you going to grow older with gusto or deteriorate with age?"[88]

We have seen the problems with framing good health as a personal choice and achievement—not the least of which is this framework's tendency to downplay how factors like wealth or poverty influence well-being. This tendency is evident in Northrup's advice to elderly women to "always refuse the senior discount because it just reinforces the false belief that you're growing older and more frail, that you can't work and need to be taken care of by others."[89] However well-intended, I wonder what this recommendation implies for senior women who are struggling to make ends meet, or who must rely on others for physical care. Are these women (and their bodies) failures? Are their age-related struggles the result of—or punishment for—a bad attitude, faulty belief, lack of willpower, or insufficient joy? Surely impoverished female elders are just as "entitled" (Northrup's word) to the rewards of ageless living—"Vibrant good health," "A fulfilling sex life," "Clarity and authenticity in…relationships"—as the aging "Alpha goddesses" who are getting massages, spending weekends at resorts, and insisting that "this is my time" to stop worrying about everybody else and start nurturing myself.[90]

Northrup's celebration of mature women as immortal goddesses aims to empower readers by challenging stereotypes of old age as a time of physical debility and cultural irrelevance for females. But the liberating potential of her message is undercut by a disturbing disregard for women whose age-related hardships are shaped by the not-so-ethereal assaults of poverty, ableism, and other systemic injustices. Interestingly, this disregard did not stop *Goddesses Never Age* from becoming an Amazon.com "best seller" in early 2016. Perhaps this popularity is not surprising given how much this book tells us what we want to hear: age-related suffering can be avoided. Northrup even admits that she "didn't want to write a health book for women that would scare them about growing older."[91] While fearing aging is hardly helpful, we need to ask: Who benefits when the narratives that shape our feelings about getting older deliver what is, at best, a partial truth? What is the price of our collective denial of the other truths about elderly bodies, namely, that they are irreducibly diverse, vulnerable, change-prone, and mortal?

When body/mind disintegrates

The shortcomings of Northrup's mind-over-matter approach to aging become clear in the experiences of people with Alzheimer's, a brain disease that causes loss of memory, cognitive disorientation, physical debility, personality changes, and eventually death. Alzheimer's exposes the error of Descartes' dualism by illustrating how our sense of self is deeply rooted in a particular bodily organ: the brain. Although this disease occurs most often in people over 65, it can develop sooner, as Thomas DeBaggio's story illustrates.

DeBaggio was diagnosed with early-onset Alzheimer's just before his 58th birthday. In *Losing My Mind*, he refuses to sugarcoat his experience of accelerated atrophy—of being "forced into old age against [his] will." Alzheimer's is "the closest thing to being eaten alive slowly," DeBaggio observes.[92] Gradually, the disease consumes his memory and ability to think clearly. "Ideas evaporate like snowflakes on a warm roof…my mind is drifting out of control. I have to wait like a hunter to capture a thought." Even writing the sentences to tell his tale is a grueling labor: "At any moment I may lose my train of thought and end up losing another neurotransmitter and the story that went with it."[93] By the end of the book, some words have missing letters, and several incidents are repeated. Still, most readers can only imagine what it's like to lose the very things our society defines as essential for human happiness, health, and virtue: a well-ordered mind and body.

For DeBaggio, the devastation of Alzheimer's unearths both regrets and lingering ambitions. He wishes he had worked less and had more fun, but money was always an issue. In fact, financial anxieties prompted DeBaggio to forego his dream of becoming a writer. Ironically, Alzheimer's frees him— albeit tentatively—to not only pursue his love of words, but to do something remarkable with what he regrettably describes as an otherwise "ordinary" life: to tell the truth about what it's like when your mind/brain disintegrate.[94]

In DeBaggio's account, this truth includes both a "sense of struggle and joy."[95] The combination of these seemingly incompatible feelings is most apparent in his effort to resist the shame assigned by a culture that worships at the altar of self-control. Immediately following his diagnosis, DeBaggio contemplates suicide. "I was facing a difficult, slow decline, leading to eventual loss of nearly everything human beings value, ending finally as a near-vegetable rotting in the sun." He decides against taking his own life, but struggles with embarrassment over his increasing debility. He's too ashamed to ask for help at a printing store when he can't remember how the copy machine works. "It was the first time I felt old, decrepit, and utterly useless."[96] Despite his desperation, however, DeBaggio carries on with his truth-telling mission, hoping "to break through the sense of shame and silence Alzheimer's has engendered." The liberation he experiences is not a triumph over the "nakedness" of his "sense of inadequacy, fear, and failure," but a reluctant embrace of that sense of vulnerability—an embrace sometimes aided by the forgetfulness Alzheimer's imposes: "It's hard to be embarrassed when you can't remember who you are, what you said, or where you are going."[97]

Alzheimer's raises questions that are relevant for persons of any age: Who are you if your brain malfunctions to the point where you can't remember who you are? How crucial are memory and orderly thought to your identity and worth as a person? According to whom? Why does aging erode brain/body functioning more in some than others? How do we—or should we—respond to bodies/minds that refuse to become "ageless?" Hopefully, we won't wait until we are old to explore such questions. For these questions can help us craft a different narrative of aging, one that enables us to welcome—rather than fear—the prospect of growing older.

Reimagining aging

The staggering popularity and profitability of the quest to vanquish the powers of aging and defy the gravity of the grave tell us something about our hunger for beliefs and rituals with which to deal with the transitory nature of our bodies and lives. Functionally, secular myths of immortality and everlasting youth resemble the religious narratives that have guided humans for millennia, proffering comfort, direction, and inspiration in the face of change, uncertainty, and finitude. The problem is not that we create and believe in stories to help us cope with our fears of aging and death. The problem happens when, in our effort to avoid adversity, the stories we tell ourselves—and the norms, expectations, and ideals they generate—put us at war with the impermanence, diversity, and vulnerability of embodied life.

What might an alternative narrative of aging look like? Instead of endorsing the salvation myths of immortality and perpetual youth, it would encourage us to work to alleviate the suffering many elders face and learn from the wisdom their long lives offer. This narrative would challenge stereotypes of older persons as decrepit, uninteresting, and unproductive by highlighting their diversity, complexity, and ingenuity, and by emphasizing the social justice dimensions of aging. Neither romanticizing nor demonizing society's elders, this narrative's perspective, images, and storyline would show and tell the truth(s) about aging flesh, honestly revealing the opportunities and limits that a finite future creates. Within this alternative narrative, the bodies/spirits of elders are resources for the self-examination and prophetic critique our society badly needs.

The diversity and complexity of aging

Reimagining aging requires us to recognize and respect older bodies' irreducible diversity. This diversity is apparent even among elders from very similar social, cultural, economic, and religious backgrounds. In *Aging with Grace*, David Snowdon describes the multiple ways and speeds with which aging affected the bodies and minds of 678 Catholic nuns, ages 74–108, whose common lifestyle made them ideal subjects for his research on Alzheimer's. Launched in 1986, Snowdon's "Nun Study" was one of the first to demonstrate that dementia "is not an inevitable consequence of aging."[98] While some elderly sisters developed Alzheimer's in their sixties, seventies, and eighties, others continued to thrive mentally and physically into their nineties and beyond. Snowdon's research revealed that multiple factors—e.g. heredity, childhood linguistic abilities, mental and physical health, diet and exercise, attitude and faith—influence brain/body functioning in old age. Though no longer groundbreaking, the Nun Study offers lingering lessons on how incredibly varied the aging process can be, even among a fairly homogenous group of elderly women.

This process is not only physiologically diverse, but psychologically complex. Some people enjoy getting older; some don't; and some are mixed. Those who have internalized ageism often experience their advanced years as a time of irredeemable loss. In *Coming into the End Zone*, Doris Grumbach paints a bleak picture of old age. For her, turning 70 feels "disastrous…without redeeming moments."[99] Yet the very honesty of Grumbach's despairing tone hints at the liberation many female elders feel: the freedom to stop pretending—to tell-it-like-it-is. In *Crones Don't Whine*, Jean Shinoda Bolen describes women's truth-telling as a path to wholeness in old age. After decades of wondering "Am I good enough or pretty enough?" mature women can stop striving for outer approval and start trusting the truth of their inner experience.[100] Along these lines, Gloria Steinem observed that women tend to become more radical with age, as they relinquish "the tyrannies of social expectation."[101] Even so, variables like health, financial status, and social support networks significantly determine whether aging feels onerous, liberating, or both. A 93-year-old female nursing home resident told Pipher: "When you get this old you have bad days, good days, and days you'd rather not be alive."[102]

Honoring the biodiversity and psychic complexity of the aging process is crucial for dismantling stereotypes about "old people." We don't challenge these stereotypes when we praise elders for being "young at heart" since such praise assumes that old is bad. "What's wrong with being old at heart…?" Moon asks. "Wouldn't you like to be loved by people whose hearts have practiced loving for a long time?"[103] Moon feels similarly annoyed when people try to counter stereotypes of seniors as lacking libido by insisting "old folks can have rich sex lives." It's not that elderly bodies can't enjoy erotic pleasure, Moon says, but when this possibility becomes a universal expectation, it feels oppressive. In the context of our hyper-sexualized culture, "It's hard for people to admit what they're *not* doing." Elders shouldn't have to feel ashamed if they're not having sex. "I claim the right to lose libido as I get older," Moon says. Still, she's not promising anything.[104]

Redemptive laughter

Moon's use of humor to unmask superficial clichés and question social expectations exemplifies the ingenious ways many older persons resist our culture's depreciation of their bodies. The biological, psychological, and social benefits of laughter have been well documented (e.g. laughing bolsters the immune system, relieves stress, and strengthens relationships). But, for elders, humor also often serves a political function as a tool for exposing/contesting ageism.[105]

Seniors' humor often playfully pokes fun at the changes in their bodies that put them at odds with our youth-adoring culture. Among the participants in Loe's study, a 93-year-old man named Glenn, who walks very slowly, wears a T-shirt that says "RETIRED: please go around me." An almost-90-year-old woman attributes her brutal honesty to the "decomposition of her frontal cortex." Ninety-one-year-old Eddie jokes that his exercise routine at the gym consists primarily of moving his jaw. When someone tells him he looks good, Eddie asks, "Compared to whom?" When someone else says, "Yeah, you look fresh and clean there Eddie," he replies, "I try to shower once a week whether I need it or not!" As he makes his way to the locker room, Eddie, who is bald, calls to his friend "I'd like to borrow your hair brush!"—to which his friend responds: "I brought hairspray for you too!"[106]

In *The Laughter of the Oppressed*, theologian Jacqueline Bussie argues that laughter can function as an ethical tool of resilience and resistance in the context of oppression. Her analysis suggests that subjugated peoples' ability to find humor in even the most disempowering situations interrupts the systems of domination and protects oppressed people from internalizing these systems' rules.[107] Seen in this light, a group of older women who laugh about hiding their "turkey necks" with turtlenecks and scarves are not endorsing—but exposing and even mocking—beauty norms that privilege sag-free flesh. To fully appreciate the ingenious ways elders use laughter to resist the shame directed at their slow, bald, or sagging bodies, we need to honor Glenn's request: "Please laugh with me and not at me."[108]

The social justice dimensions of aging

Neither the happy image of wealthy retirees living it up on golf courses, nor the pitiful picture of lonely, hunched-over elderly people languishing in nursing homes tells the whole truth about old age. The diversity and complexity of this truth is shaped by the multiple social variables that impact older people's lives. Simply put, you stand a better chance of living longer and healthier if you are white and middle- or upper-class.[109] On average, affluent males outlive poor men by 7 years, and wealthy white women live 14 years longer than poor black men.[110] Studies also correlate higher educational levels with better cognitive and physical functioning in old age.[111] This is good news if you're fortunate enough to go to college. But what if you lack access to higher education because of the multiple barriers low-income and minority persons commonly face? Narratives that celebrate "the upside of aging"[112] must also highlight how social privilege and oppression impact elders' bodies and spirits. Contrary to the claims of self-help gurus, how we age is not simply the result of personal belief, lifestyle, and attitudinal choices. Aging is fundamentally a social justice issue.

Ancient Hebrew and Christian communities emphasized the social justice dimensions of aging by advocating respect and care for the gray-haired among them, e.g. parents, widows, elders. By highlighting collective responsibility for society's marginalized, the Bible's prophetic perspective exposes the absurdity—and immorality—of the expensive/lucrative crusade for eternal youth when many older people's physical and psychic needs go unmet, and those who care for them are regularly underpaid and uninsured. This perspective compels us to ask: Who will be able to afford the technologies and medicines needed to vanquish the effects of aging? How can we justify lavishing superfluous care on some, while failing to offer rudimentary care to others?[113] What kind of society devotes enormous resources to the dream of delaying death, while many lives are cut short by racism, sexism, poverty, and other forms of structural violence?

Systemic inequalities do not dissipate—and are often magnified—in old age. Until we broaden our understanding of "health" to include attention to social justice issues, we cannot create the kind of infrastructure—the economic, medical, social, psychological, and spiritual resources—diverse elders need to be well. The Bible's prophetic voice provides guidance in this regard, with its critique of our culture's idolatrous veneration of individual autonomy—idealized in young, nondisabled bodies—and its advocacy of a *communal* ethic oriented by the common good.

Aging and the truth of interdependence

Though not its intention, the Nun Study shows us what a communal approach to aging looks like in practice. In fact, Snowdon attributes the overall good health, strong spirits, and considerable longevity of the sisters he studied to the "ever-present network of love and support" that nourishes them in their advanced years: "The community not only stimulates their minds, celebrates their accomplishments, and shares their aspirations, but also encourages their silences, intimately understands their defeats, and nurtures them when their bodies fail."[114] The nuns' capacity to give and receive care is invigorated by their "deep spirituality." This shared faith strengthens them in the face of adversity and infuses their life with a sense of purpose beyond their own personal fulfillment. For example, 104-year-old Sr. Matthia showed Snowdon a notebook in which she had written the names of the 4,378 students she had taught in her younger decades—all of whom she continued to pray for. Sr. Matthia also knitted a pair of mittens every day and donated them to local charities.[115] Of course, not all of the elderly nuns Snowdon studied experienced such vitality; but all benefited from the ethic of care pervading their community.

The rewards of caring for others in old age are evident in an experiment Bill Thomas conducted when he became medical director of a nursing home in upstate New York. Concerned about the depressing, lifeless atmosphere of the facility, he and his wife got a grant that allowed them to bring pets (dogs, cats, birds, and rabbits), plants, and children to the facility. After an initial period of chaos, both the residents and their caretakers responded enthusiastically to this innovation. Even elders with advanced Alzheimer's took an interest in caring for the animals. Formerly withdrawn and nonambulatory residents offered to take the dogs for walks. Drug prescriptions and costs declined significantly, and deaths fell by 15 percent. Reflecting on the success of Thomas's experiment, Atul Gawande observes that elders need more than a safe, sterile, controlled environment; they need a reason to live—a purpose that transcends the independent self our society worships.[116]

The hollowness of the autonomous ideal that many Westerners associate with success is apparent in the loneliness and depression elders often experience. While the relational skills and social networks many females develop throughout their lives generally serve them well in their senior years, older women are still more likely to experience depression than their male peers.[117] Elderly men are also susceptible to feeling isolated and morose given their life-long gender training to be independent, purposeful, and productive. When Loe's grandfather stopped working and his wife passed away, he straight-out asked her: "What is left to live for?" He is not alone in this query. In the United States today, white men over 65 are the highest-risk group for suicide, ahead of white males ages 20–24.[118]

Intergenerational and ancestral connections

One way to counter the ethic of autonomous individualism that sets us up to feel sad, lonely, and inadequate in old age is to cultivate intergenerational relationships. Young people can do this by investing in family and more-than-kin connections with elders (e.g. spending time with grandparents or "adopting" a grandparent at a senior living facility). Age-desegregation is more common in underprivileged communities, whose members often have to pool resources to survive in a racist, classist society. Intergenerational co-residence is higher among minorities than whites in the United States, for example, and Black and Hispanic families are less likely to put elders in nursing homes. Though not stress free,[119] such intergenerational family ties are rooted in a strong sense of communal accountability that provides a safety net for elders on society's margins. This sense of accountability also promotes cross-generational bonds beyond biological kinship. For example, a 95-year-old African-American woman that Loe interviewed refers to her church as a "second family," and a 92-year-old Latina is called *abuela* (grandmother) by members of her congregation.[120]

The meaningful connections that these intergenerational relationships proffer can also be cultivated with elders who are no longer living. Reverence for ancestors is a common feature of many nonwhite/non-Western traditions and among racial, ethnic, and religious minority communities in the United States today. By blurring the boundaries between the living and the dead, ancestral connections can make mortality less scary. Such relationships also foster a sense of rootedness amid the changes and uncertainties that old age brings. For example, an elder named Shana said she felt grounded working in her garden and knowing this work connected her to her Russian Jewish ancestors, who were farmers. Awareness of this ancestral connection emboldened her spirit even as the weakness of her 94-year-old legs made pulling weeds difficult.[121]

The meaning and strength Shana derived from her roots—both metaphorical and literal—resonates with the womanist wisdom Alice Walker articulated in *In Search of Our Mother's Gardens*.[122] In this classic text, Walker discovered her black female foremothers as empowering sources of inspiration for her writing. In turn, Walker's writing inspired a generation of third world feminist theologians who looked to their female elders and ancestors to guide their struggles for liberation and wholeness. In *Inheriting Our Mother's Gardens*, Kwok Pui-lan recalls how the older women in her childhood church in Hong Kong participated in social reforms to promote gender equality. This recollection helps Kwok see herself as part of "a long tradition of Chinese Christian women, who with tremendous self-respect, struggled not only for their own liberation but also for justice in church and society."[123] Mercy Amba Oduyoye unearthed a similar wellspring of strength when she discovered that her African mother was related to a powerful spiritual/political leader who helped unify the Asante people into a strong nation: "I knew then I had in my veins the blood of mothers who would not be ordered around."[124] Indigenous, Chicana, and Latina feminists also draw on "ancestral knowledge" to help heal the wounds of historical trauma that continue to threaten their well-being. Lara Medina writes: "When Xicana/o communities celebrate *Días de los muertos*, we are invoking the hearts of our ancestors to return to nourish the land and the dreams of the living."[125]

When Patrisse Cullors, cofounder of the Black Lives Matter movement in the United States, was asked to describe the spiritual inspiration for her activism, she immediately acknowledged her ancestors, particularly her great-grandmother, a Choctaw, Blackfoot, African-American woman who raised Cullors and her three siblings while their mother worked multiple jobs to put food on the table. In addition to providing childcare, Cullors' great-grandmother was an amazing singer, and she belonged to the NAACP (National Association for the Advancement of Colored People). Cullors recalls her recounting stories of how her great-grandfather defended their family from the Ku Klux Klan.[126] For many persons in subjugated communities, maintaining intergenerational bonds with elders and ancestors is simultaneously a survival strategy, a source of healing, and an antidote to the alienating effects of our culture's hyper-individualism.

Creating/discovering a sense of purpose in old age

In its "Study of Successful Aging," the MacArthur Foundation found that 80 percent of American seniors believe "life is not worth living if one cannot contribute to the well-being of others." In another study, 60 percent said it's extremely important to feel "valued and needed." And in his interviews with 800 older individuals, psychiatrist George Vaillant discovered that the most satisfied elders "cared about and reached out to other people, to whatever extent they could."[127] These findings suggest that old age fosters appreciation for human interdependence—not just because elderly bodies frequently require assistance from others, but also because mature adults have learned that being of service is mutually beneficial. An 87-year-man told Gawande that what buoyed his spirits, despite his physical limitations and occasional depression, was his ability to care for his blind and ailing wife. For him, this responsibility was not a burden, but a source of self-worth.[128]

All thirty of the oldest old in Loe's study on aging in place "actively embraced aging" by mobilizing resources that enabled them to balance self-care with serving others, and self-directedness with asking for help. None were passive in their acceptance of the changes in their bodies and circumstances. Nor did they seek to deny or defy such changes because they had found sources of meaning that didn't require them to be younger. These sources varied: Juana, a 92-year-old Puerto-Rican-born woman, had been an avid baseball fan for 60 years and never missed a Yankees game; Ruth, a 98-year-old Jewish woman, shared her life-long love of singing with the local Jewish community; Hy, a 92-year-old former professor, continued his educational and activist endeavors by teaching classes for retirees and working with advocacy organizations like Amnesty International and the AARP; and Shana derived immense pleasure from her garden:

> This spring I had a white rhododendron outside of my bedroom and it was just beautiful, with white flowers. I have to go and see if anything is coming up now…Oh, I think when you are gardening you can never have mental illness. It is so grounding. And you don't mind being alone.[129]

Regardless of age, everyone needs a sense of purpose—a reason to wake up in the morning. That need does not diminish with the passage of time.

Redefining "productive members of society"

Not all seniors have the physical and cognitive capacity to pursue their passions or give back to their community in explicit ways. Not all meet gerontologists' definition of "successful aging."[130] Still, all have something to contribute to the common good. For this to happen, we need to broaden our definition of what it means to be a "productive member of society" so that it encompasses more than being active in the paid workforce. Younger generations can help old people become *elders* by honoring their role as our culture's storytellers and "wisdom keepers."[131]

Storytelling can be therapeutic for elders;[132] but it can also enrich the imaginations of younger generations, who never knew a world without cell phones and Facebook—a world where not every home had a television (much less Netflix), where it wasn't unusual for kids to drop out of school to help their parents make ends meet, where blacks in the American south couldn't use the same restrooms, restaurants, and schools as whites, where diseases like polio and the measles were common. My maternal grandmother used to spark my childhood imagination with stories about skiing to school in the Swiss Alps village where she was born. She loved to recount an incident that happened the day she arrived at Ellis Island at age 10: a kind man gave her a banana but had to demonstrate how to eat it (i.e. remove the peeling) because she didn't speak English and had never seen a banana before. We need the vantage point of our elders' stories—not to paint a nostalgic picture of some golden era, but to make us wonder about the things we take for granted.

Even old people with severe physical or cognitive limitations have something crucial to contribute to our collective welfare, if we let them. Their very presence compels us to examine our beliefs about what it means to be human—to ask, as Gawande puts it, "what makes life worth living when we are old and frail and unable to care for ourselves?"[133] This unsettling question prompts both self-examination (e.g. What is the source of a person's worth?) and critical analysis of our culture's supreme values (e.g. Are productivity, autonomy, and control really the highest ends?). Ira Byock has formulated similarly soul-searching questions based on his work with elderly and dying patients: "What would be left undone if I died today?' and 'How can I live most fully in whatever time is left." [134]

Byock and Gawande represent an alternative medical approach to dying that is helpful for reimagining aging: hospice care. Hospice prioritizes providing comfort and reducing suffering over taking extreme (and often futile) measures to prolong a dying patient's life. Essentially, hospice is palliative care for people who have less than six months to live and have agreed to forego curative therapies. This approach not only challenges conventional biomedicine's view of mortality as the enemy; it assumes healing is possible even when a patient is on her deathbed. Hospice care has a crucial role to play in a new narrative of growing old. For until we are able to recognize, wrestle, and reconcile with our dread of dying, we will continue to harbor fear of aging.

"Remember that you are going to die"

I was extremely fortunate to attend a liberal arts college that encouraged me to think not just about a future career, but about the meaning of life—often in relation to death. This college is steeped in the Benedictine heritage, a Catholic monastic tradition founded by St. Benedict, who admonished monks to "Day by day remind yourself that you are going to die." [135] This instruction may sound depressing, but that's because we're conditioned to see death as the enemy and aging as failure.

In part by design, in part by chance, and in part by choice, thinking about death was an integral and enriching part of my college education. My first-year writing professor (Sr. Nancy Hynes) suggested I focus my research paper on Emily Dickinson, whom I'd never heard of, but whose two poems—"I heard a Fly buzz—when I died" and "Because I could not stop for Death"—made me think seriously about mortality for the first time in my young life. I'll spare you the details of my novice analysis. Suffice it to say that, for Dickinson, contemplating death was a source of creativity and a means for wrestling with the mystery of transience. The next year, my philosophy professor (Fr. Rene McGraw) had the class read *The Death of Ivan Ilyich*, a short novel by Tolstoy, in which the main character struggles with the reality that he is sick and dying, while everyone around him pretends it isn't true. Discussing the story, students critiqued such pretenses and expressed our aspirations to live authentically. Later that year, I hung a poster on my dorm room wall that expressed this aspiration. It pictured two people canoeing on a serene, tree-surrounded, Minnesota lake with a quote from Henry David Thoreau:

> I went to the woods because I wished to live deliberately, to front only the essential facts of life and see if I could not learn what it had to teach and not, when I came to die, discover that I had not lived.[136]

As I reflect back on the poetry, stories, and philosophies that shaped my youthful desires to live a meaningful and authentic life, I can't help but wonder if what scares us most about getting old is the possibility that we have existed without really living.

The paradox of aging

Perhaps the biggest irony of our culture's fantasies of immortality and eternal youth is that we so often fail to appreciate the lives we have—until we are forced to see their limits. By manifesting these limits, bodies nearing their final passage challenge us to wake up—to stop squandering our energy on superficial pursuits and start paying attention to what really matters. Whatever our age, realizing we won't live forever can make us more intentional about, present to, and grateful for our lives and our relationships. Jane Gross discovered the redemptive possibilities of a finite future in the final months of her mother's life. By that time, her mother's waning health forced them to use an alphabet board to communicate. Even so, those conversations were the most honest, meaningful, and healing they'd ever had.[137] The proximity of death freed them to let go of expectations, resentments, and disappointments that had previously prevented them from truly connecting.

It's easy to postpone the peace of forgiveness and the pleasure of gratitude when you think you have all the time in the world. But the vantage point of a limited future can open us to what Gloria Steinem calls the "secret of intensified life."[138] This intensity can be paradoxically subtle. Although downshifting did not come easily to Seymour, a 93-year-old white male and former high-achiever, as his future shortened, he began to appreciate the "here and now" of his everyday life, with its mundane pleasures—like the warmth of Florida winters and communicating with friends on e-mail. Another of Loe's interviewees, a 95-year-old African-American woman named Rose, said being grateful for each day is the cornerstone of her faith. She enjoys watching wildlife out the window of her son's home where she lives, and interacting with the family pets.[139] Paradoxically, Rose's and Seymour's capacity to be present to and savor the small satisfactions of daily life stems from their awareness of an ever-shrinking future. The poignancy of their perspectives explains why Cartensen's 92-year-old father told her that younger generations need to "stop talking only about how to save the old folks, and start talking about how [elders] may save us all."[140]

Elders may save us by sharing their atypical vantage point of a finite future. Awareness that life is short can make us more selective about what deserves our time, attention, anger, or worry.[141] Cartensen's research suggests that older people are generally more content and less depressed than twenty- and thirty-somethings, who, though in the "prime" of their lives, are often stressed by the infinite possibilities of an open-ended future. Cartensen refers to the emotional stability many elders experience as the "paradox of aging."

> As we age, our time horizons grow shorter and our goals change. When we recognize that we don't have all the time in the world, we see our priorities most clearly; we take less notice of trivial matters; we savor our life; we're more appreciative; we're open to reconciliation; we invest in more emotionally important parts of life, and life gets better.[142]

Whatever our age, an older person's vantage point of a limited future can prompt us to become more mindful: to stop chasing after shame-inducing fantasies of physical perfection and start investing our energy in relationships, activities, and causes that enrich our lives and benefit others. Ultimately, the paradox of aging suggests that the impermanence and frailty of elderly flesh is not shameful, but liberating.

Rethinking the resurrection

The paradox of aging provides a lens for rethinking the story of Jesus' resurrection. Rather than see this story as signaling God's cosmic triumph over sin/death, we can interpret it as a metaphor for the truth of transience: the interdependence of life and death, growth and entropy, creativity and destruction that's manifest in every body, particularly in flesh that has lived a long time. From this perspective, the hope the resurrection conveys is not the promise of immortality and eternal youth, but the potential for creating- discovering-experiencing new life—new meaning—out of the rubble of irreversible change, loss, and limits that are indelible parts of the human condition. This hope differs from denial because it isn't predicated on avoiding suffering or escaping to a picture-perfect past or future. In this retelling of the resurrection story, Jesus' crucifixion symbolizes both the nonavoidance of suffering and the murderous cruelty of a sociopolitical system that punishes nonconformity.

Interpreted through the lens of aging bodies, Jesus' resurrection is not just an event that occurred some 2000 years ago, but a story that is happening today. This drama unfolds in our struggles for redemption—our yearning for meaning, connection, healing, and dignity—in a culture that teaches us to feel ashamed of our body's noncompliance with social norms and to project that shame onto others. We miss the transformative potential to which the resurrection story points if we reduce it to an immortality myth that promises eternal life in a permanently youthful body. Our elders bear witness to this transformative potential by showing us—in the midst of inevitable entropy and limits—how to benefit ourselves by serving others, how to prioritize what matters most, appreciate what already is, and let go of what we can't control.

A theology of transience

Reimagining aging requires us to reinterpret other religious ideas as well, including our assumptions about God. Traditional images of God as a supernatural, all-powerful, *unchanging* (male) being, whose perfection is uncontaminated by the messiness, flux, and finitude of the flesh, imply that change is undesirable, particularly the developments in female bodies. Implicitly, images that reify (objectify) divine power suggest there's something impure about impermanence, and that being closer to God (or more God-like/virtuous) means rising above the chaotic, unpredictable permutations of embodied life.[143] Indirectly, such images sanction the beliefs that death is evil and senescence is shameful.

A more aging-friendly theology relinquishes the idea that God never changes in favor of a dynamic view of the Holy. In this theology, the symbol "God" calls our attention to the ever-changing, creative power of life: the mysterious movement that generates, dwells within, and continually reconfigures all life forms—e.g. atoms and amoebas, trees and rivers, birds and elephants, human bodies/spirits.[144] The image of divine creativity as the animating Spirit that pervades and interconnects life's diverse manifestations is not as familiar as depictions of God as the "Unmoved Mover," almighty Creator, or even a grandfatherly figure. But neither is this image new. Poetic references to *ruah*—the life-giving breath of God—go all the way back to the second verse of the Bible (Genesis 1.2), in which the divine spirit moves over the waters at the dawn of creation. For decades, feminist theologians of various colors and cultures have returned to this fluid image to reimagine the Sacred as a dynamic power, rather than an ageless being—a power that that dwells in earthly bodies (human and nonhuman) and makes itself known in the truths of our diverse, ever-evolving experiences.

FIGURE 8.6 *Beautiful older woman's smiling face © Daniel Berehulak.*
Source: Getty Images.

Theological images that affirm—rather than denigrate—the transitory nature of our bodies and lives are not an overnight cure for the shame, frustration, and exclusion many older people experience in a youth-obsessed culture. Still, such images can help us cultivate a less hostile/more accepting perspective on the shifts that happen in older bodies. Such a perspective not only challenges our culture's idolization of youthful physiques, but allows us to perceive graying hair, weakening muscles, and stiffening joints as evidence of accumulated wisdom, rather than signs of our body's betrayal. If we practice this perspective repeatedly, we may even start to perceive goodness, beauty, and truth in the lines of our grandmothers' faces (Figure 8.6) and in the noncompliant features of our own flesh.

A wabi-sabi perspective

To shift our perspective on aging bodies, we can cultivate a *wabi-sabi* aesthetic. As Susan Moon explains, *wabi-sabi* is a Japanese term that describes "the beauty of impermanence, the imperfection of things that are worn and frayed and chipped through use." *Wabi-sabi* names the loveliness of material objects that show the marks of time—e.g. an old barn, a giant Sequoia, a quilt made from recycled fabric, a grandfather's hands. Moon observes that teenagers take shortcuts to *wabi-sabi* when they buy designer jeans that are prefaded, tattered, ripped. But "the true wabi-sabi look can't be made in a factory" because it requires the passage of time.[145] When Sr. Matthai died at the age of 105, her caretakers found the three-inch crucifix she had received when she first became a nun. The metallic body of Christ and its surrounding wood inlay were "polished smooth by years of prayer," revealing the beauty of the sister's venerable spirit.[146]

In *Beyond the Centaur*, Margaret Miles describes an experiment in which she consciously sought to undo her socialization to see older female bodies as shameful. Each day, she spent time "looking long and intently" at a photo of Rodin's famous sculpture, *She Who Was the Helmet Maker's Once-Beautiful Wife*, in which the frail, withered, bent body of an old woman is made stunningly beautiful by the artist's craft and perspective. "I had a very personal reason for undertaking this exercise," Miles explains: "I wanted not to feel ugly as an old woman." After about a year of studying the sculpture's beauty, she was able to perceive her own aging body from a *wabi-sabi* perspective: as "the site of a lifetime of experience, as utterly beautiful."[147]

Practicing peace with aging

As Miles' experiment suggests, changing our perceptions of elderly flesh requires focused intention and repetitious effort. In a culture obsessed with looking and feeling younger, accepting and embracing the impermanence, fragility, and finitude that older bodies reveal is an ongoing practice, not a passive endeavor.

There are many ways to practice peace with aging, whatever stage of life you embody. You can appreciate the diversity, complexity, and ingenuity of elders; work for justice on their behalf; study the difference between suffering that is inevitable (e.g. the entropy in aging bodies) and suffering that can be avoided, reduced, and transformed (e.g. ageism); critique anti-aging industries and notice the fears and delusions on which they prey; challenge our culture's ideology of individual self-mastery and its idolization of youthful bodies; recognize and support the contributions elders make to our collective well-being; reflect on mortality and allow the vantage point of a limited future make you more present to your life; slow down enough to observe the truth of transience around and within you, and see if you can behold its beauty. Perhaps the most important way younger people can practice peace with aging is to spend time with elders, whose nonconforming bodies pave the way for all of us to reject the salvation myth of physical improvement and the shame it encourages, and to marvel at the mystery of the passage of time as it manifests itself in our flesh and in our lives.

Epilogue

As I listen to the daily news—reports about wars and terrorist bombings, income inequality and corporate greed, environmental destruction and unbridled consumerism, systemic violence against women and minorities, and sanctioned exclusion of immigrants and refugees—it's hard not to wonder whether it makes sense to have spent well over a year of my life writing a book about something as seemingly trivial as body shame.[1] Compared to these and other massive global problems, feelings of physical inadequacy and even the judgments we make of each other can seem pretty superficial. But that's only if we fail to connect the dots—if we neglect to notice

- how the disdain and aggression we direct at nonconforming bodies (our own and others') perpetuate a much larger, deeply entrenched, collective attitude of fear/hostility toward the diversity and vulnerability of embodied life—the same attitude that fosters the superiority complexes that lead to oppression and violence around the world

- how the better body story simultaneously stimulates and disguises this antagonistic mindset with promises of salvation (happiness, health, and healing) through physical "improvement"—defined by a singular, normative ideal

- how these promises divert our attention from the actual sources of human suffering—i.e. ignorance, greed, and malice and the systemic injustices these experiences produce—by encouraging us to fight and fix our flesh rather than work to create a more just, sane, compassionate society

In short, what connects individuals' seemingly personal struggles with body shame to broad social patterns of inequality, aggression, and exclusion is a deeply ingrained way of thinking that seeks to conquer uncertainty, homogenize difference, control change, and avoid suffering.

Since this way of thinking echoes certain narratives and norms in traditional Christianity (modified by Cartesian assumptions), Christians have an especially prominent role to play in challenging the shaming gaze the culture of physical improvement encourages. Fortunately, there are excellent resources within Christianity for developing this critique, and for constructing an alternative perspective on health, happiness, and healing. Whatever your religious affiliation, or lack thereof, you can help deescalate the animosity directed at unconventional bodies and support a less combative/more accepting approach to embodied life. You don't have to be the president or a CEO, a prestigious scientist or literary genius, a celebrity or Hollywood producer to make a difference. Whoever you are, whatever your life situation, you can do your small but significant part to create a world in which *every*body is cared for and respected,

- by thinking critically about the better body story, the dominant cultural values and assumptions this narrative embodies, the war-like mentality and strategies it promotes, and the shame it generates and triggers

- by sharing your critical awareness with others and pursuing conversations that take body shame out of the closet so it has a chance to be transformed

- by appreciating the marvelous diversity of human bodies, including your own unique form of physicality and its interdependence with others

- by doing your best to responsibly care for the body you have, while backing others' efforts to nurture their bodies wisely

- by wrestling and reconciling with the difficulties of life in the flesh—its fragility, transience, and finitude—while supporting and empathizing with the somatic frailties and struggles of others

- by practicing an attitude of fascination, wonder, and humility in face of the mystery incarnated in human flesh and in all forms of life

Ultimately, the body issues explored in this book are not only *not* trivial, but they put us in touch with profound existential questions—questions about how we make meaning and pursue a sense of purpose; how we deal with suffering in ourselves and in the world; how we relate to what we don't understand and can't control.

Whatever your age, size, ability, health status, sexuality, religion, color, class, or culture, body issues matter because the relationship you cultivate with your flesh through your everyday thoughts, feelings, and choices reverberates in your self-understanding, your perceptions of and interactions with others, and your experience of life itself.

May you approach this relationship with care and kindness, curiosity and gratitude, respect and compassion, presence and unconditional love.

Notes

Introduction

1 Paul Tillich, *Dynamics of Faith* (New York: HarperOne, 2009 [1957]).

2 Simi Linton, *My Body Politic: A Memoir* (Ann Arbor: University of Michigan Press, 2007), 81.

3 Rosemarie Garland Thomson, *Extraordinary Bodies: Figuring Physical Disability in American Culture and Literature* (New York: Columbia University Press, 1997), 137.

4 Medya Yegnoglu, "Sartorial Fabric-ations: Enlightenment and Western Feminisim," in *Postcolonialism, Feminism, and Religious Discourse*, ed. Laura E. Donaldson and Kwok Pui-lan (New York: Routledge, 2002), 93.

5 Simone de Beauvoir, *The Second Sex* (New York: Vintage, 1989 [1949]).

1 Deconstructing the "better body" story

1 Merriam-Webster Online Dictionary, accessed May 13, 2014, http://www.merriam-webster.com/dictionary/better?show=0&t=1400009693.

2 R. Marie Griffith, *Born Again Bodies: Flesh and Spirit in American Christianity* (Berkeley: University of California, 2004), 4, 8–9.

3 bell hooks, *Black Looks: Race and Representation* (Boston: South End, 1992), 63–72, 21; Delores Williams, "A Womanist Perspective on Sin," in *A Troubling in My Soul: Womanist Perspectives on Evil and Suffering*, ed. Emilie Townes (Maryknoll, NY: Orbis, 1993), 143.

4 John Berger, *Ways of Seeing* (London: Penguin, 1972), 47.

5 Sharon Betcher, *Spirit and the Politics of Disablement* (Minneapolis: Fortress, 2007), 30.

6 Michel Foucault, *The Order of Things: An Archeology of the Human Sciences* (1970; reprint, New York: Vintage, 1973).

7 I'm summarizing big ideas from Michel Foucault's analyses in *Madness and Civilization: A History of Insanity in the Age of Reason* (New York: Vintage, 1988); *Discipline and Punish: The Birth of the Prison* (New York: Vintage, 1995); and *Power/Knowledge: Selected Interviews and Other Writings, 1972–1977*, ed. Colin Gordon (New York: Vintage, 1980).

8 Iris Marion Young, *Justice and the Politics of Difference* (Princeton, NJ: Princeton University Press, 1990), 125.

9 Rosemarie Garland Thompson, *Extraordinary Bodies: Figuring Disability in American Culture and Literature* (New York: Columbia University Press), 7–8.

10 Merriam-Webster Online Dictionary, accessed June 6, 2014, http://www.merriam-webster.com/dictionary/shameful.

11 Ibid., accessed June 6, 2014, http://www.merriam-webster.com/dictionary/shame.

12 Brené Brown, *Daring Greatly: How The Courage to Be Vulnerable Transforms the Way We Live, Love, Parent, and Lead* (New York: Gotham, 2012), 68–72, 24–26.

13 Douglas wrote about the socially constructed designation of "dirt" in *Purity and Danger: An Analysis of Concepts of Pollution and Taboo* (New York: Routledge, 1992). S. Lochlann Jain reminded me of Douglas' observation that "Where there is dirt, there is a system" in *Malignant: How Cancer Becomes Us* (Berkeley: University of California Press, 2013), 204.

14 Brown, *Daring Greatly*, 27.

15 Ibid., 85–91, 130.

2 Christianity's hidden contributions to the culture of physical improvement

1 Pew Forum on Religion & Public Life. *"'Nones' on the Rise."* Washington, DC: Pew Research Center (October 2012), accessed March 10, 2016, http://www.pewforum.org/2012/10/09/nones-on-the-rise/.

2 For examples of quasi-religious secular phenomena, see Bruce Forbes and Jeffrey Mahan, eds. *Religion and Popular Culture*, Third Edition (Berkeley: University of Berkeley Press, 2017); Monica Miller, et al., *Religion in Hip Hop: Mapping the New Terrain in the U.S.* (London: Bloomsbury, 2015); Joseph Price, *From Season to Season: Sports as American Religion* (Mercer, 2002); and Bron Taylor, "Surfing into Spirituality and a New, Aquatic Nature Religion," *Journal of the American Academy of Religion* 75:4 (2007): 923–951.

3 Douglas Jacobsen and Rhonda Hustedt Jacobsen, *No Longer Invisible: Religion in University Education* (New York: Oxford, 2012), 11–14.

4 Monica Miller, *Religion and Hip Hop* (New York: Routledge, 2012), 2.

5 David Loy, "The Religion of the Market," *Journal of the American Academy of Religion* 65:2 (1997): 275, 289.

6 Ibid., 275.

7 Ibid., 281–284.

8 Sharon Betcher, *Politics and the Spirit of Disablement* (Minneapolis: Augsburg Fortress, 2007), 3.

9 Susie Orbach, *Bodies* (New York: Picador), 167; Joan Jacob Brumberg, *The Body Project: An Intimate History of American Girls* (New York: Vintage Books, 1997).

10 In *The Corinthian Body* (New Haven: Yale University Press, 1995), Dale Martin cautions against reading Paul through the lens of Cartesian dualism that modern Westerners take for granted. Yet Paul's interpreters emphasized the dangers of physical desire. See also: Lisa Isherwood and Elizabeth Stuart, *Introducing Body Theology* (Sheffield, England: Sheffield Academic Press, 1998), 62; Peter Brown, *The Body and Society: Men, Women, and Sexual Renunciation in Early Christianity* (New York: Columbia University Press, 1988).

11 Margaret Miles, *Fullness of Life: Historical Foundations for a New Asceticism* (New York: Wipf & Stock, 2006), 58.

12 Quoted in Miles, *Fullness of Life*, 25. Brown also comments on Tertullian's instruction to "Look to the body," *The Body and Society*, 81.

13 Quoted in Miles, *Fullness of Life*, 68, 76.

14 Quoted in ibid., 25, 57.

15 Ibid., 68–70.

16 Brown, *The Body and Society*, 376–377.

17 Teresa M. Shaw, *The Burden of the Flesh: Fasting and Sexuality in Early Christianity* (Minneapolis: Fortress, 1998), 3.

18 Miles, *Fullness of Life*, 43.

19 Shaw, *The Burden of the Flesh*, 162–163, 180.

20 Shaw says Jerome sees bodily desire as particularly dangerous because it is an "enemy within." *Burden of the Flesh*, 111.

21 Phyllis Trible, "Eve and Adam: Genesis 2–3 Reread," in *Womanspirit Rising: A Feminist Reader in Religion*, eds. Carol P. Christ and Judith Plaskow (New York: HarperSanfrancisco, 1979), 74–83.

22 Ambrose, "On Paradise," in *Women in the Early Church*, ed. Elizabeth Clark (Wilmington Delaware: Michael Glazier, 1983), 30.

23 Augustine, "Literal Commentary on Genesis," in *Women in the Early Church*, 40.

24 Ambrose, "On Paradise," in *Women in the Early Church*, 33.

25 Rosemary Ruether, *Women and Redemption: A Theological History* (Minneapolis: Fortress, 1998), 5.

26 Isherwood and Stuart, *Introducing Body Theology*, 18.

27 Shaw, *Burden of the Flesh*, 85.

28 Chrysostom, "The Kind of Women Who Ought To Be Taken as Wives," in *Women in the Early Church*, 36–37.

29 Isherwood and Stuart, *Introducing Body Theology*, 81.

30 C. R. Moss, "Heavenly Healing: Eschatological Cleansing and the Resurrection of the Dead in the Early Church," *Journal of the American Academy of Religion* 79:4 (December 2011): 991–1017.

31 Ibid., 993.

32 Ibid., 996, 1008–1009.

33 Virginia Burrus, *Saving Shame: Martyrs, Saints, and Other Abject Subjects* (Philadelphia: University of Pennsylvania Press, 2007), 57.

34 Betcher, *Spirit and the Politics of Disablement*, 3, 41.

3 Religious-like features of the culture of physical improvement

1 René Descartes, *Discourse on Method*, trans. Laurence Lafleur (Upper Saddle River, NJ: Prentice Hall 1956), 21.

2 Descartes, *Discourse on Method*, 21.

3 Genevieve Lloyd, *The Man of Reason: 'Male' and 'Female' in Western Philosophy* (New York: Routledge, 1993).

4 Margaret Miles, *Beyond the Centaur: Imagining the Intelligent Body* (Eugene OR: Cascade Books, 2014), 31–33.

5 Margaret Miles, *Image as Insight: Visual Understanding in Western Christianity and Secular Culture* (New York: Wipf & Stock Publishers, 2006 [reprint edition]).

6 Chris Hedges, *Empire of Illusion: The End of Literacy and the Triumph of the Spectacle* (New York: Nation Books, 2009), 17.

7 Ibid., 6, 26–27

8 This video, created by Tim Piper, is available at https://www.youtube.com/watch?v=iYhCn0jf46U (accessed July 21, 2015); Margo DeMello discusses this example in *Body Studies: An Introduction* (New York: Routledge, 2014), 180–181.

9 Susie Orbach, *Bodies* (London: Picador, 2009), 113.

10 Talal Asad, *Geneaologies of Religion: Discipline and Reasons of Power in Christianity and Islam* (Baltimore: Johns Hopkins Press, 1993), 73, 83–86.

11 See my article on this topic: "Embodying Learning: Post-Cartesian Pedagogy and the Academic Study of Religion," in *Teaching Theology and Religion* 12:2 (April 2009): 123–136.

12 Mary Douglas, *Natural Symbols: Explorations in Cosmology* (New York: Pantheon, 1982 [1970]); *Purity and Danger: An Analysis of the Concept of Pollution and Taboo* (1966; reprint, New York: Routledge, 1991).

13 Catherine Bell, *Ritual Theory, Ritual Practice* (New York: Oxford, 2009), 48–49, 83–90.

14 Michel Foucault, *Discipline and Punish: The Birth of the Prison* (New York: Vintage, 1979); Michel Foucault, *History of Sexuality: Volume 1* (New York: Vintage Books 1990 [1978]). See also Jana Sawicki, *Disciplining Foucault: Feminism, Power, and the Body* (New York: Routledge, 1991), 21–24.

15 Virginia Burrus, *Saving Shame: Martyrs, Saints, and Other Abject Subjects* (Philadelphia: University of Pennsylvania Press, 2007).

16 These examples appear on *Health* magazine's covers: July/August 2011, April 2015, March 2015, respectively.

17 Brené Brown, *Daring Greatly: How the Courage to Be Vulnerable Transforms the Way We Live, Love, Parent, and Lead* (New York: Gotham), 86.

18 MedHelp claims to be "The World's Largest Health Community," accessed July 21, 2015, http://www.medhelp.org/posts/Erectile-Dysfunction/The-shame-of-ED/show/942198.

19 Joan Jacob Brumberg, *The Body Project: An Intimate History of American Girls* (New York: Vintage, 1997), 143.

20 Jennifer Siebel Newsom and Gavin Newsom, "The Problem with Victoria Secret's Marketing," *Huffington Post* (April 5, 2013), accessed July 15, 2014, http://www.huffingtonpost.com/jennifer-siebel-newsom/the-danger-in-victorias-secrets-marketing_b_3024702.html.

21 Karen Dion, Ellen Berscheid, and Elaine Walster, "What is Beautiful is Good," *Journal of Personality and Social Psychology* 24:3 (1972): 285–290; see also Eagly, et al., "What Is Beautiful is Good, But . . .: A Meta-Analytic Review of Research on the Physical Attractiveness Stereotype" *Psychological Bulletin* 110:1 (July 1991): 109–128.

22 Doris Bazzini, et al., "Do Animated Disney Characters Portray and Promote the Beauty-Goodness Stereotype?" *The Journal of Applied Social Psychology* 40:10 (October 2010): 2687–2709.

23 Marie Griffith discusses physiognomy in *Born Again Bodies: Flesh and Spirit in American Christianity* (Berkeley: University of California Press), 57–68.

24 Brumberg, *The Body Project*, 62–65.

4 An alternative approach to embodied life

1 Nhat Hanh develops the concept of "interbeing" in his many books. Among those that have most influenced my thinking are: *Love in Action: Writings on Nonviolent Social Change* (Berkeley, CA: Parallax Press, 1993); *Peace Is Every Step: The Path of Mindfulness in Everyday Life* (New York: Bantam, 1992); *For A Future to Be Possible: Buddhist Ethics for Everyday Life* (Berkeley: Parallax, 2009), *Living Buddha, Living Christ* (New York: Riverhead, 1995); *Being Peace* (Berkeley: Parallax, 1987).

2 Bernie Glassman, *Bearing Witness: A Zen Master's Lessons in Making Peace* (New York: Bell Tower, 1998), 48–50.

3 Ibid., 36–37.

4 Thich Nhat Hanh, *Love in Action*, 65–71.

5 Pema Chödrön, *Living Beautifully with Uncertainty and Change* (Boston: Shambala, 2012), 3–7.

6 C. W. Huntington, Jr., "The Triumph of Narcissism: Theravada Buddhist Meditation in the Marketplace," *Journal of the American Academy of Religion* 83:3 (September 2015): 642.

7 The Center for Contemplative Mind in Society (http://www. contemplativemind.org) is a resource for faculty seeking to address the inner lives of students in the process of academic learning. For more on the contemplative movement in and beyond higher education, see Fran Grace and Judith Simmer-Brown, *Meditation and the Classroom: Contemplative Pedagogy for Religious Studies* (Albany: Suny Press, 2011), and *Contemplative Nation: How Ancient Practices are Changing the Way We Live*, ed. Mirabai Bush (Kalamazo, MI: Fetzer Institute, 2011).

8 See, e.g., Rita Gross, *Buddhism after Patriarchy: A Feminist History, Analysis, and Reconstruction of Buddhism* (Albany: State University of New York Press, 1992).

9 Carol Christ, "Why Women Need the Goddess: Phenomenological, Psychological, and Political Reflections," in *Womanspirit Rising: A Feminist Reader in Religion*, eds. Carol Christ and Judith Plaskow (New York: Harper & Row, 1979), 273–287.

10 Elizabeth Johnson, *Quest for the Living God: Mapping Frontiers in the Theology of God* (New York: Continuum, 2007).

11 Ivone Gebara, *Longing For Running Water: Ecofeminism and Liberation* (Minneapolis: Fortress, 1999).

12 Johnson, *Quest for the Living God*, 137.

13 "Body and Religion Group Session," Annual American Academy of Religion Conference, Baltimore, MD (November 24, 2014).

5 Disability shame

1 NPR/TED Staff, "How Do We Use Our Challenges to Live Beyond Limits?" (July 18, 2014), accessed March 31, 2016, http://www.wnyc.org/story/how-do-we-use-our-challenges-to-live-beyond-limits/.

2 Sharon Betcher, *Spirit and the Politics of Disablement* (Minneapolis: Fortress, 2007).

3 Rosemarie Garland Thomson, *Extraordinary Bodies* (New York: Columbia University Press, 1997), 22.

4 Several authors explain this distinction. See, e.g., Nancy Eiesland, *The Disabled God: Toward a Liberatory Theology of Disability* (Nashville: Abingdon, 1994), 27.

5 Alison Kafer, *Feminist, Queer, Crip* (Bloomington: Indiana University Press, 2013), 7.

6 Robert Murphy, *The Body Silent: The Different World of the Disabled* (New York: W.W. Norton, 1987), 4, vi–vii; see also Lennard Davis, *Enforcing Normalcy: Disability, Deafness, and the Body* (New York: Verso, 1995), 73.

7 Simi Linton, *My Body Politic: A Memoir* (Ann Arbor, MI: University of Michigan Press, 2007), 3.

8 Ibid., 25–26, 32.

9 Ibid., 68, 54.

10 Eli Clare, *Exile and Pride: Disability, Queerness and Liberation* (Cambridge, MA: Southend Press, 2009 [1999]), 7.

11 Ibid., 7–8. Kafer discusses similar problems with overdrawing the distinction between "impairment" and "disability," since *both* are social. See *Feminist, Queer, Crip*, 7.

12 Thomas Reynolds, *Vulnerable Communion: A Theology of Disability and Hospitality* (Grand Rapids, MI: Brazos, 2008), 27.

13 Kafer, *Feminist, Queer, Crip*, 1.

14 Betcher, *Spirit and the Politics of Disablement*, 51. See also S. Betcher, "Becoming Flesh of My Flesh: Feminist and Disability Theologies on the Edge of Posthumanist Discourse," *Journal of Feminist Studies in Religion* 26:2 (2010): 107–118.

15 Eiesland, *The Disabled God*, 121; Kafer, *Feminist, Queer, Crip*, 25.

16 Matthew Sanford, *Waking: A Memoir of Trauma and Transcendence* (New York: Rodale, 2006), xvii.

17 Center for Disease Control and Prevention, accessed May 8, 2015, http://www.cdc.gov/nchs/fastats/disability.htm.

18 Kevin Sack, "Research Finds Wide Disparities in Health Care by Race and Region," *New York Times*, June 5, 2008, accessed April 6, 2016, http://www.nytimes.com/2008/06/05/health/research/05disparities.html?_r=0..

19 Kafer, *Feminist, Queer, Crip*, 107.

20 Ibid., 8, 24.

21 This isn't to say that everyone experiences disability in some way. Such a watered down claim ignores the structural and emotional difficulties people with disabilities frequently face. Reynolds, *Vulnerable Communion*, 40.

22 Kafer, *Feminist, Queer, Crip*, 10–19; Davis, *Enforcing Normalcy*, xiv-xv.

23 Davis, *Enforcing Normalcy*, xiv; Kafer, *Feminist, Queer, Crip*, 74–75.

24 Davis, *Enforcing Normalcy*, 8.

25 Eiesland, *The Disabled God*, 23–24.

26 This phrase captures a key insight/advantage of Kafer's political/relational model of disability, *Feminist, Queer, Crip*, 11.

27 Ibid., 2.

28 Eiesland, *The Disabled God*, 71.

29 John Hull, *The Tactile Heart: Blindness and Faith* (London: SMC Press, 2013), 36–37.

30 Ibid., 42–43, 90–91.

31 Mary Lowe, "'Rabbi, Who Sinned?' Disability Theologies and Sin," in *Dialog* 51:3 (Fall 2012), 188.

32 Eiesland, *The Disabled God*, 75–81.

33 Ibid., 71–72; see also Rebecca Chopp's "Foreword" to *The Disabled God*, 11.

34 Lowe, "'Rabbi, Who Sinned?'" 185–194.

35 Hull, *The Tactile Heart*, 22–23.

36 Ibid., 60.

37 Ibid., 90–91; see also C. R. Moss, "Heavenly Healing: Eschatological Cleansing and the Resurrection of the Dead in the Early Church," *Journal of the American Academy of Religion* 79:4 (December 2011) 991–1017.

38 Hull, *The Tactile Heart*, 118–119.

39 Ibid., 67–71.

40 Betcher, *Spirit and the Politics of Disablement*, 119.

41 Eiesland, *The Disabled God*, 70–74.

42 Reynolds, *Vulnerable Communion*, 41–42.

43 Bethany Hamilton, *Soul Surfer: A True Story of Faith, Family, and Fighting to Get Back on the Board* (New York: Pocket Books), 65, 198, 207.

44 Eiesland, *The Disabled God*, 73.

45 Ibid.

46 Hull, *The Tactile Heart*, 23–24.

47 Reynolds, *Vulnerable Communion*, 16, 38–39.

48 Harriet McBryde Johnson, *Too Late To Die Young: Nearly True Tales from A Life* (New York: Picador, 2005), 11.

49 Hull, *The Tactile Heart*, 85.

50 Reynolds, *Vulnerable Communion*, 28.

51 Joan Tollifson, "Enjoying the Perfection of Imperfection," in *Being Bodies: Buddhist Women on the Paradox of Embodiment*, eds. Lenore Friedman and Susan Moon (Boston: Shambala Press), 18–19.

52 McBryde Johnson, *Too Late To Die Young*, 2.

53 Tollifson, "Enjoying the Perfection of Imperfection," 18–19.

54 Ibid., 22.

55 Betcher, *Spirit and the Politics of Disablement*, 19.

56 Garland Thomson, *Extraordinary Bodies*, 63.

57 Ibid., 56–57, 64–66, 80.

58 Davis, *Enforcing Normalcy*, 90. Garland Thomson, *Extraordinary Bodies*, 63.

59 An advertisement for Heth and photos of other freaks appear in unnumbered pages between Chapters 2 and 3 of Garland Thomson's *Extraordinary Bodies*.

60 Ibid., 59–65.

61 Ibid., 65.

62 McBryde Johnson, *Too Late to Die Young*, 1–2.

63 Ibid., 224–225, 219.

64 Ibid., 205, 220–221, 214.

65 Ibid., 230–239.

66 Reynolds, *Vulnerable Communion*, 25–26.

67 Garland Thomson, *Extraordinary Bodies*, 70–77.

68 Davis, *Enforcing Normalcy*, 87.

69 Ibid., 24–25, 28–30, 35; see also Kafer, *Feminist, Queer, Crip*, 30.

70 Susan Schweik, *The Ugly Laws: Disability in Public* (New York: New York University Press, 2009), 1–2, 34–39.

71 Ibid., 59.

72 Davis, *Enforcing Normalcy*, 41–43, 150–157.

73 Ibid., 35–38.

74 Garland Thomson, *Extraordinary Bodies*, 78–79.

75 McBryde Johnson, *Too Late to Die Young*, 176.

76 Clare, *Exile and Pride*, 107.

77 Ibid., 112–113, 151.

78 Sanford, *Waking*, 59, 82–84.

79 Ibid., 98–104, 109–115.

80 Linton, *My Body Politic*, 183.

81 Clare, *Exile and Pride*, 2–3, 8–9.

82 Ibid., 9.

83 Kafer, *Feminist, Queer, Crip*, 88.

84 Ibid., 93.

85 Clare, *Exile and Pride*, 130.

86 Sanford, *Waking*, 95–96, 112.

87 Quoted from the Christopher and Dana Reeve Foundation website, accessed June 19, 2015, http://www.christopherreeve.org/site/c.ddJFKRNoFiG/b.5048263/k.7A2C/Campaign_to_Cure_Paralysis.htm. See also McBryde Johnson, *Too Late to Die Young*, 120.

88 Davis, *Enforcing Normalcy*, 93–96.

89 Linton, *My Body Politic*, 28.

90 Clare, *Exile and Pride*, 120–121.

91 Ibid., 134.

92 Amy Purdy, *On My Own Two Feet: From Losing My Legs to Learning the Dance of Life* (New York: William Morrow, 2014), 27, 126, 108, 7, 13, 18–22, 135.

93 Ibid., 223, 89–91.

94 Ibid., 106, 151.

95 Ibid., 73–76, 214, 82–85, 145.

96 Ibid., 2, 125, 74–75.

97 Ibid., 93, 164–165, 69, 2.

98 Ibid., 6–7, 53, 163.

99 Ibid., 211.

100 Ibid., 67, 23.

101 Betcher, "Becoming Flesh of My Flesh," 107.

102 Sanford, *Waking*, 124, 180, 243, xvii.

103 McBryde Johnson, *Too Late to Die Young*, 7–10.

104 Murphy, *The Body Silent*, 117.

105 Lowe, "'Rabbi, Who Sinned?'" 187–188.

106 Julia Watts Belser, "God on Wheels: Disability and Jewish Feminist Theology," *Tikkun* 29:4 (Fall 2014): 28.

107 Deborah Beth Creamer, *Disability and Christian Theology: Embodied Limits and Constructive Possibilities* (New York: Oxford University Press, 2010).

108 McBryde Johnson, *Too Late to Die Young*, 208.

109 Kafer, *Feminist, Queer, Crip*, 1–2.

110 McBryde Johnson, *Too Late to Die Young*, 2.

111 Ibid., 255.

112 Karen Armstrong, *Twelve Steps to A Compassionate Life* (New York: Alfred A. Knopf, 2010) 118.

113 Ivone Gebara, *Longing for Running Water: Ecofeminism and Liberation* (Minneapolis: Fortress, 1999), 101–135.

114 Bernie Glassman, *Bearing Witness: A Zen Master's Lessons in Making Peace* (New York: Bell Tower, 1998) xiv; 67–68.

115 Armstrong, *Twelve Steps*, 128.

116 Garland Thomson, *Extraordinary Bodies*, 46; see also Betcher, "Becoming Flesh of My Flesh," 108.

117 Sanford, *Waking*, 4.

118 Kafer, *Feminist, Queer, Crip* 16. It's the "curative imaginary" that Kafer takes issue with—a mentality stuck in anticipation of a cure and unable to imagine fulfillment short of a cure (27).

119 Linton, *My Body Politic*, 69, 39–40.

120 Clare, *Exile and Pride*, 122–123.

121 Lowe, "'Rabbi, Who Sinned?'" 185–194.

122 Monica Coleman, *Making a Way Out of No Way: A Womanist Theology* (Minneapolis, MN: Fortress, 2008).

123 McBryde Johnson, *Too Late to Die Young*, 208.

124 Ibid., 256.

125 Eiesland, *The Disabled God*, 96.

126 In her classic definition, Alice Walker identifies a "womanist" as a black feminist or feminist of color who "Loves herself. *Regardless.*" See *In Search of Our Mother's Garden: Womanist Prose* (New York: Harcourt Brace

Javanovish, 1983) xii. Coleman develops the theological implications of this definition in *Making a Way Out of No Way*.

127 Hull, *The Tactile Heart*, 31–34.

128 Clare, *Exile and Pride*, 12–13, xiii.

129 Tollifson, "Enjoying the Perfection of Imperfection," 22–23.

130 Joan Tollifson, *Nothing to Grasp* (Salisbury, UK: Non-Duality Press, 2012), 57.

131 Tollifson, "Enjoying the Perfection of Imperfection," 22–23.

132 Betcher, "Becoming Flesh of My Flesh," 106–108, 111–112.

133 Betcher, *Spirit and the Politics of Disablement*, 200.

134 McBryde Johnson, *Too Late to Die Young*, 179, 251.

135 Betcher, "Becoming Flesh of My Flesh," 115.

136 McBryde Johnson, *Too Late to Die Young*, 228.

137 Betcher, *Spirit and the Politics of Disablement*, 203.

138 Kafer, *Feminist, Queer*, Crip, 26–27.

139 Betcher, *Spirit and the Politics of Disablement*, 194.

140 Ibid., 204.

6 Fat shame

1 Lizzie Crocker, "Britain's Crazy Decision to Ban 'Beach Body' Ads," *The Daily Beast*, accessed October 12, 2015, http://www.thedailybeast.com/articles/ 2015/04/30/britain-s-crazy-decision-to-ban-beach-body-ads.html; Change. Org figure reflects tally as of April 7, 2016, https://www.change.org/p/ proteinworld-arjun-seth-remove-are-you-beach-body-ready-advertisements.

2 Crocker, "Britain's Crazy Decision"; Caroline Davies, "'Beach Body Ready' Tube Advert Protests Planned for Hyde Park," *The Guardian* (April 28, 2015), accessed October 12, 2015, http://www.theguardian.com/media/2015/apr/27/ mass-demonstration-planned-over-beach-body-ready-tube-advert.

3 Brogan Driscoll, "'Two Wrongs Don't Make A Right'," *Huffington Post*, UK, accessed October 12, 2015, http://www.huffingtonpost.co.uk/2015/ 04/25/renee-somerfield-protein-worlds-beach-body-model-responds- to-backlash_n_7141520.html; Brogan Driscoll, "'Your Body Is Not A Commodity': Controversial Beach Body Adverts Vandalised on London Underground," *The Huffington Post*, UK (April 23, 2015), accessed October 12, 2015, http://www.huffingtonpost.co.uk/2015/04/23/beach-body-advert- vandalised_n_7124444.html;

4 Crocker, "Britain's Crazy Decision."

5 Davies, "'Beach Body Ready' Tube Advert Protests."

6 Sophie Gadd, "'Why Make Your Insecurities Our Problem?' Beach Body Poster Scandal Gets Worse," *Mirror Online*, accessed May 11, 2015, http:// www.mirror.co.uk/usvsth3m/why-make-your-insecurities-problem-5573256

(April 24, 2015); Natasha Hinde, "Plus-Size Model Ashley Graham Delivers Perfect Response to Protein World's 'Beach Body' Advert," *The Huffington Post*, UK (May 5, 2015), accessed October 12, 2015, http://www.msn.com/en-us/lifestyle/whats-hot/plus-size-model-delivers-perfect-response-to-beach-body-advert/ar-BBiY0dIto-beach-body-advert/ar-BBiY0dI.

7   My books on this topic are *The Religion of Thinness: Satisfying the Spiritual Hungers behind Women's Obsession with Food and Weight* (Carlsbad, CA: Gurze, 2009) and *Starving for Salvation: The Spiritual Dimensions of Eating Problems among American Girls and Women* (New York: Oxford University Press, 1999).

8   Marilyn Wann, "Foreword: Fat Studies: An Invitation to Revolution," *The Fat Studies Reader*, eds. Esther Rothblum and Sondra Solovay (New York: New York University Press, 2009), ix.

9   Wann, "Foreword," xii-xiii

10 The indexes of many works by fat studies scholars cited in this chapter indicate the paucity of attention to traditional religion. Meanwhile, scholars of religion have paid more attention to appetite control than body size. A special issue of *Fat Studies: An Interdisciplinary Journal of Body Weight and Society* 4 (2015), edited by Lynn Gerber, Susan Hill, and LeRhonda Manigault-Bryant, signals an important step in exploring the multiple intersections between religious studies and fat studies.

11 Mycroft Masada, "Good News: A Sermon on Fat Justice," *Fat Studies*, 198–203.

12 Ibid., xii.

13 Annemarie, quoted by Susan Greenhalgh, *Fat-Talk Nation: The Human Costs of America's War on Fat* (Ithaca: Cornell University Press, 2015), 116.

14 Linda Bacon, *Health at Every Size: The Surprising Truth about Your Weight* (Dallas: Benbella Books, 2010 [2008]), 151.

15 Wann, "Foreword," xiv.

16 Greenhalgh, *Fat-Talk Nation*, 289.

17 Ibid., 40–41.

18 Ibid., 109, 102, 174, 241.

19 U.S. Department of Health and Human Services, "Overweight and Obesity Statistics," http://www.niddk.nih.gov/health-information/health-statistics/Pages/overweight-obesity-statistics.aspx; World Health Organization, Regional Office for Europe, "Data and Statistics," http://www.euro.who.int/en/health-topics/noncommunicable-diseases/obesity/data-and-statistics. Both sites accessed October 15, 2015.

20 Food and Agriculture Organization of the United Nations, "The State of Food and Agriculture," (Rome, 2013), accessed November 20, 2015, http://www.fao.org/docrep/018/i3300e/i3300e.pdf.

21 Mary Douglas, *Natural Symbols: Explorations in Cosmology* (New York: Pantheon, 1982 [1970]), xii, 115.

22 Virgie Tovar, "Pecan Pie, Sex, and Other Revolutionary Things," in *Hot and Heavy*, ed. Tovar (Berkeley: Seal Press, 2012), 175

23 Susan Hill, *Eating to Excess: The Meaning of Gluttony and the Fat Body in the Ancient World* (Santa Barbara, CA: Praeger, 2011), 2–5, 13, 63.

24 Ibid., 14, 21–22; Lisa Isherwood *The Fat Jesus: Christianity and Body Image* (New York: Seabury Books, 2008), 39.

25 Hill, *Eating to Excess*, 22–23, 26

26 Karl Olav Sandnes, *Belly and Body in the Pauline Epistles* (Cambridge: Cambridge University Press, 2012).

27 Hill, *Eating to Excess*, 40–42; Isherwood, *The Fat Jesus*, 41.

28 Hill, *Eating to Excess*, 59, 3.

29 I discuss the "legacy of Eve" in relation to contemporary women's attitudes toward food and body more in depth in *The Religion of Thinness*, 165–205.

30 Christina Less, "Reluctant Appetites: Anglo-Saxon Attitudes towards Fasting," *Saints and Scholars: New Perspectives on Anglo-Saxon Literature and Culture in Honour of Hugh Magennis*, ed. Stuart McWilliams (Cambridge: D.S. Brewer, 2012), 170; Isherwood, *The Fat Jesus*, 47.

31 Theresa Shaw, *The Burden of the Flesh: Fasting and Sexuality in Early Christianity* (Minneapolis: Augsburg Fortress, 1998), 25, 163; 174–176; 223–224

32 Ibid., 53–64, 99.

33 Ibid., 9, 21–24, 133–137, 236.

34 Carolyn Walker Bynum, *Holy Feast and Holy Fast: The Religious Significance of Food for Medieval Women* (Berkeley: University of California Press, 1987).

35 Raymond of Capua, *The Life of Catherine of Siena*, trans. George Lamb (New York: P.J. Kennedy, 1960). For a discussion of the term "anorexia mirabilis," see Joan Jacob Brumberg, *Fasting Girls: The History of Anorexia Nervosa* (New York: Plume Books, 1988), 41.

36 R. Marie Griffith, *Born Again Bodies: Flesh and Spirit in American Christianity* (Berkeley: University of California Press, 2004), 24–32, 45; quote from p. 33.

37 Quoted in Laura Fraser, "The Inner Corset: A Brief History of Fat in the United States," in *The Fat Studies Reader*, 13.

38 Griffith, *Born Again Bodies*, 32–37, 40–41, 47; Hillel Schwartz, *Never Satisfied: A Cultural History of Diets, Fantasies and Fat* (New York: Free Press, 1986), 25–28.

39 Amy Erdman Farrell, *Fat Shame: Stigma and the Fat Body in American Culture* (New York: New York University Press, 2011), 4.

40 Griffith, *Born Again Bodies*, 57–68.

41 Erdman Farrell's account builds on previous work on the history of dieting, especially Hillel Schwartz, *Never Satisfied* and Peter Stearns, *Fat History: Bodies and Beauty in the Modern West* (New York: New York University Press, 1997), whose arguments she summarizes in p. 44.

42 Quoted in Erdman Farrell, *Body Shame*, 35. See also Joyce L. Huff, "A 'Horror of Corpulence': Interrogating Bantingism and Mid-Nineteenth-Century Fat-Phobia," in *Bodies Out of Bounds: Fatness and Transgression*, eds. Jana Evans Braziel and Kathleen LeBesco (Berkeley: University of California Press, 2001), 39–59.

43 Erdman Farrell, *Fat Shame*, 26–27, 112.

44 Ibid., 34–35; Fraser, "The Inner Corset," 11.

45 Erdman Farrell, *Fat Shame*, 26–29; Levy-Navarro, "Fattening Queer History," in *The Fat Studies Reader*, 16; Hillel Schwartz, 142–143, 248–249; Roberta Pollack Seid, *Never Too Thin: Why Women Are at War with Their Bodies* (New York: Prentice Hall, 1989), 91, 226.

46 Sander L. Gilman, *Fat Boys: A Slim Book* (Lincoln: University of Nebraska Press, 2004), 49.

47 Griffith describes the form of Christianity that most influenced Americans' pursuit of physical perfectibility as "white, middle-class Protestantism," noting that many of the "somatic disciplines and devotions" that characterize this pursuit "draw their source and momentum from specific Protestant patterns." *Born Again Bodies*, 4, 8–9.

48 Clifford Putney, *Manhood and Sports in Protestant America, 1880–1920* (Cambridge, MA: Harvard University Press, 2003).

49 Erdman Farrell, *Fat Shame*, 46–49, 83, 52–53.

50 Ibid., 59–81, especially 62–63, 68–72.

51 My discussion of evangelical dieting draws heavily on Griffith, *Born Again Bodies*, 160–250.

52 Isherwood, *The Fat Jesus*, 77.

53 Griffith, *Born Again Bodies*; Lynn Gerber, *Seeking the Straight and Narrow: Weight Loss and Sexual Reorientation in Evangelical America* (Chicago: University of Chicago, 2011).

54 Emily Contois "Guilt-Free and Sinfully Delicious: A Contemporary Theology of Weight Loss Dieting," *Fat Studies*, 112–125.

55 The Pro Ana Lifestyle, accessed October 26, 2015, http://theproanalifestyle. weebly.com/the-ana-religion–lifestyle.html. A Google search for "Pro-Ana" yields numerous "thinspirational" images and other web pages promoting this subculture.

56 See, e.g., Alyssa Brown, "American's Desire to Shed Pounds Outweigh Effort," November 29, 2013, accessed October 26, 2015, http://www. gallup.com/poll/166082/americans-desire-shed-pounds-outweighs-effort. aspx. A *Bliss* magazine survey documents body-dissatisfaction among females in England, cited in Isherwood, *The Fat Jesus*, 15–16. For studies indicating high levels of concern with body image among boys, see "Exploring Disordered Eating During Early Adolescence," and "Body Image in Young Adult Men," in *Eating Disorders Review* 25:3 (May/June 2014).

57 Susan Bordo, "The Empire of Images in Our World of Bodies," *Chronicle of Higher Education* 50 (December 19, 2003): B6–B10.

58 Lynn Mabel-Lois and Alderbaran, "Fat Women and Women's Fear of Fat," in *Shadow on a Tightrope: Writings by Women on Fat Oppression*, eds. Lisa Schoenfielder and Barb Wieser (San Francisco: Aunt Lute Books, 1983), 55.

59 Feminist scholarship that critiques the mandate for female slenderness is too extensive to list here. My own work is influenced by feminists who employ a Foucauldian analysis of disciplinary power embedded in weight-loss practices, e.g. Sandra Bartky, *Femininity and Domination: Studies in the Phenomenology of Oppression* (New York: Routledge, 1990); Susan Bordo, *Unbearable Weight: Feminism, Western Culture, and the Body* (Berkeley: University of California Press, 1993); Frigga Haug, *Female Sexualization: A Collective Work of Memory* (London: Verso, 1987).

60 Andrea Elizabeth Shaw, *The Embodiment of Disobedience: Fat Black Women's Unruly Political Bodies* (New York: Lexington Books, 2006).

61 Kwok Pui-lan, "Unbinding Our Feet: Saving Brown Women and Feminist Religious Discourse," in *Postcolonialism, Feminist, and Religious Discourse*, eds. Laura Donaldson and Kwok Pui-lan (New York: Routledge, 2002), 63.

62 I discuss the neocolonial dynamics of the religion of thinness in greater depth in "Spreading the Religion of Thinness from California to Calcutta: A Postcolonial Feminist Analysis," in *The Journal of Feminist Studies in Religion* 25:1 (April 2009): 19–42.

63 Cheryl Townsend Gilkes, "The 'Loves' and 'Troubles' of African American Women's Bodies: A Womanist Challenge to Cultural Humiliation and Community Ambivalence," in *A Troubling in My Soul: Womanist Perspectives on Evil and Suffering*, ed. Emilie Townes (Maryknoll, NY: Orbis, 1993), 243–245.

64 Becky Thompson, *A Hunger So Wide and So Deep: American Women Speak Out on Eating Problems* (Minneapolis: University of Minnesota Press, 1994), 39, 92, 25–45.

65 Erdman Farrell, *Fat Shame*, 5, 131.

66 Winfrey quoted in Ibid., 126. Erdman Farrell discusses both Winfrey and Obama (among others). See pp. 124–127, 131–136.

67 Rosemarie Garland Thomson, *Extraordinary Bodies: Figuring Physical Disability in American Culture and Literature* (New York: Columbia University Press, 1997); see also Erdman Farrell, 32–34.

68 Edward Wyatt, "On 'The Biggest Loser,' Health Can Take Back Seat," *New York Times* (November 24, 2009), accessed October 25, 2015, http://www.nytimes.com/2009/11/25/business/media/25loser.html?_r=0; Rachel Arndt, "'The Biggest Loser' Cashes in on the Screen and On the Ranch," *Fast Company*, accessed October 28, 2015, http://www.fastcompany.com/1826836/biggest-loser-cashes-screen-and-ranch.

69 Alessandra Stanley makes this point at the beginning of "Plus-Size Sideshow," *The New York Times* (August 24, 1008), accessed March 30, 2016, http://www.nytimes.com/2008/08/24/arts/television/24stan.html?_r=0.

70 Wyatt, "On 'The Biggest Loser'"; Sophie Jan Evans, "'We Are All Fat Again!' Former Biggest Loser Contestants Admit 'Almost All of Them'

Have Regained Their Weight," *Dailymain.com* (January 26, 2015), accessed October 29, 2015, http://www.dailymail.co.uk/femail/article-2927207/We-fat-Former-Biggest-Loser-contestants-admit-controversial-regained-weight-endure-lasting-health-issues.html.

71 Glenn Gaesser, "Is 'Permanent Weight Loss' an Oxymoron? The Statistics on Weight Loss and the National Weight Control Registry," in *The Fat Studies Reader*, 37–39.

72 Bacon, *Health at Every Size*, 24, 67, 140.

73 Eric Oliver, *Fat Politics: The Real Story Behind America's Obesity Epidemic* (New York: Oxford University Press, 2006), 37.

74 Charlotte Biltekoff, in "The Terror Within: Obesity in Post 9/11 U.S. Life," *American Studies*, 48:3 (Fall 2007): 29, 34; Greenhalgh, *Fat-Talk Nation*, 8; Linda Bacon and Lucy Aphramor, *Body Respect: What Conventional Health Books Get Wrong, Leave Out, and Just Plain Fail to Understand about Weight* (Dallas: BenBella Books, 2014), 11; Linda Bacon, *Health at Every Size*, xxiii.

75 Marketdata Enterprises, Inc., "Weight Loss Market Sheds Some Dollars in 2013," Press Release (February 4, 2014), accessed March 30, 2016, http://www.marketdataenterprises.com/wp-content/uploads/2014/01/Diet-Market-2014-Status-Report.pdf.

76 "The U.S. Surgeon General's Call To Action To Prevent and Decrease Overweight and Obesity," accessed November 1, 2015, http://www.ncbi.nlm.nih.gov/books/NBK44206/. Greenhalgh uses the concept of the fit, thin "biocitizen" to describe how the war on fat works by enticing people to see fighting fat as a moral/civic duty. *Fat-Talk Nation*, 18–28; on fat as a "disease," see 27, 31.

77 Greenhalgh, *Fat-Talk Nation*, 27–29, viii.

78 Ibid., 105–109.

79 Ibid., 81–83.

80 Ibid., 50, 217.

81 Abby Weintraub, "Truce," in *Hot and Heavy*, 42–47.

82 Ibid.

83 Greenhalgh defines fat talk as "Comments and conversations about weight, diet, exercise, and related topics" that function as "a common language with which people strike up friendships, argue, and generally engage one another," *Fat-Talk Nation* 24–25. Greenhalgh distinguishes between "biopedagogical" and "biobullying" fat-talk (35), both of which generate fat shame.

84 Paul Ernsberger, "Does Social Class Explain the Connection between Weight and Health?" in *The Fat Studies Reader*, 25–36; Department of Health and Human Services, "Overweight and Obesity Statistics," accessed November 3, 2015, http://www.niddk.nih.gov/health-information/health-statistics/documents/stat904z.pdf.

85 Even the US government admits that social and environmental differences play a greater role in determining health than individual lifestyle choices. Bacon and Aphramor, *Body Respect*, 22–23.

86 Greenhalgh, *Fat-Talk Nation*, 59–61, 212–213. On mother-blaming, see also Natalie Boero, "Fat Kids, Working Mom, and the 'Epidemic of Obesity': Race, Class, and Mother Blame," in *The Fat Studies Reader*, 115–119.

87 Many of Greenhalgh's students who struggle intensely with weight issues are of Asian ancestry. See *Fat-Talk Nation.*

88 Bacon, *Health At Every Size*, 125–127; Wann, "Foreword," xvi; Pat Lyons, "Prescription for Harm: Diet Industry, Public Health Policy, and the 'Obesity Epidemic,' " in *The Fat Studies Reader*, 82–83.

89 Bacon and Aphramor, *Body Respect*, 12–26; Bacon, *Health at Every Size*, 68, 124–130, 137–140.

90 Lyons, "Prescription for Harm," 82; Greenhalgh, *Fat-Talk Nation*, 239.

91 Bacon, *Health at Every Size*, 101–122.

92 David Kessler, *The End of Overeating: Taking Control of the Insatiable American Appetite* (New York: Rodale, 2009).

93 Oliver, *Fat Politics;* Kathleen LeBesco, *Revolting Bodies: The Struggle to Redefine Fat Identity* (Amherst: University of Massachusetts Press, 2004); Paul Campos, *The Obesity Myth: Why America's Obsession with Weight Is Hazardous to Your Health* (New York: Gotham Books, 2004); Glenn A. Gaesser, *Big Fat Lies: The Truth About Your Weight and Your Health* (Carlsbad, CA: Gurze, 2002); Michael Gard and Jan Wright, *The Obesity Epidemic: Science, Morality and Ideology* (London and New York: Routledge, 2005); Laura Fraser, *Losing It: False Hopes and Fat Profits in the Diet Industry* (New York: A Plume Book, 1997).

94 Bacon, *Health at Every Size*, 152–155; Pat Lyons, "Prescription for Harm," 77–80; Kate Cohen, "Fen Phen Nation," *PBS Frontline* (Nov. 13, 2003), accessed November 4, 2015, http://www.pbs.org/wgbh/pages/frontline/shows/prescription/hazard/fenphen.html.

95 Erdman Farrell, *Fat Shame*, 12.

96 E. Dellinger Flum, "Impact of Gastric Bypass Operation on Survival: A Population-based Analysis, *Journal of the American College of Surgeons* 199:4 (2004): 543–551.

97 Lyons uses the phrase "by any means" to describe the mentality of the "obesity" war's leaders in "Prescription for Harm," 78.

98 Greenhalgh, *Fat-Talk Nation*, 197, 212.

99 Bacon and Aphramor, *Body Respect* 17–19; Greenhalgh, *Fat-Talk Nation*, 239.

100 Greenhalgh, *Fat-Talk Nation* 8.

101 U.S. Department of Health and Human Services, "NIH Categorical Spending: Estimates of Funding for Various Research, Condition, and Disease Categories (RCDC)" (February 5, 2015), accessed November 4, 2015, http://report.nih.gov/categorical_spending.aspx. For more on the war's hidden costs, see Part 3 of Greenhalgh's *Fat-Talk Nation*.

102 Bacon and Aphramor identify these principles (pp. 81–82) and elaborate them throughout *Body Respect.*

103 Deb Burgard, "What Is 'Health at Every Size?'" in *The Fat Studies Reader*, 42.

104 Bacon and Aphramor, *Body Respect*, 82–85.

105 Ibid., 17.

106 Marylin Wann, *Fat!So? Because You Don't Have to Apologize for Your Size* (Berkeley, CA: Ten Speed Press, 1998), 41, 52.

107 Bacon and Aphramor, *Body Respect*, 87–88.

108 Thich Nhat Hanh discusses this precept in *For A Future To Be Possible: Buddhist Ethics for Everyday Life* (Berkeley: Parallax Press, 2007), 57–69.

109 Bacon and Aphramor, *Body Respect*, 184–185.

110 Ibid., 88.

111 C. W. Huntington, Jr., "The Triumph of Narcissism: Theravada Buddhist Meditation in the Marketplace," *Journal of the American Academy of Religion* 83:3 (Sept 2015), 642.

112 For example, Shawn Copeland proffers a womanist critique of the Enlightenment/Cartesian version of selfhood in *Enfleshing Freedom: Body, Race, and Being* (Minneapolis: Fortress, 2010), 88–89.

113 Isherwood, *The Fat Jesus*, 105, 111–112.

114 Ibid., 134–135, 7, 21, 141–143.

115 "Revolting Bodies" is the title of Kathleen LeBesco's book (see footnote 92); see also LeBesco's essay "Queering Fat Bodies/Politics," in *Bodies Out of Bounds*, 74–87.

116 Paraphrasing Tovar, "Epilogue" *Hot and Heavy*, 173.

117 Tovar, "Pecan Pie, Sex…", 230.

118 Delores Williams develops this theme in "Womanist Theology: Black Women's Voices," in *Weaving the Visions: New Patterns in Feminist Spirituality*, eds. Judith Plaskow and Carol Christ (New York: HarperSanFrancisco, 1989), 179–186.

119 Beverly Wildung Harrison, "The Power of Anger in the Work of Love: Christian Ethics for Women and Other Strangers," in *Weaving the Visions*, eds. Plaskow and Christ, 220–221.

120 Tovar, "Introduction," *Hot and Heavy*, 7, 10–11.

121 Ibid., 7–11, and Tovar, "Pecan Pie, Sex…", 174.

122 Wann, *Fat!So?*, 69.

123 Jess Baker, "Why People Hate Tess Munster (and Other Happy Fat People)" *The Militant Baker* (January 28, 2015), accessed November 19, 2015, http://www.themilitantbaker.com/2015/01/why-people-hate-tess-munster-and-other.html.

124 Wann, *Fat!So?*, 25.

125 Copeland's phrase, in *Enfleshing Freedom*, 2.

126 Masada, "Good News," 199–200.

127 Ibid., 200, 197–207.

128 Tovar, "Love," 94; "Life," 8–9, 11; "Pecan Pie, Sex…", 176, in *Hot and Heavy*.

129 Emma Corbett-Ashby, "Public Stretch Mark Announcement," in *Hot and Heavy*, 30–31.

130 Emily Anderson, "Fat at the Gym," in *Hot and Heavy*, 20–24.

7 The shame of chronic pain and illness

1 David B. Morris, *The Culture of Pain* (Berkeley: University of California Press, 1993), 1–7.

2 David L. Katz, "We Can Be Disease-Proof," *Huffington Post* (September 17, 2013), accessed August 17, 2015, http://www.huffingtonpost.com/david-katz-md/how-to-be-disease-proof_b_3938307.html.

3 Arthur Kleinman, *The Illness Narratives: Suffering, Healing, and the Human Condition* (New York: Basic Books, 1988).

4 The American Chronic Pain Association, accessed December 15, 2015, http://theacpa.org; U.S. National Center for Health Statistics, accessed July 28, 2015, http://www.nationalhealthcouncil.org/sites/default/files/AboutChronicDisease.pdf.

5 Laurie Edwards, *In the Kingdom of the Sick: A Social History of Chronic Illness in America* (New York: Walker & Company, 2013), 11.

6 Melanie Thernstrom, "Pain: The Disease," *New York Times Magazine* (December 16, 2001), accessed April 2, 2016, http://www.nytimes.com/2001/12/16/magazine/pain-the-disease.html?pagewanted=all; Morris, *The Culture of Pain*, 74–78.

7 Aviva Brandt, quoted in Edwards, *In the Kingdom of the Sick*, 49.

8 Ibid., 50

9 Janet Geddis, quoted in ibid., 84.

10 Susan Sontag, *Illness as Metaphor* (New York: Farrar, Straus, and Giroux, 1977), 3.

11 Edwards, *In the Kingdom of the Sick*, 11.

12 Ibid., 52–54; Susan Wendell, "Unhealthy Disabled: Treating Chronic Illnesses as Disabilities," *Hypatia* 16:4 (2001): 17–33.

13 Edwards, *In the Kingdom of the Sick*, 52–58.

14 Deanna Thompson, *Hoping for More: Having Cancer, Talking Faith, and Accepting Grace* (Eugene, OR: Cascade Books, 2012), 88–89.

15 Wendell, "Unhealthy Disabled," 21; Jessica Leigh Hester, "Living With Invisible Illness," *The Atlantic* (July 17, 2015) 1–9, accessed August 5, 2015, http://www.theatlantic.com/health/archive/2015/07/invisible-illness-chronic-disease-fibromyalgia/398393/.

16 Edwards, *In the Kingdom of the Sick*, 55.

17   Bruce Kramer (with Kathy Wurzer), *We Know How This Ends: Living While Dying* (Minneapolis: University of Minnesota, 2015), 25.

18   Alison Kafer, *Feminist, Queer, Crip* (Bloomington: Indiana University Press, 2013), 11–13.

19   Gary Ferngren, *Medicine and Health Care in Early Christianity* (Baltimore: John Hopkins Press, 2009), 59–60.

20   Elaine Scarry, *The Body in Pain: The Making and Unmaking of the World* (New York: Oxford University Press, 1985), 16.

21   John Pilch, "Disease," in *The New Interpreter's Dictionary of the Bible D-H*, Volume 2, eds. Katharine Doob Sakenfeld, et al. (Nashville: Abingdon Press, 2007), 137–138.

22   Linda Smith, "Searching for the Roots of Healing," in *Good is the Flesh: Body, Soul, and Christian Faith*, ed. Jean Denton (London: Morehouse Publishing, 2005), 13–22; Gary Ferngren, *Medicine and Religion: A Historical Introduction* (Baltimore: John Hopkins Press, 2014), 210.

23   Pilch, "Disease," 138–139.

24   Gary Ferngren, *Medicine and Religion*, 59; Pilch, "Disease," 138.

25   David B. Morris, *Illness and Culture in the Postmodern Age* (Berkeley: University of California Press, 2000), 53. In "The Paradox of Healing Pain," *Religion* 39 (2009): 22–33, Rebecca Sachs Norris helpfully observes that "Pain may be seen as a problem to be healed or as a means for healing" (22). While she does not develop these two perspectives as options *within* Christianity, I see them as coexisting, and to some extent comingling, throughout Christian history.

26   Virginia Burrus, *Saving Shame: Martyrs, Saints, and Other Abject Subjects* (Philadelphia: University of Pennsylvania, 2007), 85–87, 104–105.

27   Carolyn Walker Bynum, "Religious Women in the Later Middle Ages," *Christian Spirituality: High Middle Ages and Reformation*, ed. Jill Raitt (New York: Crossroad, 1989), 131–132.

28   Elizabeth Clark and Herbert Richardson, eds. *Women and Religion: The Original Sourcebook of Women Christian Thought* (New York: Harper Sanfrancisco, 1996), 95, 102–103; Leigh Gilmore; *Autobiographies: A Feminist Theory of Self-Representation* (Ithaca: Cornell University Press, 1994), 139.

29   C. R. Moss, "Heavenly Healing: Eschatological Cleansing and the Resurrection of the Dead in the Early Church," *Journal of the American Academy of Religion* 79:4 (December 2011), 991–1017.

30   Dean VanDruff, "Sickness, Disease, Healing," *Archives*, accessed August 5, 2015, http://www.acts17-11.com/dialogs_sickness.html.

31   A. A. Allen, "Health, Healing, Holiness: Lesson-2," Preministerial and Christian Workers' Bible College Correspondence Courses, accessed September 9, 2015, http://www.holiness-preaching.com/history/aa_allen/health%20healing%20holiness%202.html.

32 See, e.g., Mark Mincolla, *Whole Health: A Holistic Approach to Healing for the 21st Century* (New York: Tarcher, 2015).

33 Rachel Benedict, quoting her doctor in Paula Kamen, *All in My Head: An Epic Quest to Cure an Unrelenting, Totally Unreasonable, and Only Slightly Enlightening Headache* (Cambridge, MA: Da Capo Press, 2005), 312.

34 Ivone Gebara, *Longing for Running Water: Ecofeminism and Liberation* (Minneapolis: Fortress, 1999), 89–95.

35 Stuart S. Kassan, et al., *Chronic Pain for Dummies* (Hoboken, NJ: Wiley Publishing, 2008), 1, 12.

36 Edwards, *In the Kingdom of the Sick*, 110–111.

37 Kassan, et al., *Chronic Pain for Dummies*, 1, 29–32, 211.

38 Reflecting a search on April 1, 2016; numbers fluctuate daily.

39 "Unite and Fight Cancer," accessed August 6, 2015, http://www. uniteandfight.org.

40 Advertisement for Warriors in Pink merchandise in *Health* (October 2011): 83; see also "Warriors in Pink," accessed April 1, 2016, http://www. warriorsinpink.ford.com/we-are-warriors/

41 S. Lochlann Jain, *Malignant: How Cancer Becomes Us* (Berkeley, University of CA, 2013), 31, 59.

42 "American Cancer Society," accessed August 6, 2015, http://www.cancer.org.

43 Aviva Patz, "Breast Cancer: What You Must Know Now," *Health* (October 2011), 77.

44 Lochlann Jain, *Malignant*, 8–12.

45 Laura Beil, "The Enemy Inside You," *Women's Health* (March, 2014), accessed August 4, 2014, http://www.womenshealthmag.com/health/ chronic-inflammation.

46 "American Lung Association," accessed August 7, 2015, http://www.lung. org/lung-disease/asthma/taking-control-of-asthma/; "MedHelp" blog by "curiousasheck" (September 7, 2013), accessed August 7, 2015, http://www. medhelp.org/posts/Asthma/Battling-Asthma/show/2005573.

47 "Arthritis Foundation," accessed April 2, 2016, http://www.arthritis.org and http://www.arthritis.org/fighting-for-you/.

48 "New Age," accessed August 25, 2015, http://shop.destroydiseases.com/ GUARANTEED-to-Destroy-Disease-Quickly-Original-Version-DWNLD-NEW-AGE-Health-Guide.htm.

49 Kramer, *We Know How This Ends*, 24

50 Kate Granger, "Having Cancer is Not a Fight or a Battle," *Guardian* (April 25, 2014), accessed August 12, 2015, http://www.theguardian.com/society/2014/ apr/25/having-cancer-not-fight-or-battle.

51 Lochlann Jain, *Malignant*, 35.

52 Ibid., 68–69.

53 Sontag, *Illness as Metaphor*, 58.

54 Sharon Betcher, *Spirit and the Politics of Disablement* (Minneapolis: Fortress, 2007), 8, 22.

55 Lochlain Jain, *Malignant*, 205–209, 212, 219.

56 Ibid, 207–209.

57 Edwards, *In the Kingdom of the Sick*, 28–47, 88–89.

58 Ibid., 13, 27; Lochlann Jain, *Malignant*, 57.

59 David L. Katz, *Disease-Proof: The Remarkable Truth About What Makes Us Well* (New York: Hudson Street Press, 2013), 8–14, x–xvi.

60 Ibid., 48, 174, 43.

61 Katz, "We Can Be Disease-Proof."

62 Thompson, *Hoping for More*, 79.

63 This phrase comes from the title of Arthur Frank's book: *At the Will of the Body: Reflections on Illness* (New York: Houghton Mifflin, 2002).

64 The U.S. Centers for Disease Control and Prevention provides statistics on chronic illnesses that include demographic information, accessed April 8, 2016, http://www.cdc.gov/DataStatistics/. In *Body Respect: What Conventional Health Books Get Wrong, Leave Out, and Just Plain Fail to Understand about Weight* (Dallas, TX: Bella Books, 2014), Linda Bacon and Lucy Aphramor note: "People lower on the social ladder usually run twice the risk of serious illness and premature death as those near the top," 22. See also Lochlann Jain, *Malignant*, 39; Edwards, *In the Kingdom of the Sick*, 194–195.

65 Lochlann Jain, *Malignant*, 39.

66 Kamen, *All In My Head*, 280.

67 Katz, *Disease-Proof*, 16, 229, 24.

68 Katz, "We Can Be Disease-Proof."

69 Janet Geddis, quoted in Edwards, *In the Kingdom of the Sick*, 72–73.

70 Alicia Cornwell, quoted in ibid., 71.

71 Kamen makes this point throughout *All in My Head*; see also Edwards, *In the Kingdom of the Sick*, 69–86.

72 Diane Hoffman and Anita Tarzian, "The Girl Who Cried Pain: A Bias Against Women in the Treatment of Pain," *Journal of Law, Medicine, & Ethics* 29 (2001): 21.

73 Kamen, *All in My Head*, 161, 164.

74 Eve Ensler, *In the Body of the World* (New York: Henry Holt and Company, 2013), 39.

75 Feminists have critically analyzed Victorian discourses on hysteria. See, e.g., Elaine Showalter, *Hystories: Hysteria, Gender and Culture* (New York: Pan Books, 1997); Barbara Ehrenriech and Deirdre English, *For Her Own Good: Two Centuries of the Experts' Advice to Women* (New York: Anchor Books, 2005); Jane Gallop, *Thinking Through the Body* (New York: Columbia University Press, 1988); Kamen, *All In My Head*, 97–112.

76   Kamen, *All in My Head*, 80.

77   Edwards, *In the Kingdom of the Sick*, 115–117.

78   Brené Brown, *Daring Greatness: How the Courage to Be Vulnerable Transforms the Way We Live, Love, Parent and Lead* (New York: Gotham, 2012), 91–94.

79   Melissa McLaughlin, quoted by Edwards, *In the Kingdom of the Sick*, 27.

80   Frank, *At the Will of the Body*, 58.

81   Kamen, *All in My Head*, 212.

82   Beth Eddy, "Stress Tested," *Religious Studies News* (September 8, 2015), accessed September 17, 2015, http://rsn.aarweb.org/guide-guild/stress-tested.

83   Sandy Boucher, *Hidden Spring: A Buddhist Woman Confronts Cancer* (Boston: Wisdom Publications, 2000), 147.

84   Lochlann Jain, *Malignant*, 22.

85   Ensler, *In the Body of the World*, 65.

86   Lochlann Jain, *Malignant*, 55.

87   Carolyn Johnson, "How an Obscure Drug's 4000% Price Increase Might Finally Spur Action on Soaring Health Care Costs," *Washington Post Online* (September 21, 2015), accessed September 23, 2015, http://www.washingtonpost.com/news/wonkblog/wp/2015/09/21/how-an-obscure-drugs-4000-price-increase-might-finally-spur-action-on-soaring-health-care-costs/.

88   Kamen, *All in My Head*, 57–59, 48.

89   Kristine Chip, quoted by Lochlann Jain, *Malignant*, 32.

90   "Duncan Cross" (pseudonym), quoted by Edwards, *In the Kingdom of the Sick*, 90.

91   Frank, *At the Will of the Body*, 110–111.

92   Kamen, *All in My Head*, 8.

93   Sontag, *Illness as Metaphor*, 53–57, 22–23.

94   Ensler, *In the Body of the World*, 54–57.

95   Ibid., 27, 20.

96   Ibid., 41–42.

97   Ibid., 7.

98   Ibid., 68–69, 38, 75–76.

99   Margaret Mohrmann, "The Idolatry of Health and the Idolatry of Life," in *Good is the Flesh*, ed. Denton, 35–37.

100   Kramer, *We Know How This Ends*, 24.

101   Ibid., 29–32, 58.

102   Ibid., 24.

103   Gebara, *Longing for Running Water*, 146–147.

104 Gebara, *Out of the Depths: Women's Experience of Evil and Salvation* (Minneapolis: Augsburg Fortress, 2002) 109–132.

105 Ibid., 113.

106 Audre Lorde, *The Cancer Journals* (San Francisco: Aunt Lute Books, 1997 [1980]), 49. See, e.g., Delores Williams' womanist critique of redemptive suffering in *Sisters in the Wilderness: The Challenge of Womanist God-Talk* (Maryknoll, NY: 1993), 161–167.

107 Thompson, *Hoping for More*, 87–88.

108 Ibid., 86–87, 129.

109 Lorde *The Cancer Journals*, 8, 56.

110 Gebara, *Out of the Depths*, 114.

111 Ibid., 116, 119.

112 Lorde, *The Cancer Journals*, 8, 56, 16–22.

113 Ibid., 49–52, 42, 60–63.

114 Ibid., 62–66.

115 Ibid., 49, 53, 62–68.

116 Ibid., 8, 67–68.

117 Ibid., 14.

118 Gebara, *Out of the Depths*, 123.

119 Boucher, *Hidden Spring*, 61–62.

120 Kramer, *We Know How This Ends*, 147–148.

121 Lorde, *The Cancer Journals*, 75; Ensler, *In the Body of the World*, 183.

122 Lorde, *The Cancer Journals*, 11, 15, 18, 79, 61; Ensler, *In the Body of the World*, 196.

123 Lorde, *The Cancer Journals*, 24.

124 Gebara, *Longing for Running Water*, 30, 152.

125 Thompson, *Hoping for More*, 51-52.

126 Ibid., xiv, 81.

127 Ibid., xiv-xv.

128 Kramer, *We Know How This Ends*, 17–20, 25, 54–56.

129 Gebara, *Longing for Running Water*, 159.

130 Thompson, *Hoping for More*, 21, xiii–xiv. For Thompson, this communal incarnation of love extends to the "virtual body of Christ," which communicates support through Internet websites like CaringBridge (57).

131 Lorde, *The Cancer Journals*, 18–19, 10, 29.

132 Ensler, *In the Body of the World*, 162–169.

133 Thompson, *Hoping for More*, 24.

134 Frank, *At The Will of the Body*, 118.

135 Virginia Woolf, *On Being Ill* (Ashfield, MA: Paris Press, 2012 [1883]), 3–5, 11–12.

136 Ibid., 12–13. See Hermione Lee, "Introduction," to Woolf's *On Being Ill*, xxxi-xxviii.

137 Frank, *At The Will of the Body*, 119–120.

138 Ensler, *In the Body of the World*, 214–216.

139 Lorde, *The Cancer Journals*, 76.

140 Ibid., 76–78.

141 Jo Hilder, "9 Things Not to Say to Someone with Cancer. Please," *Mamamia* blog (September 20, 2012), accessed Sept. 21, 2015, http://www.mamamia. com.au/wellbeing/9-things-not-to-say-to-someone-who-has-cancer/.

142 Ensler, *In the Body of the World*, 88–89.

143 Gebara, *Longing for Running Water*, 161–164.

8 The shame of getting old

1 National Stroke Association, "What is TIA?" accessed Jan. 6, 2016, http://www.stroke.org/understand-stroke/what-stroke/what-tia

2 Susan Moon, *This is Getting Old: Zen Thoughts on Aging with Humor and Dignity* (Boston: Shambala, 2010), ix.

3 Quoted in Mary Pipher, *Another Country: Navigating the Emotional Terrain of Our Elders* (New York: Riverhead Books, 1999), 15.

4 Ibid., 39.

5 Thesaurus.com, accessed January 12, 2016, http://www.thesaurus.com/browse/stereotype?s=t.

6 Sheree Kwong See and E. Nicoladis, "Impact of Contact on the Development of Children's Positive Stereotyping about Aging Language Competence," *Educational Gerontology* 36 (2010): 52–66.

7 David Oliver, "A Holistic Approach to Ministry," in *Religion and Aging: An Anthology of the Poppele Papers*, ed. Derrel Watkins (New York: Haworth, 2001), 6.

8 Meika Loe, *Aging Our Way: Independent Elders, Interdependent Lives* (New York: Oxford University Press, 2011), 210, 214.

9 Ehud Bodner, "On the Origins of Ageism among Older and Younger Adults," *International Psychogeriatrics* 21:6 (2009): 1006–1008.

10 Ibid., 1003–1004.

11 Margo DeMello, *Body Studies: An Introduction* (New York: Routledge, 2014), 46.

12 Muriel Gillick, *The Denial of Aging: Perpetual Youth, Eternal Life, and Other Dangerous Fantasies* (Cambridge: Harvard University Press, 2006), 4.

13 Richard Hays and Judith Hays, "The Christian Practice of Growing Old: The Witness of Scripture," in *Growing Old in Christ*, ed. Stanley Hauerwas, et al. (Grand Rapids, MI: William B. Eerdman's Publishing, 2003), 11.

14 J. Gordon Harris, "Aging," *The New Interpreter's Dictionary of the Bible A-C*, Volume 1, ed. Katherine Doob Sakenfeld (Nashville, TN: Abingdon, 2006), 70–71; D. J. W., "Age, Old Age," in *The New Bible Dictionary*, Third Edition, ed., D. R. W. Wood (Downers Grove, IL: Intervarsity Press, 1996), 18.

15 Jason Bembry, *Yahweh's Coming of Age* (Winona Lake, IN: Eisenbrauns, 2011).

16 D. J. W., "Age, Old Age," 18.

17 Linda Maloney, "The Pastoral Epistles," in *Searching the Scriptures, Volume Two: A Feminist Commentary*, ed. Elisabeth Schüssler Fiorenza (New York: Crossroad, 1994), 371–372.

18 Rowan A. Greer, "Special Gift and Special Burden," in *Growing Old in Christ*, 31–32.

19 Harris, "Aging," 70–71; D .J. W., "Age, Old Age," 18.

20 World Health Organization, "Definition of an Older or Elderly Person," accessed January 12, 2016, http://www.who.int/healthinfo/survey/ageingdefnolder/en/; Loe, *Aging Our Way*, 10–11.

21 Gary F. Merrill, *Our Aging Bodies* (New Brunswick, NJ: Rutgers University Press, 2015), 4–28; American Association of Retired Persons, "Chronic Care: A Call to Action for Health Reform" (2009), accessed January 13, 2016, http://assets.aarp.org/rgcenter/health/beyond_50_hcr_conditions.pdf.

22 Merrill discusses these and other physiological changes in *Our Aging Bodies*.

23 Gillick, *The Denial of Aging*, 8–9.

24 Jane Gross, *A Bittersweet Season: Caring for Our Aging Parents – and Ourselves* (New York: Vintage, 2011), 285.

25 Loe, *Aging Our Way*, 5.

26 Gross, *A Bittersweet Season*, 15.

27 Ibid., 306, 314–15.

28 Laura Cartensen, *A Long Bright Future: Happiness, Health, and Financial Security in an Age of Increased Longevity* (New York: Crown Publishers, 2011), 16–17.

29 Merrill, *Our Aging Bodies*, 1–30; Loe, *Aging Our Way*, 11–12.

30 Gillick, *The Denial of Aging*, 221–222; 267.

31 Loe, *Aging Our Way*, 21–22.

32 Atul Gawande, *Being Mortal: Medicine and What Matters in the End* (New York: Henry Holt and Company, 2014), 17, 71–75.

33 Pipher, *Another Country*, 44–45.

34 Gross, *A Bittersweet Season*, 6, 11–13.

35 Merrill, *Our Aging Bodies*, 2.

36 DeMello, *Body Studies*, 44.

37 Gawande, *Being Mortal*, 48; "Annual Median Cost of Long Term Care in the Nation," *Genworth*, accessed Feb 18, 2016, https://www.genworth.com/corporate/about-genworth/industry-expertise/cost-of-care.html.

38 Ann Neumann, "Dying in America," *Harvard Divinity Bulletin* (Summer/ Autumn, 2015): 7.

39 Laura Talarsky, "Defining Aging and the Aged: Cultural and Social Constructions of Elders in the U.S." *Arizona Anthropologist* 13 (1998): 103–104.

40 Ibid., 102.

41 DeMello, *Body Studies*, 45–46; see also Arlene Weintraub, *Selling the Fountain of Youth: How the Anti-Aging Industry Made a Disease Out of Getting Old – and Made Billions* (New York: Basic Books, 2010), 111.

42 Merrill, *Our Aging Bodies*, 143–145.

43 Gawande, *Being Mortal*, 36, 46.

44 Elizabeth O'Brien, "10 Secrets of the Anti-Aging Industry," *MarketWatch* (Feb. 13, 2014), accessed January 19, 2016, http://www.marketwatch.com/story/ 10-things-the-anti-aging-industry-wont-tell-you-2014-02-11.

45 The American Academy of Anti-Aging Medicine, "What is Anti-Aging Medicine?" Accessed January 19, 2016, http://www.a4m.com; for an accessible article on anti-aging research, see Stephen Hall, "On Beyond 100," *National Geographic* (May, 2013), accessed, March 7, 2016, http://ngm. nationalgeographic.com/2013/05/longevity/hall-text.

46 Gillick, *The Denial of Aging*, 195–224; Weintraub, *Selling the Fountain of Youth*, 3–19.

47 Stephen Cave, *Immortality: The Quest To Live Forever And How It Drives Civilization* (New York: Crown Publishers, 2012), 4, 118.

48 DeMello, *Body Studies*, 27.

49 Gawande, *Being Mortal*, 9.

50 Moon, *This Is Getting Old*, 26–39.

51 Gillick, *The Denial of Aging*, 46–47, 63–67.

52 Gawande, *Being Mortal*, 259.

53 "The Cost of Dying," *60 Minutes*, CBS News (November 20, 2009).

54 Cave, *Immortality*, 67–77.

55 Gillick, *The Denial of Aging*, 205, 124.

56 Gawande, *Being Mortal*, 149, 220.

57 Ibid., 177–182, 243.

58 Gross, *A Bittersweet Season*, 12.

59 Gillick, *The Denial of Aging*, 225–226, 5.

60 Greer, "Special Gift and Special Burden," 23–24; Hays and Hays, "The Christian Practice of Growing Old," 3–4.

61 Cave, *Immortality*, 88–102.

62 Margaret Miles, *Beyond the Centaur: Imagining the Intelligent Body* (Eugene, OR: Cascade Books, 2014), 26.

63 Augustine, *City of God*, 22.15, quoted in Greer, "Special Gift and Special Burden," 25.

64 Bede, *On Genesis* 1.1.11-13, CCSL 118A, ed. C. W. Jones (Turnout: Brepols, 1967), 14–15.

65 Augustine, *City of God*, 22.15, quoted in Greer, 25. Historian Carolyn Walker Bynum says early and medieval theologians' preoccupation with resurrected bodies expressed both a belief that human souls needed flesh to be complete, and revulsion at the impurity of physical decay. *The Resurrection of the Body in Western Christianity* (New York: Columbia University Press, 1995).

66 David Aers, "The Christian Practice of Growing Old in the Middle Ages," in *Growing Old in Christ*, 33–35, 40–42.

67 Quoted in ibid., 44.

68 Helen Rodnite Lemay, *Women's Secrets: A Translation of Pseudo-Albertus Magnus'* De Secretis Mulierum *with Commentaries* (Albany, NY: State University of New York Press, 1992).

69 Aers, "The Christian Practice of Growing Old in the Middle Ages," 41; quotes from "On Women's Secrets" are from Aers's essay.

70 Cave, *Immortality*, 102; Pew Research Center, "America's Changing Religious Landscape" (May, 12, 2015), accessed January 28, 2016, http://www.pewforum.org/2015/05/12/americas-changing-religious-landscape/#fn-23198-1.

71 DeMello, *Body Studies*, 45; Bodner, "The Origins of Ageism," 1011.

72 Ibid., 46.

73 Anabelle Gurwitch, *I See You Made an Effort: Compliments, Indignities, and Survival Stories from the Edge of 50* (New York: Plume, 2014), 24–34.

74 Katherine Newman, *A Different Shade of Gray: Midlife and Beyond in the Inner City* (New York: The New Press, 2003), 113–143.

75 DeMello, *Body Studies*, 48.

76 O-Brien, "10 Secrets of the Anti-Aging Industry"; see also Weintraub, *Selling the Fountain of Youth*, 14-15.

77 Philosophy, "Hope in a Jar," accessed January 21, 2016, http://www.philosophy.com/original-formula-moisturiser-for-all-skin-types/hope-in-a-jar,default,pd.html.

78 Elemér Hankiss explores trivial/existential nexus in *The Toothpaste of Immortality: Self-Construction in the Consumer Age* (Baltimore, MA: Johns Hopkins University Press, 2006).

79 Alexandra Petrie, "With Hillary Clinton's *People* Cover, Sometimes a Chair is Just a Chair," *Washington Post* (June 4, 2014) http://www.washingtonpost.com/blogs/compost/wp/2014/06/04/with-hillary-clintons-people-cover-sometimes-a-chair-is-just-a-chair/; Matt Murray, "Hillary Clinton's Magazine Cover Inspires 'Walker' Meme," *Today* (June 5, 2014) http://www.today.com/money/hillary-clintons-magazine-cover-inspires-walker-meme-2D79758918; Catherine Thompson, "Drudge Suggests Hillary Is 'Holding A Walker' On *People* Magazine Cover," *TPMLivewire* (June 4, 2014) http://talkingpointsmemo.com/livewire/drudge-hillary-clinton-people-cover-walker; Adam Auriemma, "Solved: *People* Magazine's Hillary Clinton Cover Mystery,"

The Wall Street Journal (June 4, 2014) http://blogs.wsj.com/washwire/2014/06/04/solved-people-magazines-hillary-clinton-cover-mystery/. All websites accessed Jan. 5, 2016.

80 DeMello, *Body Studies*, 48.

81 Moon, *This is Getting Old*, 103–105.

82 Ibid., 104.

83 Laura Hurd Clarke and Melanie Griffin, "Visible and Invisible Ageing: Beauty Work as a Response to Ageism," *Ageing and Society* 28 (2008): 653–674.

84 Christiane Northrup, *Goddesses Never Age: The Secret Prescription for Radiance, Vitality, and Well-Being* (Carlsbad, CA: Hay House, 2015), xi–xiv, 17.

85 Ibid., 356, book jacket, back cover.

86 Ibid., x-xvi.

87 Ibid., x-xiii, book jacket, 334–343.

88 Ibid., xv, 3–7.

89 Ibid., xi.

90 Ibid., 13–14, book jacket.

91 Ibid., xvi.

92 Thomas DeBaggio, *Losing My Mind: An Intimate Look at Life with Alzheimer's* (New York: The Free Press, 2003), 41.

93 Ibid., 48, 68.

94 Ibid., 44–47, 136.

95 Ibid., 29.

96 Ibid., 181–182, 116.

97 Ibid., 141, 48, 162, 184.

98 David Snowdon, *Aging with Grace: What the Nun Study Teaches Us about Leading Longer, Healthier, More Meaningful Lives* (New York: Bantam, 2001), 100.

99 Doris Grumbach, *Coming into the End Zone: A Memoir* (New York: W. W. Norton & Company, 1991).

100 Jean Shinoda Bolen, *Crones Don't Whine: Concentrated Wisdom for Juicy Women* (San Francisco: Conari, 2003), 75–76.

101 Gloria Steinem, *Doing Sixty and Seventy* (Berkeley, CA: Elders Academy, 2006), 5, 22.

102 "Sonja," quoted by Mary Pipher, *Another Country*, 44.

103 Moon, *This Is Getting Old*, xi.

104 Ibid., 100.

105 Loe, *Aging Our Way*, 146–147.

106 Quoted in ibid., 145–149, 10.

107 Jacqueline Bussie, *The Laughter of the Oppressed: Ethical and Theological Resistance in Wiesel, Morrison, and Endo* (London: Bloomsbury, 2007).

108 Loe, *Aging Our Way*, 152, 146.

109 Ibid., 11.

110 Michael A. Fletcher, "Research Ties Economic Inequality to Gap in Life Expectancy," *Washington Post* (March 10, 2013) accessed February 17, 2016, https://www.washingtonpost.com/business/economy/research-ties-economic-inequality-to-gap-in-life-expectancy/2013/03/10/c7a323c4-7094-11e2-8b8d-e0b59a1b8e2a_story.html; Cartensen, *A Long Bright Future*, 41.

111 Snowdon, *Aging with Grace*, 41–42.

112 Paul Irving, ed. *The Upside of Aging: How Long Life is Changing the World of Health, Work, Innovation, Policy, and Purpose* (Hoboken, NJ: Wiley, 2014).

113 Cave, *Immortality*, 67–78; Gillick, *The Denial of Aging*, 12.

114 Snowdon, *Aging with Grace*, 202.

115 Ibid., 214.

116 Gawande, *Being Mortal*, 111–128.

117 Loe, *Aging Our Way* 143; Lisa Barry, et al., "Higher Burden of Depression among Old Women: The Effect of Onset, Persistence and Mortality Over Time," *Archives of General Psychiatry* 65:2 (February 2008): 172–178, accessed February 29, 2016, http://www.ncbi.nlm.nih.gov/pmc/articles/PMC2793076/

118 Loe, *Aging Our Way*, 20–26.

119 Newman, *A Different Shade of Gray*, 22–23, 141–142.

120 Loe, *Aging Our Way*, 180–181, 193–196, 219.

121 Ibid., 85, 232–233.

122 Alice Walker, *In Search of Our Mother's Gardens: Womanist Prose* (New York: Harcourt Brace Jovanovich, 1983).

123 Kwok Pui-lan, "Mothers and Daughters, Writers and Fighters," in *Inheriting Our Mothers Gardens: Feminist Theology in Third World Perspective*, eds. Letty Russell, et al (Louisville: The Westminster Press, 1988), 29.

124 Mercy Amba Oduyoye, "Be a Woman, and Africa Will Be Strong," in *Inheriting Our Mothers Gardens*, 36.

125 Lara Medina, "Napantla Spirituality: My Path to the Source(s) of Healing," in *Fleshing the Spirit: Spirituality and Activism in Chicana, Latina, and Indigenous Women's Lives*, eds. Elisa Facio and Irene Lara (Tucson: University of Arizona Press, 2014), 170.

126 Patrisse Cullors and Robert K. Ross, interview with Krista Tippett, "The Resilient World We're Building Now," *On Being*, National Public Radio (February 18, 2016), accessed February 28, 2016, http://www.onbeing.org/program/patrisse-cullors-and-robert-ross-the-resilient-world-were-building-now/8425.

127 Gillick, *The Denial of Aging*, 235, 268.

128 Gawande, *Being Mortal*, 50.

129 Loe, *Aging Our Way*, 7, 33–41, 85.

130 John Rowe and Robert Kahn, "Successful Aging," *The Gerontologist* 37:4 (1997): 433.

131 Pipher, *Another Country*, 52; Pacific Institute website, accessed February 29, 2016, http://pacificinstitute.org/index.php

132 Loe, *Aging Our Way*, 101.

133 Gawande, *Being Mortal*, 92.

134 Ira Byock, *Dying Well: Peace and Possibilities at the End of Life* (New York: Riverhead, 1997), 34.

135 St. Benedict, *The Rule of St. Benedict in English*, ed. Timothy Fry, O.S.B. (Collegeville, MN: Liturgical Press, 1982), 28.

136 Henry David Thoreau, *Walden and Civil Disobedience* (New York: Signet, 2012 [1854]), 64–65.

137 Gross, *A Bittersweet Season*, 337–359.

138 Steinem, *Doing Sixty and Seventy*, xiv.

139 Loe, *Aging Our Way*, 87–88, 276–277.

140 Laura Cartensen, "Our Aging Population—It May Just Save Us All," in *The Upside of Aging*, 3–4.

141 Cartensen, *A Long Bright Future*, 5, 16–17.

142 Laura Cartensen, "Why Should We Look Forward to Getting Older?" *TED Radio Hour* interview with Guy Raz (June 22, 2015), accessed February 21, 2016, http://www.npr.org/templates/transcript/transcript.php?storyId=414999589

143 Lisa Isherwood and Elizabeth Stuart, *Introducing Body Theology* (Sheffield, UK: Sheffield Academic, 1998), 65, 81.

144 Monica Coleman, *Making a Way Out of No Way: A Womanist Theology* (Minneapolis: Fortress, 2008), 45.

145 Moon, *This Is Getting Old*, xii-xiii.

146 Snowdon, *Aging with Grace*, 214.

147 Miles, *Beyond the Centaur*, 116–118.

Epilogue

1 Eve Ensler asked a similar question in *The Good Body*, a play about her tormented relationship with her less-than-flat stomach (New York: Villard, 2004), ix.

Selected bibliography

Aers, David. "The Christian Practice of Growing Old in the Middle Ages." In Hauerwas et al., *Growing Old in Christ*, 38–59.

Armstrong, Karen. *Twelve Steps to a Compassionate Life*. New York: Alfred A. Knopf, 2010.

Bacon, Linda. *Health at Every Size: The Surprising Truth about Your Weight*. Dallas: Benbella Books, 2010 (2008).

Bacon, Linda and Lucy Aphramor. *Body Respect: What Conventional Health Books Get Wrong, Leave Out, and Just Plain Fail to Understand about Weight*. Dallas: BenBella Books, 2014.

Barry, Lisa C. and Heather G. Allore, Zhenchao Gue, Martha Bruce, and Thomas Gill. "Higher Burden of Depression among Old Women: The Effect of Onset, Persistence and Mortality Over Time." *Archives of General Psychiatry* 65 no. 2 (February 2008): 172–178.

Bartky, Sandra. *Femininity and Domination: Studies in the Phenomenology of Oppression*. New York: Routledge, 1990.

Betcher, Sharon. *Spirit and the Politics of Disablement*. Minneapolis: Fortress, 2007.

Betcher, Sharon. "Becoming Flesh of My Flesh: Feminist and Disability Theologies on the Edge of Posthumanist Discourse." *Journal of Feminist Studies in Religion* 26 no. 2 (2010): 107–118.

Biltekoff, Charlotte. "The Terror Within: Obesity in Post 9/11 U.S. Life." *American Studies* 48 no. 3 (Fall 2007): 29–48.

Bodner, Ehud. "On the Origins of Ageism among Older and Younger Adults." *International Psychogeriatrics* 21 no. 6 (2009): 1003–1014.

Bordo, Susan. *Unbearable Weight: Feminism, Western Culture, and the Body*. Berkeley: University of California Press, 1993.

Boucher, Sandy. *Hidden Spring: A Buddhist Woman Confronts Cancer*. Boston: Wisdom Publications, 2000.

Braziel, Jana Evans and Kathleen LeBesco, eds. *Bodies Out of Bounds: Fatness and Transgression*. Berkeley: University of California Press, 2001.

Brown, Brené. *Daring Greatness: How the Courage to Be Vulnerable Transforms the Way We Live, Love, Parent and Lead*. New York: Gotham, 2012.

Brown, Peter. *The Body and Society: Men, Women, and Sexual Renunciation in Early Christianity*. New York: Columbia University Press, 1988.

Brumberg, Joan Jacob. *The Body Project: An Intimate History of American Girls*. New York: Vintage Books, 1997.

Brumberg, Joan Jacob. *Fasting Girls: The History of Anorexia Nervosa*. New York: Plume Books, 1988.

Burgard, Deb. "What Is 'Health at Every Size?'" In Rothblum and Solovay, *The Fat Studies Reader*, 42–53.

Burrus, Virginia. *Saving Shame: Martyrs, Saints, and Other Abject Subjects*. Philadelphia: University of Pennsylvania Press, 2007.

Bussie, Jacqueline. *The Laughter of the Oppressed: Ethical and Theological Resistance in Wiesel, Morrison, and Endo*. London: Bloomsbury, 2007.

Bynum, Carolyn Walker. *Holy Feast and Holy Fast: The Religious Significance of Food for Medieval Women*. Berkeley: University of California Press, 1987.

Bynum, Carolyn Walker. *The Resurrection of the Body in Western Christianity*. New York: Columbia University Press, 1995.

Byock, Ira. *Dying Well: Peace and Possibilities at the End of Life*. New York: Riverhead, 1997.

Campos, Paul. *The Obesity Myth: Why America's Obsession with Weight Is Hazardous to Your Health*. New York: Gotham Books, 2004.

Cartensen, Laura. *A Long Bright Future: Happiness, Health, and Financial Security in an Age of Increased Longevity*. New York: Crown Publishers, 2011.

Cartensen, Laura. "Our Aging Population—It May Just Save Us All." In Irving, *The Upside of Aging*, 3–18.

Cave, Stephen. *Immortality: The Quest to Live Forever and How It Drives Civilization*. New York: Crown Publishers, 2012.

Chödrön, Pema. *Living Beautifully with Uncertainty and Change*. Boston: Shambala, 2012.

Christ, Carol P. and Judith Plaskow, eds. *Womanspirit Rising: A Feminist Reader in Religion*. New York: Harper & Row, 1979.

Clare, Eli. *Exile and Pride: Disability, Queerness and Liberation*. Cambridge, MA: South End Press, 2009 (1999).

Clark, Elizabeth, ed. *Women in the Early Church*. Wilmington, DL: Michael Glazier, 1983.

Clark, Elizabeth and Herbert Richardson, eds. *Women and Religion: The Original Sourcebook of Women in Christian Thought*. New York: HarperCollins, 1996 (1977).

Coleman, Monica. *Making a Way Out of No Way: A Womanist Theology*. Minneapolis, MN: Fortress, 2008.

Contois, Emily. "Guilt-Free and Sinfully Delicious: A Contemporary Theology of Weight Loss Dieting." In Gerber, Hill, and Manigault-Bryant, *Fat Studies*, 112–125.

Copeland, Shawn. *Enfleshing Freedom: Body, Race, and Being*. Minneapolis: Fortress, 2010.

Creamer, Deborah Beth. *Disability and Christian Theology: Embodied Limits and Constructive Possibilities*. New York: Oxford University Press, 2010.

Davis, Lennard. *Enforcing Normalcy: Disability, Deafness, and the Body*. New York: Verso, 1995.

DeBaggio, Thomas. *Losing My Mind: An Intimate Look at Life with Alzheimer's*. New York: The Free Press, 2003.

DeMello, Margo. *Body Studies: An Introduction*. New York: Routledge, 2014.

Denton, Jean, ed. *Good is the Flesh: Body, Soul, and Christian Faith*. London: Morehouse Publishing, 2005.

Descartes, René. *Discourse on Method*. Translated by Laurence Lafleur. Upper Saddle River, NJ: Prentice Hall, 1956.

Donaldson, Laura E. and Kwok Pui-lan, eds. *Postcolonialism, Feminist, and Religious Discourse*. New York: Routledge, 2002.

Douglas, Mary. *Purity and Danger: An Analysis of Concepts of Pollution and Taboo.* New York: Routledge, 1992 (1966).

Douglas, Mary. *Natural Symbols: Explorations in Cosmology.* New York: Routledge, 2003 (1970).

Edwards, Laurie. *In the Kingdom of the Sick: A Social History of Chronic Illness in America.* New York: Walker & Company, 2013.

Ehrenriech, Barbara and Deirdre English. *For Her Own Good: Two Centuries of the Experts' Advice to Women.* New York: Anchor Books, 2005.

Eiesland, Nancy. *The Disabled God: Toward a Liberatory Theology of Disability.* Nashville: Abingdon, 1994.

Ensler, Eve. *In the Body of the World.* New York: Henry Holt and Company, 2013.

Erdman Farrell, Amy. *Fat Shame: Stigma and the Fat Body in American Culture.* New York: New York University Press, 2011.

Ernsberger, Paul. "Does Social Class Explain the Connection between Weight and Health?" In Rothblum and Solovay, *The Fat Studies Reader,* 25–36.

Ferngren, Gary. *Medicine and Health Care in Early Christianity.* Baltimore: John Hopkins Press, 2009.

Ferngren, Gary. *Medicine and Religion: A Historical Introduction.* Baltimore: John Hopkins Press, 2014.

Foucault, Michel. *The Order of Things: An Archeology of the Human Sciences.* New York: Vintage, 1973 (1970).

Foucault, Michel. *Discipline and Punish: The Birth of the Prison.* New York: Vintage, 1995 (1977).

Foucault, Michel. *Power/Knowledge: Selected Interviews and Other Writings, 1972–1977.* Edited by Colin Gordon. New York: Vintage, 1980.

Frank, Arthur. *At the Will of the Body: Reflections on Illness.* New York: Houghton Mifflin, 2002.

Fraser, Laura. "The Inner Corset: A Brief History of Fat in the United States." In Rothblum and Solovay, *The Fat Studies Reader,* 11–14.

Fraser, Laura. *Losing It: False Hopes and Fat Profits in the Diet Industry.* New York: A Plume Book, 1997.

Gaesser, Glenn A. *Big Fat Lies: The Truth About Your Weight and Your Health.* Carlsbad, CA: Gurze, 2002.

Gard, Michael and Jan Wright. *The Obesity Epidemic: Science, Morality and Ideology.* London and New York: Routledge, 2005.

Garland Thomson, Rosemarie. *Extraordinary Bodies: Figuring Physical Disability in American Culture and Literature.* New York: Columbia University Press, 1997.

Gawande, Atul. *Being Mortal: Medicine and What Matters in the End.* New York: Henry Holt and Company, 2014.

Gebara, Ivone. *Longing for Running Water: Ecofeminism and Liberation.* Minneapolis: Fortress, 1999.

Gebara, Ivone. *Out of the Depths: Women's Experience of Evil and Salvation.* Minneapolis: Augsburg Fortress, 2002.

Gerber, Lynn. *Seeking the Straight and Narrow: Weight Loss and Sexual Reorientation in Evangelical America.* Chicago: University of Chicago, 2011.

Gerber, Lynn, and Susan Hill, and LeRhonda Manigault-Bryant, guest editors of *Fat Studies: An Interdisciplinary Journal of Body Weight and Society* 4 (2015), 82–91.

Gilkes, Cheryl Townsend. "The 'Loves' and 'Troubles' of African American Women's Bodies: A Womanist Challenge to Cultural Humiliation and Community Ambivalence." In Townes, *A Troubling in My Soul*, 323–349.

Gillick, Muriel. *The Denial of Aging: Perpetual Youth, Eternal Life, and Other Dangerous Fantasies*. Cambridge: Harvard University Press, 2006.

Gilman, Sander. *Fat Boys: A Slim Book*. Lincoln, NE: University of Nebraska Press, 2004.

Glassman, Bernie. *Bearing Witness: A Zen Master's Lessons in Making Peace*. New York: Bell Tower, 1998.

Greenhalgh, Susan. *Fat-Talk Nation: The Human Costs of America's War on Fat*. Ithaca: Cornell University Press, 2015.

Greer, Rowan A. "Special Gift and Special Burden: Views of Old Age in the Early Church." In Hauerwas et al., *Growing Old in Christ*, 19–37.

Griffith, R. Marie. *Born Again Bodies: Flesh and Spirit in American Christianity*. Berkeley: University of California, 2004.

Gross, Jane. *A Bittersweet Season: Caring for Our Aging Parents—and Ourselves*. New York: Vintage, 2011.

Grumbach, Doris. *Coming into the End Zone: A Memoir*. New York: W.W. Norton & Company, 1991.

Gurwitch, Anabelle. *I See You Made an Effort: Compliments, Indignities, and Survival Stories from the Edge of 50*. New York: Plume, 2014.

Hanh, Thich Nhat. *For A Future to Be Possible: Buddhist Ethics for Everyday Life*. Berkeley: Parallax, 2009.

Hanh, Thich Nhat. *Love in Action: Writings on Nonviolent Social Change*. Berkeley, CA: Parallax Press, 1993.

Hanh, Thich Nhat. *Peace Is Every Step: The Path of Mindfulness in Everyday Life*. New York: Bantam, 1992.

Hankiss, Elemér. *The Toothpaste of Immortality: Self-Construction in the Consumer Age*. Baltimore, MA: Johns Hopkins University Press, 2006.

Harrision, Beverly Wildung. "The Power of Anger in the Work of Love: Christian Ethics for Women and Other Strangers." In Plaskow and Christ, *Weaving the Visions*, 214–225.

Hauerwas, Stanley, and Carole Bailey Stoneking, Keith G. Meador, and David Cloutier, eds. *Growing Old in Christ*. Grand Rapids, MI: William B. Eerdman's Publishing, 2003.

Haug, Frigga. *Female Sexualization: A Collective Work of Memory*. London: Verso, 1987.

Hays, Richard and Judith Hays. "The Christian Practice of Growing Old: The Witness of Scripture." In Hauerwas et al., *Growing Old in Christ*, 3–18.

Hill, Susan E. *Eating to Excess: The Meaning of Gluttony and the Fat Body in the Ancient World*. Santa Barbara, CA: Praeger, 2011.

Hoffman, Diane E. and Anita J. Tarzian. "The Girl Who Cried Pain: A Bias Against Women in the Treatment of Pain." *Journal of Law, Medicine, & Ethics* 29 (2001): 13–27.

hooks, bell. *Black Looks: Race and Representation*. Boston: South End, 1992.

Hull, John. *The Tactile Heart: Blindness and Faith*. London: SMC Press, 2013.

Huntington, C. W. "The Triumph of Narcissism: Theravada Buddhist Meditation in the Marketplace." *Journal of the American Academy of Religion* 83 no. 3 (September 2015): 624–648.

Hurd Clarke, Laura and Melanie Griffin. "Visible and Invisible Ageing: Beauty Work as a Response to Ageism." *Ageing and Society* 28 (2008): 653–674.

Irving, Paul, ed. *The Upside of Aging: How Long Life is Changing the World of Health, Work, Innovation, Policy, and Purpose.* Hoboken, NJ: Wiley, 2014.

Isherwood, Lisa. *The Fat Jesus: Christianity and Body Image.* New York: Seabury Books, 2008.

Isherwood, Lisa and Elizabeth Stuart. *Introducing Body Theology.* Sheffield, England: Sheffield Academic Press, 1998.

Johnson, Elizabeth. *Quest for the Living God: Mapping Frontiers in the Theology of God.* New York: Continuum, 2007.

Kafer, Alison. *Feminist, Crip, Queer.* Bloomington: Indiana University Press, 2013.

Kamen, Paula. *All in My Head: An Epic Quest to Cure an Unrelenting, Totally Unreasonable, and Only Slightly Enlightening Headache.* Cambridge, MA: Da Capo Press, 2005.

Kleinman, Arthur. *The Illness Narratives: Suffering, Healing, and the Human Condition.* New York: Basic Books, 1988.

Kramer, Bruce, with Kathy Wurzer. *We Know How This Ends: Living While Dying.* Minneapolis: University of Minnesota, 2015.

Kwong See, Sheree and E. Nicoladis. "Impact of Contact on the Development of Children's Positive Stereotyping about Aging Language Competence." *Educational Gerontology* 36 (2010): 52–66.

Kwok, Pui-lan. "Unbinding Our Feet: Saving Brown Women and Feminist Religious Discourse." In Donaldson and Kwok, *Postcolonialism, Feminist, and Religious Discourse,* 62–81.

Kwok, Pui-lan. "Mothers and Daughters, Writers and Fighters." In Russell et al., *Inheriting Our Mothers Gardens,* 21–34.

LeBesco, Kathleen. *Revolting Bodies: The Struggle to Redefine Fat Identity.* Amherst: University of Massachusetts Press, 2004.

Lelwica, Michelle. "Spreading the Religion of Thinness from California to Calcutta: A Postcolonial Feminist Analysis." In *The Journal of Feminist Studies in Religion* 25 no. 1 (April 2009): 19–42.

Lelwica, Michelle. *The Religion of Thinness: Satisfying the Spiritual Hungers behind Women's Obsession with Food and Weight.* Carlsbad, CA: Gurze, 2009.

Lelwica, Michelle. *Starving for Salvation: The Spiritual Dimensions of Eating Problems among American Girls and Women.* New York: Oxford University Press, 1999.

Levy-Navarro, Elena. "Fattening Queer History." In Rothblum and Solovay, *The Fat Studies Reader,* 15–22.

Linton, Simi. *My Body Politic: A Memoir.* Ann Arbor, MI: University of Michigan Press, 2007.

Lochlann Jain, S. *Malignant: How Cancer Becomes Us.* Berkeley: University of California Press, 2013.

Loe, Meika. *Aging Our Way: Independent Elders, Interdependent Lives.* New York: Oxford University Press, 2011.

Lorde, Audre. *The Cancer Journals.* San Francisco: Aunt Lute Books, 1997 (1980).

Lowe, Mary. "'Rabbi, Who Sinned?' Disability Theologies and Sin." In *Dialog* 51 no. 3 (Fall 2012): 185–194.

Loy, David. "The Religion of the Market." *Journal of the American Academy of Religion* 65 no. 2 (1997): 275–290.

Masada, Mycroft. "Good News: A Sermon on Fat Justice." In Gerber, Hill, and Manigault- Bryant, *Fat Studies*, 197–207.

McBryde Johnson, Harriet. *Too Late To Die Young: Nearly True Tales from A Life*. New York: Picador, 2005.

Medina, Lara. "Napantla Spirituality: My Path to the Source(s) of Healing." In Elisa Facio and Irene Lara (eds), *Fleshing the Spirit: Spirituality and Activism in Chicana, Latina, and Indigenous Women's Lives*, 167–185. Tuscon: University of Arizona Press, 2014.

Merrill, Gary F. *Our Aging Bodies*. New Brunswick, NJ: Rutgers University Press, 2015.

Miles, Margaret R. *Fullness of Life: Historical Foundations for a New Asceticism*. New York: Wipf & Stock, 2006.

Miles, Margaret R. *Beyond the Centaur: Imagining the Intelligent Body*. Eugene OR: Cascade Books, 2014.

Mohrmann, Margaret E. "The Idolatry of Health and the Idolatry of Life." In Denton, *Good is the Flesh*, 33–43.

Moon, Susan. *This is Getting Old: Zen Thoughts on Aging with Humor and Dignity*. Boston: Shambala, 2010.

Morris, David B. *Illness and Culture in the Postmodern Age*. Berkeley: University of California Press, 2000.

Morris, David B. *The Culture of Pain*. Berkeley: University of California Press, 1993.

Moss, Candida R. "Heavenly Healing: Eschatological Cleansing and the Resurrection of the Dead in the Early Church." *Journal of the American Academy of Religion* 79 no. 4 (December 2011): 991–1017.

Murphy, Robert. *The Body Silent: The Different World of the Disabled*. New York: W. W. Norton, 1987.

Newman, Katherine S. *A Different Shade of Gray: Midlife and Beyond in the Inner City*. New York: The New Press, 2003.

Oduyoye, Mercy Amba. "Be a Woman, and Africa Will Be Strong." In Russell et al., *Inheriting Our Mothers Gardens*, 33–53.

Oliver, Eric. *Fat Politics: The Real Story Behind America's Obesity Epidemic*. New York: Oxford University Press, 2006.

Pipher, Mary. *Another Country: Navigating the Emotional Terrain of Our Elders*. New York: Riverhead Books, 1999.

Plaskow, Judith and Carol P. Christ, eds. *Weaving the Visions: New Patterns in Feminist Spirituality*. New York: HarperSanFrancisco, 1989.

Purdy, Amy. *On My Own Two Feet: From Losing My Legs to Learning the Dance of Life*. New York: William Morrow, 2014.

Reynolds, Thomas. *Vulnerable Communion: A Theology of Disability and Hospitality*. Grand Rapids, MI: Brazos, 2008.

Rothblum, Esther and Sondra Solovay, eds. *The Fat Studies Reader*. New York: New York University Press, 2009.

Rowe, John and Robert Kahn. "Successful Aging." *The Gerontologist* 37 no. 4 (1997): 433–440.

Russell, Letty, and Kwok Pui-lan, Ada Maria Isasi-Diaz, and Katie Geneva Cannon, eds. *Inheriting Our Mothers Gardens: Feminist Theology in Third World Perspective*. Louisville: The Westminster Press, 1988.

Sachs Norris, Rebecca. "The Paradox of Healing Pain." *Religion* 39 (2009): 22–33.

Sanford, Matthew. *Waking: A Memoir of Trauma and Transcendence.* New York: Rodale, 2006.

Scarry, Elaine. *The Body in Pain: The Making and Unmaking of the World.* New York: Oxford University Press, 1985.

Schoenfielder, Lisa and Barb Wieser, eds. *Shadow on a Tightrope: Writings by Women on Fat Oppression.* San Francisco: Aunt Lute Books, 1983.

Schwartz, Hillel. *Never Satisfied: A Cultural History of Diets, Fantasies and Fat.* New York: Free Press, 1986.

Schweik, Susan. *The Ugly Laws: Disability in Public.* New York: New York University Press, 2009.

Seid, Roberta Pollack. *Never Too Thin: Why Women Are at War with Their Bodies.* New York: Prentice Hall, 1989.

Shaw, Andrea Elizabeth. *The Embodiment of Disobedience: Fat Black Women's Unruly Political Bodies.* New York: Lexington Books, 2006.

Shaw, Teresa M. *The Burden of the Flesh: Fasting and Sexuality in Early Christianity.* Minneapolis: Fortress, 1998.

Shinoda Bolen, Jean. *Crones Don't Whine: Concentrated Wisdom for Juicy Women.* San Francisco: Conari, 2003.

Snowdon, David. *Aging with Grace: What the Nun Study Teaches Us about Leading Longer, Healthier, More Meaningful Lives.* New York: Bantam, 2001.

Sontag, Susan. *Illness as Metaphor.* New York: Farrar, Straus, and Giroux, 1977.

Stearns, Peter. *Fat History: Bodies and Beauty in the Modern West.* New York: New York University Press, 1997.

Steinem, Gloria. *Doing Sixty and Seventy.* Berkeley, CA: Elders Academy, 2006.

Talarsky, Laura. "Defining Aging and the Aged: Cultural and Social Constructions of Elders in the U.S." *Arizona Anthropologist* 13 (1998): 101–107.

Thompson, Becky. *A Hunger So Wide and So Deep: American Women Speak Out on Eating Problems.* Minneapolis: University of Minnesota Press, 1994.

Thompson, Deanna A. *Hoping for More: Having Cancer, Talking Faith, and Accepting Grace.* Eugene, OR: Cascade Books, 2012.

Tillich, Paul. *Dynamics of Faith.* New York: HarperOne, 2009 (1957).

Tollifson, Joan. "Enjoying the Perfection of Imperfection." In Lenore Friedman and Susan Moon (eds), *Being Bodies: Buddhist Women on the Paradox of Embodiment*, 18–24. Boston: Shambala, 1997.

Tollifson, Joan. *Nothing to Grasp.* Salisbury, UK: Non-Duality Press, 2012.

Tovar, Virgie, ed. *Hot and Heavy.* Berkeley: Seal Press, 2012.

Townes, Emilie, ed. *A Troubling in My Soul: Womanist Perspectives on Evil and Suffering.* Maryknoll, NY: Orbis, 1993.

Walker, Alice. *In Search of Our Mother's Garden: Womanist Prose.* New York: Harcourt Brace Javanovich, 1983.

Wann, Marilyn. "Foreword: Fat Studies: An Invitation to Revolution." In Rothblum and Solovay, *The Fat Studies Reader*, ix–xxv.

Watkins, Derrel, ed. *Religion and Aging: An Anthology of the Poppele Papers.* New York: Haworth, 2001.

Watts Belser, Julia. "God on Wheels: Disability and Jewish Feminist Theology." *Tikkun* 29 no. 4 (Fall 2014): 27–29.

Weintraub, Arlene. *Selling the Fountain of Youth: How the Anti-Aging Industry Made a Disease Out of Getting Old—and Made Billions.* New York: Basic Books, 2010.

Wendell, Susan. "Unhealthy Disabled: Treating Chronic Illnesses as Disabilities."
    Hypatia 16:4 (2001): 17–33.
Williams, Delores. *Sisters in the Wilderness: The Challenge of Womanist God-
    Talk*. Maryknoll, New York: 1993.
Williams, Delores S. "Womanist Theology: Black Women's Voices." In Plaskow
    and Christ, *Weaving the Visions*, 179–186.
Woolf, Virginia. *On Being Ill*. Ashfield, MA: Paris Press, 2012 (1883).
Young, Iris Marion. *Justice and the Politics of Difference*. Princeton, NJ: Princeton
    University Press, 1990.

Index